Born in Belfast, Tony Canavan moved to Newry i
museum for Newry & Mourne District Council. Shc
Frontier Town in 1989 he moved to Belfast to take up ε , ...ιι ιne Federation for
Ulster Local Studies. On getting married in 1996 he moved to Dublin where he still
lives working as an editor and writer. He is assistant publisher with *Books Ireland* and
museums editor with *History Ireland*. He still has contacts with the Newry area
dividing his time between Dublin and Carlingford where he is a member of the
Carlingford Lough Heritage Trust.

FRONTIER TOWN

An *Illustrated History of*
NEWRY

TONY CANAVAN

Second Edition Published in Ireland 2009
in co-operation with Choice Publishing Ltd.
Drogheda, County Louth, Republic of Ireland

ISBN: 978-1-907107-08-5

First published in 1989 by
The Blackstaff Press Limited with assistance from the Northern Ireland Community Relations Council
© Tony Canavan, 1989, 2009 All rights reserved

British Library Cataloguing in Publication Data Canavan, Tony
Frontier town : an illustrated history. I. (District) Newry and Mourne, history
I. Title
941-6'58

ISBN 0-85640-430-6

CONTENTS

Introduction to the 2009 Edition

Much has happened to Newry since this book was first published in 1989, but some things do not change. Although officially now a city, Newry is still 'a very old town', as my grandmother used to say. It is one of the oldest in Ireland and unusual in being a native Irish foundation. It is still true to say that in many ways to know the history of Newry is to know the history of Ireland. The earliest Irish settlers lived in this area, and, withstanding invasions by the Vikings and the Normans, people have been living there for several thousand years. Such continuity has given the local citizens a unique sense of history.

As I said in my introduction to the first edition –

"To study Newry is to learn that local history need not be parochial or introspective. The great events of Irish history — such as the Norman invasion of 1167, Henry Grattan's 'constitution of 1782', or the Home Rule crisis and the partition of Ireland in 1921 — have all had a direct bearing on the town. But, perhaps more importantly, Newry itself has had a significant influence on the course of events in Ireland as a whole. Sitting in the Gap of the North, the town has been the focal point at decisive moments in the country's history and all too often it has been on the frontier in Ireland's wars. It has produced citizens who have played an influential role in Irish history, such as John Mitchel, the great republican writer, and Isaac Corry, the last chancellor of the exchequer in the Irish parliament before the Act of Union in 1801."

The first edition of this book sold out very quickly and copies made their way around the world. Soon people were asking that it be republished and the clamour has continued in the two decades since then. Unfortunately my own career took me away from Newry and into directions that it made it difficult for me to take up the issue of republishing and Blackstaff Press continued to be uninterested. This publication has been undertaken by me now that the opportunity has arisen,

This new edition is not a simple reprint as I have taken the opportunity to correct some errors that crept into the original and occasionally add new information. However it is essentially the same. As I stated in the 1989 edition, "the story of Newry is a rich one. The town grew up around a medieval abbey and in the eighteenth century, with the opening of its canal, the first in the British Isles, it became the foremost port in Ulster. The development of the town includes the strange institution of the lay abbot and 'exempt jurisdiction', the establishment of the police commissioners, and the great debate over the 'water question'. In fact, to chronicle all of its history would take volumes and to those whose interest has been aroused sufficiently to find out more, I refer them to my bibliography."

The acknowledgments are the same as in 1989. I would like to thank the following, which have been of assistance in my writing of this book: Armagh County Museum; Belfast Central Library; Linen Hall Library, Belfast; Main Library, Queen's University Belfast; Newry Library; Newry Museum; Public Record Office, London; Public Record Office of Northern Ireland, Belfast; Southern Education and Library Board, Local History Department, Armagh; State Paper Office, Dublin, and the members of the 1989 Newry Museum sub-committee for their advice. Thanks are still due to my family for their encouragement, my wife, Isolde, and especially to Janet, my sister, who converted the bulk of my original manuscript into type. For the current edition, I would also like to thank everyone at Choice Publications who assisted in publishing this edition.

A NEW AND
Correct MAP of ye County of
DOWN
Partly by an Actual Survey &c
Partly by Observation
1743

Notes of Reference.
Borough Towns.
Bishop's See.
Village or Seat.
Barracks.
N. or C. for Castle
Bridge
Charter School.
Spaw Well.
B. for Bally.
L. for Lough.
Large Towns.
Churches.

LOUGH NEAGH

ANTRIM COUNTY

Carrickfergus
CARICKFER
Whitehouse
Belfast

Maghergall
Lisburn
Trumery
Moyragh
Maralin
Maze
Coslets Br.
Hill Hall
Lisnasrean

Lurgan
Portadown
Lagan
Kircashock
LOWER
Hillsborough
Annahill
CASTLE
Lisburn

Truman's Lock
Isles Derry
IVEAGH
Dromore
L. Henry

Tandragee
Madenhon
Gill Hall
Drumbony
L. Erin
B. Dun
Kilinchy

Cusher R.
Terryhogan
3 Locks
Scarvagh pass
Bann Br.
Waringsford
Dromarioh
Maghnin

Acton
L. Bricklan
Garvaghy
Sulphur Spaw
Marybrook
Kilmore
Kilkleagh

Point z pass
Hanlon's Lock
McQuelan's L.
Gilbert's L.
Tuscan pass
Scofield's L.
Glen Wood
Drum Antine
4 Mile House
UPPER
Anaghelone
Knock Troagh
Makaye Br.
KINALEARTY
Loughin Island
Anna Cloun
Downpatrick

LORDSHIP OF
Rathfryland
Lurgan
B. Green
Tiekelly
B. Rona
Lisnisky
Kilco
Cabran
Castle Wellan
LECALE
Erinagh
Ballee
Seatfield

Newry
NEWRY
Drumgath
B. Goshen
Murdack Br.
Bryansford
Maghart
DourPark
B. Kinlar
B. Dargan
Rathmullen

IVEAGH
Slieve Donard
Newcastle
NEWRY BAY
Clannahery
Rathmullen
St. John's Pt.

COUNTY LOUTH
Clonallan
Bingan
Brian Bingan
Old Church
Midpace R.

Half Bar of MOURNE
Annalong
Kilkeel
Cranfield

ST GEORGE

Scale of Irish Miles

THE GAP OF THE NORTH

It was nine thousand years ago that the first settlers came to Ireland, probably crossing by boat from northern Britain. The landscape that met these people was largely the heritage of the last ice age, which had ended about five thousand years before. This had lasted almost one hundred thousand years and during it, northern Europe was covered in great sheets of ice. Ireland, in particular the north, was affected by two ice sheets: one originated in Scotland and pushed into Ireland from there; the other pushed down through the Donegal highlands. As Professor Estyn Evans has pointed out, these two ice giants struggled for supremacy, like the Irish and Scottish giants of legend, picking up huge boulders, scraping soil and rock off the land, shouldering against each other in the mountain ranges of Mourne and Cooley.

It took thousands of years for the ice to retreat and as it melted, the waters left behind made Ireland an island. The natural point of entry for these first settlers was through the bays and inlets of the Irish coast. One such bay was a large U-shaped valley that formed an inlet between the Mourne and Cooley Mountains, which would have taken the settlers to where a river entered the bay. This bay is known to us as Carlingford Lough and the place where sea and river met is where the town of Newry now stands.

The retreating ice left behind the bare granite domes of the Mournes, the broken and shattered gabbro of the Cooley range, and farther west a great dyke, or chain, of granite hills centred on Slieve Gullion that buttressed on to the plains to the south. To the north of the mountains the ice left behind a rich top soil that was often deposited in mounds or clumps known as drumlins (from the Irish word for a little hill, *droimin),* which run in a broad belt across Ireland, from Donegal Bay in the west to County Down in the east till they reach the Irish Sea. Drumlins would later form ready-made sites for settlement, but they were also an obstacle to the advancement of man and nature through south-east Ulster. The Clanrye river, for example, takes a dramatic turn from west to south because of these drumlins. Left behind too were the glacial erratics, huge stones carried and then dropped here and there by the ice. They are found scattered all over Ireland, but the Mourne Mountains have many fine examples. The most famous is the Cloughmore (the big stone) above Rostrevor, on Carlingford Lough. For centuries onlookers have marvelled at this enormous boulder perched on the hillside, and the legend has grown that the Irish giant, Finn MacCool, had thrown it across the lough against his Scottish opponent.

Map of County Down 1743, from W.Harris's *The Antient and Present State of the County of Down*.

Carlingford Lough is also the work of the ice. The steep sides of the lough and its deep basin were gouged out by it. Pushing down the river valley, the ice scraped out all the loose soil and rocks to form the u-shaped inlet, and as the ice melted and the water rose this valley was flooded to become a bay. It is similar in appearance to the inlets and bays of Scandinavia, and as such was immediately recognisable to the Vikings when they came to Ireland in the ninth century and who first called it a fiord. The landward end of Carlingford Lough consisted of a sandy marsh through which the Clanrye river meandered to the sea. Beyond the marsh a wide valley opened the way to the drumlin landscape farther inland. The low-lying ground was marshy and the uplands were often peat bog. Heavy clay soil harboured great dark forests of oak and the lighter soil was home to forests of elm, birch and holly.

Centuries earlier the melting ice had filled Lough Neagh to overflowing and the excess water flowed south to the sea at Carlingford. This great draining from Lough Neagh followed a line through modern-day Portadown, to Poyntzpass and then on to Newry and the sea. Just as the melting ice found this the surest route out of Ulster, so too would the earliest settlers have found this the surest route inwards. These earliest settlers, the people of the Mesolithic period (middle Stone Age), have left us few traces of their existence. Indeed for many decades archaeologists doubted if the Mesolithic people had reached Ireland at all. From what little that does remain, we know that they lived by hunting game and gathering food. When Ireland, like Britain, had been joined to the Continental landmass, animals and many plants had migrated there. The rising of the sea cut the country off from the rest of Europe, and while this curtailed further development of flora and fauna in line with the Continent, what there was flourished unaffected by human activity. So there was plenty of game for Mesolithic man to hunt, not least of which was the great Irish elk, which had evolved unhindered until this

time. We know nothing of the language, social organisation, or culture of these people. However, we do know that they lived simple lives, using tools made of flint and bone; they travelled in dug-out canoes and they sheltered in huts made of wood and wattle.

The first truly settled communities were those of the Neolithic, or new Stone Age, people who arrived in Ireland about 3000 BC. They had travelled along the Atlantic seaboard - the coasts of Spain and France - bringing with them a farming culture that had originated in the Middle East. For the first time man had control over his food supply: he cultivated rather than gathered cereals and fruits, and raised animals for meat and milk instead of relying on hunting. These farming people had a culture distinct from the earlier settlers and had made social as well as technological developments. They cleared away the lighter forests of elm, birch and holly in order to plant the seeds and to raise the livestock — cows, pigs, sheep — they had brought with them. These people lived in homesteads and tilled the arable soil, especially on the slopes of drumlins. For food they grew rye, barley and oats, and herded cattle and sheep. They lived in houses made of wicker over frames of wood, with thatched roofs. They used animal skins for clothes and also sheared their sheep to weave wool. They brought with them to Ireland their own pottery; round-bottomed pots of clay were used to store food and flat-bottomed pots were used for cooking. They ate fruit and ground their cereals to make flour, using the simple technique of placing the cereal between two flat stones and rubbing the top stone against the bottom one. They took an interest in their appearance and adorned themselves with necklaces and bracelets of beads and shells. Neolithic tools were a refinement on those of the Mesolithic period.

We find a greater variety of implements in stone, wood and bone.

Remarkably, the production of tools was a highly organised affair, and there were established factories that produced tools and weapons of flint and porcellanite. The people who lived in the Newry region would have acquired many of their weapons and tools from these factories, such as Tievebulliagh in County Antrim, and Rathlin Island. Not only were these traded throughout Ireland but they were also exported abroad. Porcellanite tools from the Antrim coast are found as far afield as Aberdeenshire, Dorset and Kent. This in itself is an indication that Neolithic society was complex and did not simply consist of isolated settlements with little or no contact between each other. Further proof is offered by the monuments that were built. These great structures in stone, megaliths, which are found along the Mediterranean, the Atlantic seaboard, and in the British Isles, are similar in design and construction. These, the first buildings in Ireland, were elaborate graves, often containing the remains of more than one person. Usually they are aligned to the stars or on an axis following the rising and setting of the sun.

The Carlingford Lough region was a major area of settlement. Where the town of Newry now stands was once home to these ancient Irish people of five thousand years ago. So abundant are megaliths in the vicinity that this stone-building culture was once named the Carlingford Culture, and some archaeologists believed that Neolithic man came to Ireland through the lough.

The most prominent monument left by these inhabitants is the court grave or court cairn. As the name implies, this consisted of a forecourt, marked out in stone, leading to the cairn — that is a man-made mound of stones — under which the cremated remains of the dead were buried. The burial gallery itself consisted of large stones aligned to form walls with stones set across them to form a roof. Unfortunately, few of these graves still remain intact. Above the slopes of Newry, to the south-west of the town, is a fine example of such a grave at Ballymacdermot. Four miles from Newry, at Clonlum in County Armagh, can be seen two further examples.

More visually impressive are the remains of the portal graves, commonly called dolmens. These consist of a single burial chamber made by placing one capstone on a tripod of three large stones. The capstones can be many tons in weight and great effort must have been expended to place them there. A number of dolmens are found around Newry, such as the Ballykeel dolmen at the foot of Slieve Gullion, and the Kilfeaghan dolmen near Rostrevor. To give some idea of the size of these monuments, the capstone at Kilfeaghan has been estimated to weigh thirty-five tons.

The largest type of monument our forebears have left us is the passage grave. The typical passage grave has its burial chamber set in a round cairn and is reached by an intricately constructed passage. The finest example in Ireland is at Newgrange in the Boyne valley in County Meath, but in the north of Ireland the two largest passage graves were built on the slopes of Slieve Gullion, five miles from Newry, and on the summit of Slieve Donard in the Mournes. Unfortunately, little remains of the Slieve Donard passage grave, but the one at Slieve Gullion remains largely intact, a spectacular monument to ancient man.

The number of ancient monuments within easy reach of modern-day Newry is evidence of its importance in Neolithic society. That the area of activity stretched over a wide area is shown by the number of monuments to be found in south Armagh and in the Mournes. The valley of the Clanrye river was the natural route for any movement into the north of Ireland from the sea, or across the country by land, as it afforded a passage through the mountains of the region. The geographical factors that today place Newry on the main route into and out of Ulster are just the same factors that placed it at the centre of the area of activity of ancient man in this part of Ireland.

Even as the early inhabitants of the Clanrye valley were building Ballymacdermot cairn, developments were taking place on the Continent that were to make stone obsolete as a material for tools, and to have it replaced by bronze — an alloy of tin and copper. Bronze was introduced to Ireland around 2000 BC. The change was gradual and so there was no sudden break between the use of stone and the use of bronze.

A fine example of a standing stone dating from the Bronze Age at Kilnasaggart, Co. Armagh. It is the oldest Christian inscribed stone in Ireland

5

Cloughmore, the large stone, above Rostrevor, is an example of a glacial erratic. Local legend is that Finn McCool threw it there. (Lawrence Collection)

Indeed it would appear that bronze never penetrated into the more remote region of the Mournes and stone continued to be used there until superseded by iron. Nevertheless, bronze did come to predominate to such an extent that bronze axe-heads were exported from Ireland to Britain, just as stone axe-heads previously had been.

A second wave of bronze-users came to Ireland about eight hundred years later. These were a quite distinct people with their own culture. It would appear that, like the earlier settlers, they came as immigrants rather than as invaders, as there are no signs of any major disruptions, and to judge from the gold ornaments and jewellery left from this period, Ireland enjoyed wealth and peace. The manner of burial that the bronze-users employed was significantly different from earlier peoples. There was a shift from mass graves to individual burial. The body was often buried intact, although cremation still occurred. Usually the remains of the dead were placed in a cist — that is a box or small chamber made of stones — over which a monument was placed. Some evidence of continuity with previous settlers is suggested by the Bronze Age use of earlier grave types such as cairns and dolmens. The characteristic Bronze Age grave was the round barrow and the round cairn, the former made of earth, the latter of stones. A second cairn on Slieve Gullion is such a Bronze Age burial. It is believed that standing stones — of ritual or territorial significance — and other stone alignments were also the work of the bronze-users. Like earlier monuments, these too were aligned with the sun and the stars.

The two most significant settlements of the Bronze Age people in the north both lay within easy reach of the Clanrye valley. One was at Downpatrick, and the other at Emain Macha (Navan Fort), outside Armagh city. These were obviously important centres to the bronze-users and continued to be relevant for centuries afterwards. Indeed Emain Macha was used as the capital of the kings of Ulster until the fifth century. As in previous ages, the Clanrye valley was at the heart of an important area of activity, lying between the region centred on Emain Macha and the region of which Downpatrick was the capital.

Ballykeel dolmen, an impressive example of a portal grave. (Crown copyright. Reproduced with the permission of the Controller of Her Majesty's Stationery Office)

The Bronze Age inhabitants of the Clanrye valley are recognisable as a society. The evidence of individual burial, the finely wrought jewellery, and the significance of certain settlements indicate a people who were organised in a hierarchical and territorial society. This society of kings, warriors and peasants was a direct forerunner to the social organisation that would dominate Europe until modern times. Yet these people are really just as unknown to us as the Stone Age settlers. We can infer their social organisation from the material they have left behind, but what they called themselves, their language, or their culture, we cannot know. They do not belong to history or even to legend.

The first 'historical' people to inhabit the Clanrye valley and, of course, Ireland were those who brought a new and better metal with them. However, we do not refer to them as the Iron Age people because we know their name: they were the Celts, to be known centuries later as the Gaels. To those people we owe the name 'Ireland' and most of its placenames. To them also we owe the earliest stories of this island, the legends of kings and warriors that are the forerunners of history. The early Gaels, who came to Ireland *c.* 250 BC, have left us little in the way of monuments or remains of settlements, yet what they have left is impressive. They occupied and built on the Bronze Age settlement at Emain Macha and it became an important religious and political centre for Ulster until the middle of the fifth century AD. It is also the centre of the Ulster Cycle of tales. In this Gaelic 'Camelot' ruled Conor MacNessa, and from Emain Macha rode the Curraidh na Craobhe Ruaide, the Red Branch Knights, to perform great deeds.

Another important monument left us by the early Gaels is the Dorsey Entrenchment, or Black Pig's Dyke, an earth embankment that begins to the west of Slieve Gullion, not far from Newry, and although littleremains, it once stretched across the southern frontiers of Ulster all the way to the west coast.

Archaeology tells us that it was built at the same time as the great fort at Emain Macha, in the second century BC. The exact nature and purpose of its construction will never be known, but we can suppose that it was meant to mark out the frontiers of Ulster and to regulate movement into and out of the kingdom. As the word 'Dorsey' comes from the Irish word *doras,* meaning 'door' or 'gate', it seems likely that this great entrenchment was meant to control the 'gates' of Ulster - the gaps or passes between the mountains, not least of which was the 'Gap of the North' between the Mournes and the Cooleys in which Newry sits.

More important than the physical remains are the legends and myths that the Gaels have left to us. The many tales and poems which come from this period are undoubtedly the oldest corpus of secular literature in western Europe. Greatest among them are the tales of the Red Branch Knights, and in particular the *Tain Bo Cuailgne* (the Cattle Raid of Cooley). These tales may be based on actual events but they are not 'real' history as it is understood. Nevertheless they are real in another way, for the landscape of these epics is the landscape of today. The placenames given in these tales over two thousand years ago are largely the same names we still use. We will never know where Camelot was but we can visit Emain Macha, follow the path of the army of Queen Maeve of Connacht into Ulster, and know the very place where Cuchulain, the greatest of these epic heroes, died.

The mountain to the west of Newry, Slieve Gullion, is said to be named after Culain, the smith to King Conor. In Lady Gregory's life of Cuchulain, *Cuchulain of Muirtheimne,* we are told that it was here that the boy Setanta, arriving late for a feast at the house of Culain, was met by the smith's watchdog, a large and ferocious hound that

'MAEV RIDES FORTH TO SPEAK WITH HER DRUID."

'began such a fierce yelling that he might have been heard through all Ulster, and so he sprang at him as if he had a mind not to stop and tear him up at all, but to swallow him at one mouthful. Setanta had no weapon but his stick and ball, but when he saw the hound coming at him he struck the ball with such force that it went down his throat and through his body. Then he seized him by the hind legs and dashed him against a rock until there was no life in him.'

When the king and the smith discovered what had happened, Culain bewailed the fate of his hound as there was no equal in all of Ireland. The boy Setanta then swore: 'I myself will be your watchdog, to guard your goods, and your cattle and your house.' At this point Cathbad the Druid stepped forward:

'And from this out,' he said, 'your name will be Cuchulain, the Hound of Culain.'
'I am better pleased with my own name of Setanta, son of Sualtim,' said the boy.
'Do not say that,' said Cathbad, 'for the men in the whole world will some day have the name of Cuchulain in their mouths.'

So it was that the greatest hero of Gaelic legend found his name.

To the north of Newry is Loughbrickland, which derives its name from another character of the Ulster Cycle, Bricriu, known as Neamh Theanga, the 'bitter tongue'. It was in Bricriu's fort that the great dispute over the championship of Ulster — between Cuchulain, Laegaire

9

Buadach and Conall Cearnach — began. After deeds to equal the labours of Hercules, Cuchulain proved himself to be the true champion. Many tales from the Ulster Cycle that took place near Newry could be told, but one in particular is centred on Iubhair Cinn Tragh, the 'yew tree at the head of the strand', the Irish name for Newry. It so happened that Cuchulain had fallen in love with Fand, the wife of Manannan MacLir, the king of the sea. Cuchulain had been with Fand for some time but knew that he had to return to Ulster, and to his own wife Emer.

> He bade her farewell, and she said to him, 'In whatever place you tell me to go and meet you, I will go there.' And the place they settled to meet was at Ibar Cinn Tracta. . . But when all this was told to Emer, there was great anger on her, and she had knives made ready to kill the woman with, and she came, and fifty young girls with her, to the place where they had settled to meet.

The tale goes on to tell of the confrontation between Emer and Fand at Iubhair Cinn Tragh and of the battle that ensued. Fand is saved from death by the intervention of Manannan MacLir, who takes her away with him.

The greatest epic from this period tells of the cattle raid of Cooley and the war that followed. The battles fought in this war were within earshot of Newry, and when Queen Maeve led her army into Ulster, she did so through the Gap of the North, past Iubhair Cinn Tragh, and along the ancient route that more or less parallels the present road from Newry to the city of Armagh.

The reason that this corpus of Gaelic literature still survives is that it was written down at an early date. Although the ancient Irish had a purely oral culture, writing was introduced and readily adopted when Christianity came to Ireland. Saint Patrick, the Apostle of Ireland, began his work in the fifth century, mainly in the north of the island. His mission marks a new departure for Ireland and also the real beginning of the history of Iubhair Cinn Tragh. Although Patrick challenged pagan authority wherever he found it and established Ard Macha (the modern-day Armagh) as the Christian capital on the hill opposite Emain Macha, he was not successful everywhere. Tradition has it that he was refused entry into the Mournes, the ancient kingdom of Boirche. At its borders he took off one of his sandals and threw it over the mountains. One version of the story says that it landed at Kilhornan, near Annalong in County Down, another that it fell in Carlingford Lough. As he threw it he uttered a prophecy: 'The length of that there will never be blood spilled.'

On the whole it would seem that the Irish took readily to Christianity and quickly found an accommodation between it and the old pagan culture. So it was that Christian monks, far from banishing the ancient tales, committed them to writing, so ensuring their survival to this day.

It may have been shortly after his rebuff from the kingdom of Mourne that Patrick came to the Glen Righe, the original name for the Clanrye river, where he found a hill overlooking a sandy stretch of marshland through which the river flowed. Here Patrick set up a camp and before leaving he planted a yew tree as a symbol of the new living

The legend of Saint Patrick planting the yew tree at the site of the abbey is commemorated in the seal of Newry.

faith. That, at least, is the legend, but it is this tree which gave its name to the place as the 'yew tree at the head of the strand', in Gaelic, Iubhair Cinn Tragh. Of course we have no proof that Patrick actually planted a yew tree, but we do know that such a tree was venerated at this site from an early date. In the twelfth century the Annals of the Four Masters refer to the ancient yew tree at Newry that Saint Patrick had planted. The reference to Iubhair Cinn Tragh in relation to Cuchulain might indicate a pre-Christian origin of the name, or it may have been that when the tale was written down, the only name known was the Christian one.

Whether Patrick planted the yew tree or not, it did exist, and it did give its name to the place where the abbey and later the town were to be situated. It was with the coming of Patrick that the name of Iubhair Cinn Tragh came into use and that the history of the town began. The name itself was not constant in form until modern times. As well as Iubhair Cinn Tragh, it was sometimes called Iubhair Cinn Coiche Mac Neachtain and it was Latinised as Ibar Cinn Tracta, Nyvorcintracta, and even as Viride Ligno (the flourishing tree). However, the Gaelic form of the name persisted, and its abbreviation, Na Iubhair, gave rise to the English, The Newries, The Newry, and ultimately Newry. For the sake of clarity it is referred to as Newry in this history except where the context demands otherwise.

A problem more intractable than the origin of the yew tree is the question of whether or not a monastery was founded at Newry by Saint Patrick or his disciples. As the present town is built on the site of the earlier settlements, archaeology has been unable to reveal anything of Newry's origins. Maps did not come into use until much later and the earliest map of Newry dates from the sixteenth century, so there is no evidence to be gleaned from it. We have to rely on the written word and tradition, which has it that a monastery did grow around the yew tree, dedicated to carrying on Patrick's work. It would seem strange if so venerated a tree did not attract some sort of monastic settlement. When the Cistercian abbey was established at Newry in 1144 there was a strong inference that it was founded on an older monastery and that it represented an unbroken tradition going back to the Apostle of Ireland himself. Therefore, although there is no conclusive proof, it may be safe to assume that some type of monastic community had already existed at Newry.

The introduction of writing meant that for the first time Gaelic culture was preserved for future generations. Recorded also were the contemporary conditions of Irish society, and although we cannot be certain of actual events, we do have a large amount of material on the social history of this period. For example, we have a clear picture of what a monastery was like - whether at Newry or elsewhere in the region. In this early Christian period a monastery would not have looked much different from the settlement of an Irish noble. It was not built like monasteries on the Continent; the buildings would have followed native Irish design and been made of timber, wattle and thatch. The monastery would have been surrounded by a ditch or palisade: the main building was the church, where religious services were held, and it usually had a cemetery beside it and was surrounded by little huts which were the monks' cells; larger buildings would have housed the kitchen and the refectory. Most monastic settlements would also have a library and a scriptorium, where the monks would study the Scriptures and copy them. Some of these copies were elaborate and very beautiful, taking great skill and patience to produce. The most famous of all the illustrated manuscripts produced by Irish monks is the Book of Kells, now housed in Trinity College Dublin.

One interesting feature of Irish monasticism is that sometimes nuns and monks shared the same monastery, both living under the same rule. This rule was a very strict one and was so harsh that life in a monastery was called a 'white martyrdom' ('red martyrdom' being death). Saint Columbanus exhorted his followers to 'pray Daily, fast Daily, study Daily, work Daily', and this was the basis for monastic life. Praying was done at intervals throughout the day and night. Each Wednesday and Friday were fast days, which meant going for hours without food; during Lent every day was a fast day. A monk would not only study the Scriptures but he would also be required to engage in agricultural labour or to practise a craft, such as making the clothes, furniture, candles, or tools needed by the monastery.

A monk's appearance was markedly different from that of a layman. He wore a simple tunic over which was a cape or hood of coarse undyed wool. Usually he went barefoot, unless travelling when he wore sandals. His head was shaved in a tonsure that began at the forehead and was shaved to the back, quite unlike the Continental tonsure. Despite this destitute appearance, a monk or any other cleric was ranked among the nobility, and it was considered a great honour for a son of a king or great lord to enter monastic life. Saint Colum Cille, for example, was of royal blood.

The records kept from these times onwards give detailed accounts of monastic life, and thanks to the writing down of the law tracts of the Brehons, we also know much about secular society. If there was a monastery at Newry it would have survived within a kingdom, surrounded by laymen of different ranks, from farmer to king. There were many kingdoms in Ireland at this time; the basic political unit was a *tuath,* a term that described both the territory and the people, and each *tuath* had its own king. In modern County Down there were several *tuatha,* the most important being Boirche (Mourne), Leth Cathal (Lecale), UiDubchrian (Dufferin), Ui Echach Arda (the Ards peninsula), Ui Derco Chein (the area around Belfast), and Dal mBuinne (lying east of Lough Neagh). A number of *tuatha* were bound together under another king, the *ri ruire.* Above this rank of kingship was the *ri ruirech,* the over-king of a province, such as Ulaid, the modern-day Ulster. While the higher-ranking king would claim allegiance from those under him, his authority extended only to levying troops and to exacting tribute. The internal affairs of each kingdom, no matter how big or small, were regulated by the people of the *tuath* through their own king and judges, the Brehons.

In Irish society the king shared the highest rank of nobility with the *ollamh,* the learned man, who could be a law-giver or poet; at the very bottom of the social scale were the slaves, who were labourers and certain types of entertainers. Between these two levels were the freemen and nobles. A man could rise in rank by increasing the number of cattle he owned or the number of clients he had. If someone in a lower rank became skilled in a respected craft — such as smiths, physicians or harpers — they might also rise. Although the different ranks in society were clearly defined, and the divisions rigidly adhered to, it was possible to rise — or fall — in status by one's own efforts, epitomised in the principle espoused by the Brehons that 'a man is better than his birth'.

This then was the social organisation of the inhabitants of the Clanrye valley around Newry in the ninth century. They would have lived in homesteads called raths or ringforts, which varied in size depending on the wealth and size of the family of the inhabitants. For instance, the higher-ranking noble, the *boaire,* would have had a substantial rath. Raths were as common as whitewashed cottages in the nineteenth century, and there are thousands of their remains (the 'faery' forts) throughout Ireland. A rath usually consisted of a circular enclosure surrounded by a ditch — depending on the rank of the owner, there might be two or more ditches — and a palisade, within which were one or more houses. The enclosed area served as a farmyard, and the livestock would be kept there at night. There was also a water-based counterpart to the rath, a crannog; this was a similar structure built on a man-made island set in a lough or marsh. Springhill fort, off the Newry-Belfast road, is a complete rath and the remains of many more can be seen in the hills near the town. The best example of a crannog in this area is in Loughbrickland.

Unfortunately, we know little about Newry in the early Christian age. We can only assume that the absence of Newry from the Annals means that these were uneventful years. No battle of note was fought here and no great man died. There are sporadic references, however, which indicate that it continued to be a place of importance to any traveller into or out of Ulster. Newry was included in any circuit which an over-king might take. Just as three centuries later, Murtagh, the high-king of Ireland, would stop at Newry, so too did an earlier king of Ulster reign from there for a while, as a poem, dated to 568, tells us:

When Maelcobha of the Minstrels reigned,
In yonder lubhair Cinn Tragh,
Twelve hundred bards then shelter found
Beside his tall north-eastern Yew.
To them Maelcohba of the Head
Gave maintenance for three bright years,
And till Doom's pale day may the generous chiefs
Of Deman's comely sons still reign.

The isolation of Ireland had been breached by Christianity and in the eighth century was broken yet again by a violent and destructive incursion,

The shallow draft of Viking ships enabled them to sail inland beyond Carlingford Lough and attack places even as far inland as Armagh

— the Vikings. By the closing decade of the eighth century Viking raids on the Irish coast were becoming frequent occurrences, and in the following century they were viewed by contemporaries as being the greatest scourge to have befallen Ireland. Being on the coast, Newry was vulnerable to Viking attacks. James Stuart, in his *Historical Memoirs of Armagh,* published in 1819, informs us that in 832 an army of Danes

> which had disembarked at a place named 'Inbher Chinn Tragha', the River at the Head of the Strand, subsequently called 'Na Yur', or Newry, was for a time more successful. This body of daring adventurers marched from Newry towards Armagh, and miserably wasted the country in every direction. The city which Colgan [one of the early annalists] says had never before been occupied by strangers was taken by storm, and here the Danes and the Norwegians established their headquarters for the space of a month.

In the early decades of the Viking era most of their attacks were concentrated on north-east Ireland, and so Newry suffered from direct raids or from Viking armies marching through the Clanrye valley. The Viking longships were swift vessels, each carrying between thirty and forty men, which could sail in quite shallow water. This meant that they could follow a river far inland before disembarking to ravage the surrounding country. To begin with there was little the Irish kings could do against them. There was no way of predicting when a raid would take place, and if news of a landing did come, it was not always possible to muster forces quickly enough. When the nature of the attacks changed and the Vikings sought places to settle in, the Irish began to contain the problem. Once they had permanent bases and settlements that they lived in all year round, then they were vulnerable to attack by the Irish.

One of the earliest places in which the Vikings settled was on the southern shore of Carlingford Lough. As the lough was similar in appearance to a Scandinavian fiord, this is what they called it, adding *fjord* to the Irish name Cairlinn to give us Cairlinnfjord. The Danes settled in a sheltered bay at the foot of Slieve Foy. Centuries later a town was to grow here, and was the basis for the present town of Carlingford. With the establishment of this settlement the lough and its hinterland came to be dominated by the Vikings.

Newry itself remains clouded in obscurity during this period. Having no evidence to draw on, we are left to speculate on what was happening. Being so often on the route of marching armies and hence falling within the sphere of foreign influence, it seems unlikely that a settlement of any kind — whether monastic or secular — was left at the yew tree at the head of the strand. No doubt the adaptability of Gaelic society meant that the Gaels did return to occupy the Clanrye valley. A rath abandoned in the face of a Viking army could easily be reoccupied. We find no mention of a monastic community at Newry at this time and it seems likely that any monks living in the shade of Saint Patrick's tree would have withdrawn from the coast and found refuge inland, as was happening elsewhere in Ireland.

By the beginning of the tenth century an equilibrium had been reached in Carlingford Lough, as throughout Ireland. The Viking community at Carlingford had become part of the local political scene and played an increasingly important role as a centre for trade. So influential were the Vikings that their sea and river craft largely replaced those of the Irish, and both Gael and *Gall* (foreigner) used them in trade and warfare. Irish kings had used boats in battle before, but the arrival of the Vikings heralded not only an increased use of navies but also a supply of better ships. This adoption of Viking naval techniques was of great importance in the tenth century, when a second wave of Viking incursions began, this time with the primary aim of taking land. Once again Newry was to be in the middle of the area of conflict.

Many battles were fought around Newry. In 917 the Danes were defeated on the shores of Carlingford Lough. Five years later the Annals tell us that 'Killeavy was wasted by the Foreigners of Lough Carlingford, and Dubliter, priest of Armagh, was crowned with martyrdom'. The fighting around Newry culminated in a fierce battle, fought in 926, when the Vikings were defeated by King Murtagh with the loss of two hundred men. This was a prelude to an even more serious blow when Murtagh again brought the Vikings to battle at Strangford Lough in the same year, inflicting a crushing defeat. Murtagh was typical of the new kind of king emerging at this time. It was a process that had been going on for some years, but was certainly encouraged by the Viking wars, by which the smaller *tuatha* were merging into petty kingdoms and these petty kingdoms were becoming subject to an undisputed over-kingship dominating an entire province, such as Ulster or Munster, under the control of one dynasty - in Ulster that of the O'Neills. From about the eighth century onwards the title *ri* (king) was rarely used for a leader of a *tuath* or even of a petty kingdom, who was more often referred to as *tigerna,* or lord, for a *tuath,* and *tuisech,* or the Latin *dux,* for the ruler of a petty kingdom. From the tenth century, the idea of a high-king, *ard ri,* for all Ireland began to take shape, and the most powerful over-king made claim to be the 'high-king of the Irish'.

Murtagh, the over-king in Ulster, made such a claim to the high-kingship and in 940 he made a royal circuit, commemorated in a poem composed by the royal poet, Cormacan:

> We were a night at the level Magh Rath,
>
> A night at the bright Glionn-Righe. . .

Magh Rath is the area north-east of Newry, and the bright Glionn-Righe is the Clanrye river. At Clanrye, Murtagh would have received the submission of the local nobles, and also taken hostages from them. It is interesting to note that in a curious reversal of roles, the following year Murtagh led an Irish fleet in an expedition, across the Sea of Moyle, against the Viking settlements in Scotland and the Isles.

By the eleventh century the threat of a Viking conquest was over and their settlements had become no more than petty kingdoms on the Irish scene. Even the Battle of Clontarf in 1014 was not a great struggle against the invaders but rather the final act of Brian Boru establishing himself as high-king of Ireland and in consequence making the high-kingship a political reality. Nevertheless, the Vikings had made a significant impact upon Irish society. Boatcraft was now dominated by Viking technology and new words from their language were absorbed into Gaelic, such as *marged* for market and *mangaire* for dealer. The Irish mode of warfare had been greatly influenced by the Vikings and from now on the war-axe, for example, was an essential part of a warrior's armoury. When Giraldus Cambrensis came to Ireland with the Normans in the twelfth century, he recorded:

> From an old and evil custom they always carry an axe in their hand as if it were a staff. . . Wherever they go they drag this along with them. When they see the opportunity, and the occasion presents itself, this weapon has not to be unsheathed as a sword, or bent as a bow, or poised as a spear. Without further preparation, beyond being raised a little, it inflicts a mortal blow.

The decline of Viking power was followed by a period of turbulence during which ruling dynasties asserted their authority over the provincial kingdoms, and the over-kings of provinces fought one another to secure the domination of all Ireland. During this period of confusion there is no direct evidence relating to Newry but it would seem that a monastery of some sort had been established there.

A Benedictine monk.
This order came to Ireland to implement
church reforms and is associated with
the abbey at Newry

Being the gateway to Ulster, it was a place of commercial intercourse and exchange. It is probably from this time that regular markets and fairs were held at Newry. The Irish may not have had towns before the arrival of the Vikings but seasonal markets and fairs fulfilled the same functions for trade, social gatherings and political assemblies. To the houses of the monks were probably added those of craftsmen and traders who settled at this busy crossroads. We do not know the size of the monastery at Newry, but we do know that it was considered important enough to warrant the attention of the reform movement that was affecting the church at the end of the eleventh century.

The movement to reform the church was a part of, and an incentive for, the wider movement that was taking place to bring Ireland into line with the rest of Europe. There was a strengthening belief that the archaic institutions of Irish society had to be reformed and replaced by more cohesive structures. The disappearance of minor kingships and the foundation of dynastic provincial kingdoms were the results of developments within Irish society, but the Irish were well aware of developments in the rest of Europe and some kings consciously imitated Continental modes at their own courts, establishing new offices or renaming old ones in line with the practice on the Continent.

Ireland was already part of a European institution, the church, and this was to be a major channel for new ideas. Leading churchmen sought the support of kings in reforming the church, which had fallen into bad practice during the Viking era and was organised on monastic rather than episcopal lines, and in turn supported, and influenced, these kings in their attempts to introduce political reform. In 1111 the high-king, Murtagh O'Brien, was patron of the synod of the church that divided Ireland into episcopal sees to replace the old monastic organisation. A

A Cistercian monk. This order played a major role in church reform and established the abbey at Newry in 1144

significant factor in the reform movement was the introduction of the Continental monastic orders, and these orders were important agents of change in Irish church and society.

In 1135 many Benedictine monks came to Ireland, and there is evidence to suggest that some settled in Newry. Whether or not they moved into an existing monastery to work alongside the Patrician monks or whether the monastery completely converted to the Benedictine order, we do not know. What we do know is that their influence was strong enough to ensure that the blessing of Saint Benedict was invoked in the charter that established the Cistercian abbey at Newry. The Cistercians had come to Ireland at the prompting of Mael Maedoc, the archbishop of Armagh, better known as Saint Malachy. Their first home was at Mellifont in County Louth and from this mother-house numerous daughters sprang up. The accepted date on which they arrived in Newry is 1144. The Cistercians banished the old order of monasticism with its harsh practices and later corruptions. Newry was now an abbey in the Continental manner. Gone were the old Irish habit and tonsure; these monks wore the white and black Cistercian habit and had only the centre of their heads shaved. The older monastery must have had some land but this was extended when King Dermot O'Carroll of Oirghiall (Oriel) endowed the abbey in 1153.

However, this endowment of Dermot's was superseded by the far more important charter granted to the abbey by Murtagh MacLoughlin, high-king of Ireland, in 1157. This charter granted to the monastery the lands and privileges that laid the foundation for its growth and for the special status it was to enjoy in the coming centuries. In a sense Murtagh's charter marked the official foundation of the abbey at Iubhair Cinn Tragh and marks the beginning of a new chapter in Newry's history.

2

THE YEW TREE FLOURISHES

'Murtagh MacLoughlin, king of all Ireland to all his Kings, Princes, Nobles, Leaders, Clergy and Laity, and to all each the Irish present and to come, greeting' — so begins the charter granted by Murtagh MacLoughlin to the abbey at Newry in 1157. The charter lists in detail all the lands he was granting to 'the Monks serving God in Nyvorcintracta as a perpetual and pure donation'. The list is a long one, clearly defining an area covering present-day Newry and the surrounding hinterland. The territories were granted with their 'lands, woods and water'; this was a symbolic way of saying that the monastery was to have full possession of them and all the rights pertaining to them. The rights of the monks to hold and rule over the lands is further clarified and guaranteed in a paragraph of the charter:

> And because I have founded the Monastery of Ybar-Cin-Tragha, of my own mere will, I have taken the monks so much under my protection as sons and domestics of the faith that they may be safe from the molestations and incursions of all men.

In other words, the monks held these territories directly from the king and owed no obligations to other men. The monks were granted this land to hold outside the jurisdiction of all other kings or lords, as if the abbey was a *tuath* and this was their home territory. Thus the abbey at Newry was established as a separate entity within the kingdom in which Murtagh MacLoughlin exercised over-lordship. The abbey was to retain its exempt status in one form or another throughout the time of its existence.

These lands were extended within a relatively short period of time to include large areas in present-day counties Armagh, Down and Louth. In the charter Murtagh gives permission, and thereby encouragement,

> that as Kings and Nobles of O'Neach or of Oirghiall may wish to confer certain lands upon this Monastery for the health of their souls, they may do so in my lifetime, while they have my free will and licence, that I may know what and how much of my earthly kingdom the King of Heaven may possess for the use of his poor monks.

Murtagh's charter is important not only in the history of Newry but also of all Ireland. It is one of the few royal charters to survive from the pre-Norman period and gives us an interesting insight into the nature of kingship at this time. It is written in Latin and in its style could have come from a contemporary European king. It is interesting to note that Murtagh does not use the traditional title of high-king but instead king of all Ireland. Similarly, there are clear distinctions drawn in the ranks of the nobles named between kings, princes and leaders *(duces)*. In a previous age all these nobles would have claimed to be 'kings' of some degree. The fact that Murtagh could dispense territory — in a society where land traditionally belonged to the family or *tuath* — by his 'own mere will' is a clear illustration of how the nature of royal authority had developed by this time. That the abbey at Newry retained these lands and the rights granted with them is proof of how much this was a reality and not just a formula of words.

It is significant that the charter is dated 115 7, for in that year the abbey at Mellifont in County Louth — the mother-house of the Cistercian order in Ireland — was solemnly consecrated in a ceremony at which Murtagh MacLoughlin was present as high-king of Ireland. This was the final proof that the reform movement had been accepted by Irish church and society. It is not too much to suppose that Murtagh wished to be personally associated with this movement by endowing the Cistercian abbey in his own kingdom. Although he claims in the charter that 'I have confirmed to the aforesaid Monks of my own proper gift for the health of my soul', the political advantages of such an association cannot have been far from his mind. Likewise among the other kings and lords of Ulster; it was not simply devotion to the church that prompted them to grant lands to the abbey but also a wish to do the right thing politically. Whatever the motives of their benefactors, the Cistercian monks at Newry were endowed with land the size of a small kingdom and enjoyed full rights within this territory.

The importance of the charter to Murtagh is illustrated by the status of the people he chose to witness it. They range from Giolla Mac Liag, archbishop of Armagh; Hugh O'Killedy, bishop of Oriel; and Muriach O'Coffay, bishop of Tir Eoghain; to great men such as the king of Fearnacrinn and Kennacta; Gilla Christ Ó Dubhdara, king of Fermanagh; and Aedh, the Magennis Mór; as well as 'many other clerics and laity'. Murtagh offended many minor lords during his over-lordship; they finally rebelled and deposed him, and he was murdered by his own people in 1166. But the charter he granted to Newry remained inviolate and was to survive the troubles of the coming centuries as the most permanent deed of this king of all Ireland.

Not long after the granting of this charter, calamity struck the abbey when in 1162, as the Annals of the Four Masters relate, 'the monastery of the Monks at lubhar Chinntrochta was burned, with all its furniture and books, and also the Yew Tree which Patrick himself had planted'. It is not surprising that fire should prove so destructive to an establishment whose buildings were made of wood and thatch. Although the buildings could be replaced, Saint Patrick's yew tree could not. A later tradition consoles us for the loss of this venerated relic with the story that an offshoot had been planted and flourished. This tree survived until the town's destruction in the seventeenth century, and probably provides the second yew on the arms of Newry.

This 14th century drawing shows Dermot MacMurrough and his chieftains wearing Norman style armour and fighting on horseback

While the abbey was recovering from this setback, forces were being brought into play in Ireland, and also in England and France, that were to change irrevocably the course of history in this country.

Murtagh MacLoughlin's successor to the high-kingship, Rory O'Connor, in imposing his will on the recalcitrant kingdom of Leinster, had driven its king, Dermot MacMurrough, to seek foreign aid in regaining his kingdom. Having achieved an audience with Henry II, king of England, in France in 1166, Dermot returned to England with a royal licence to recruit mercenaries for a campaign in Ireland and he found them in the Earl of Strigoil, known better as Strongbow, and other Cambro-Norman knights. Dermot returned to Leinster with a force of mercenaries in 1167, and so began the Norman invasion of Ireland. Strongbow himself, accompanied by a force of Normans, did not arrive in Ireland until 1170.

Although the monks at Newry probably heard of these foreigners and of their successes against Irish armies, they did not know them at first hand until early in 1177, when John de Courcy led twenty-two knights and a mixed force of some three hundred Norman and Irish soldiers against Rory MacDunlevy, king of Dun da Lethglass (modern Downpatrick). Like his fellow Normans, de Courcy, who had come to Ireland in search of adventure and land, chafed at the restrictive control imposed by Henry II's arrival in 1171, after Strongbow. So when the invitation came from a dissident faction in the kingdom of Down (or Ulidia), he seized the chance to escape from Dublin. His arrival at Downpatrick caught MacDunlevy off guard, who was forced to flee. In June 1177 MacDunlevy returned with Irish allies, including a contingent of clerics with holy relics, to do battle with de Courcy. The Normans completely defeated the Irish, even capturing all the clerics, and subsequently established their own lordship centred on Downpatrick. Within this, de Courcy came to an arrangement with the local Irish who accepted his over-lordship and even served alongside the Normans in their campaigns.

Norman knight of the twelfth century

The Normans' territory was firmly established between the River Bann and the east coast, but any attempts by de Courcy to extend his dominion beyond these limits usually ended in defeat. One battle in the

John de Courcy led the Norman invasion of Ulster and established a lordship at Downpatrick

attempt to widen the Norman frontier was fought at Newry, probably in 1178.

Giraldus Cambrensis, the chronicler of the Normans in Ireland, makes mention of this battle, saying it 'was fought at Newry Bridge (pontem Ivor) on [de Courcy's] return from England'. From other sources we know that at this time de Courcy had made a raid into Machaire Conaille (northern County Louth) but was met and defeated by an Irish army commanded by Murrough O'Carroll, king of Oriel, at Glen Righe — the Clanrye river, on which Newry sits.

This Irish victory did nothing to stop the Normans in the long run. John de Courcy may not have been able to extend his lordship west but the Irish could not evict him from the territories he held, and Cambrensis tells us that 'he erected castles throughout Ulster in suitable places, and established it in a most firm peace, not without the greatest labour and privation and many perils'. Two of these castles were within the vicinity of the abbey at Newry. One was down by the river, where it could guard the bridge and the ford. If the ancient road crossed the river at or near the present Ballybot Bridge, then this castle probably stood at the end of Mill Street, the site upon which a stone castle was erected some centuries later. The castle built by de Courcy was an earth structure of the motte-and-bailey type, consisting of a large mound and a palisaded enclosure. The second castle that was built, probably at this time, was some five or six miles further along the Clanrye river at a ford called Ath Cruithne. It too was a motte and bailey and it still survives as the Crown Mount in the townland of Sheeptown, north of Newry, an impressive mound of earth some hundred feet tall, surrounded by a very deep ditch with the bailey alongside. Both these castles were vital to the Normans of Down if they were to keep open their channels of communication with the main Norman stronghold to the south.

The abbey at Newry would appear to have been relatively unaffected by the warfare around it. Admittedly the armies marching across their land, with their demands for supplies and the accompanying disruption that any army brings, must have interrupted the normal routine of the monks' lives. However, beyond this the abbey was respected as neutral ground by both sides. We have seen how the native lords respected the position conferred on the abbey by Murtagh, the high-king, while in turn the Normans, who now claimed to be in Ireland under licence of the papal bull, *Laudabiliter* — a right granted by Pope Adrian IV to any king of England to invade Ireland and reform the church - showed a respect for religious establishments and often took over the patronage of a monastery in place of a deposed Irish king. John de Courcy, in particular, in order to add legitimacy to his enterprise and to win over local support, encouraged the veneration of Saint Patrick and proved himself a friend to religious orders. In return the Irish church largely welcomed the Normans as lay support for their reform movement, and the French-based order of the Cistercians was initially sympathetic to the invaders.

De Courcy may have hoped to evade royal control in Downpatrick but as the Norman colony spread from the east coast so too did royal authority. In 1177 Henry H appointed his ten-year-old son John as lord of Ireland and through his son, Henry intended to extend his control over the whole island. Later as King John he quarrelled with de Courcy, removing him from his lordship and elevating Hugh de Lacy as Earl of Ulster in his stead.

Hugh de Lacy was made Earl of Ulster by King John in place of John de Courcy

Newry was to witness a Norman invasion of Ulster of quite a different kind in 1210. This was an expedition led by King John against Hugh de Lacy, who had shown himself to be so independent of his king as to be treasonable. King John decided to take action against the earl himself, and July 1210 found him at Carlingford, preparing to cross into the lordship of Ulster. It was probably at this time that he gave licence for the building of the castle at Carlingford that still stands today bearing his name. Despite de Courcy's castle at Newry, it was decided not to risk a march by the overland route since this area was once again dominated by the Irish. John's earlier grants of land in Ulster had come to nothing. Instead he sailed from Carlingford to Ardglass on the County Down coast and from there conducted his successful campaign against de Lacy. On the return journey John travelled by land; however he again avoided Newry and the Gap of the North by turning off at the Crown Mount towards Narrow Water, where he and his army crossed Carlingford Lough. John's campaign in Ulster seems to have been a purely internal Norman affair, neither touching on the Irish monks in Newry nor the Irish kings west of the River Bann.

The Normans' use of armour and cavalry gave them a decisive advantage over the Irish forces opposing them.

Foot soldiers garrisoned the castles at Newry and the Crown Mount

King John's visit does give us an insight into the Norman lordship in Ulster. Among the records of his reign kept in the Pipe Rolls there are references to his expedition against de Lacy and in particular to the Newry area. For example, among the royal accounts there is this entry: 'And for the maintenance of 240 foot-soldiers who went into Iveagh to plunder MacKouecan, 66s.4d. [£3.32]'. Iveagh was the Irish part of south Down and was of some concern to the Normans based at Downpatrick as witnessed by this entry in the Pipe Rolls: 'And wages of 10 men-at-arms and 20 foot-soldiers who kept guard in the city and district of Downpatrick against the Irish of Iveagh for 20 days after the King's departure, 63s.4d. [£3.17].' There is also an entry referring to the castle at the Crown Mount, called Moy Cove by the Normans from the Irish name for the area in which it stands, Magh Cobha. It has been suggested that Moy Cove Castle was in fact Dundrum Castle, but this seems unlikely. Even if this were so, the entry is still relevant, being a castle and garrison of similar size. The Pipe Rolls tell us that John set aside 30s. (£1.50) 'for a new bridge at Moycove and for the repair of the paling and of a new palisade'. Also for the garrison, the entry reads, 'and as wages for one knight, one chaplain, 5 men-at-arms and 6 unarmed men at Moycove for [2 years], 152. cows, and as wages for 10 soldiers guarding the district of Moycove for the same period, 80 cows. . . and for the larder of Moycove for 2, years, 26 cows'. Despite the security of the Norman dominance within the earldom, there was a real threat from the neighbouring parts of Ulster still under Irish control.

The internal affairs of the Cistercian order were next to affect the monks at Newry. For some time dissatisfaction had been growing among its authorities in France over the conduct of the order in Ireland. Following the arrival of the Normans in 1167, the order had become divided between those houses which were daughters of Mellifont, such as Newry, and those attached to St Mary's Abbey in Dublin. The Mellifont houses were dominated by the Irish and those of St Mary's were dominated by the Normans. In 1227 two abbots from France made a visitation to the order in Ireland and they came to some sensational conclusions. They said that the houses of Mellifont had assumed a singularly Irish character and that there was a conspiracy to remove them completely from the Cistercian order. As a result of the charges brought by the French abbots, the cellarer of Mellifont and the abbot of Baltinglass were deposed from their positions for being the main instigators of the conspiracy. The abbots of five other houses, including Newry, were also accused of complicity and deposed from office. In an attempt to ensure the continuing conformity of the Irish houses, Stephen of Lexington, abbot of Stanley, commanded that no Irishman could be elected abbot in the important houses and specifically stated that Irishmen might be elected abbot only at Abbeyshrule, Concomroe and Newry. This concession was probably a recognition that these abbeys were beyond English control in any case. Newry was on the uneasy frontier between Gaelic and Norman influence, and for much of the time was considered, quite literally, to be 'beyond the Pale', that is, outside the control of Dublin, which at this time would have covered most of Leinster, the eastern area of Munster and parts of south-east Ulster.

All was not completely black for Newry at this time. The accusations of involvement in the Mellifont conspiracy and the shame of the abbot's deposition did not stop Gerard of Newry being elected to the bishopric of Dromore in 1227. The monks of Newry seemed to have had a particular say in this election, for when Gerard died, the abbey at Newry claimed a special privilege in choosing his successor. However, their claim was not upheld and if the monks had any further involvement in the election of the bishops of Dromore, we do not hear of it.

Norman control was limited to a well-defined area centring on Downpatrick and stretching south towards Dundalk in County Louth. Newry was on the western edge of this area and control was to pass between Norman and Gael. In 1236, the Annals tell us, the O'Donnell Mór, ruler of Tyrconnell, advanced at the head of his army to Iubhair Cinn Tragh and took hostages. The following year the English earl, Hugh de Lacy, occupied Newry and assuming the role of the abbey's patron, claimed it for himself. He issued a new charter recognising the abbot of Newry as a mitred prelate and confirming the abbey's existing rights. Within the feudal system Newry was granted much the same status that the abbey had enjoyed under the Gaelic order. This charter from de Lacy was not simply a new grant or a new creation but rather a confirmation of what had existed under the charter of King Murtagh. Hugh de Lacy was redefining and extending the status and powers of the abbot in the terms of the feudal order that the Normans had brought with them. It is in this charter of de Lacy's that the later legal and ecclesiastical exempt jurisdiction of Newry and Mourne owes its direct origin.

De Lacy's fragile lordship over this section of his earldom was demonstrated almost immediately after his granting of the charter, when Newry was attacked by Tadgh O'Connor Ruadth, the king of Connacht, and his ally Tadgh M'Tuathal. It is significant that there is mention of damage being done, not to the abbey, but to the town at Newry, which was burned to ashes. This is the first mention we have of

a town, and we can imagine that a settlement of traders and craftsmen had been attracted to the abbey and the river crossing.

Whatever hopes there were of securing the abbey for the Hiberno-Norman influence appeared to have died with Hugh de Lacy in 1243, when his earldom reverted to the Crown and no strong lord took his place to dominate or extend the earldom of Ulster. Six years later Maurice FitzGerald built a castle at Narrow Water and this is perhaps indicative that Newry was not considered part of the safe route into the earldom by the Normans. However, a new line of earls of Ulster was created in 1263 with the elevation of Walter de Burgo to the title by Henry III of England. The abbey seemed to have found a compromise between the competing Gaelic and Norman forces and it remained one of the Irish houses of the Cistercians, yet was accepted by the Normans to fall within their sphere of influence. In 1306 Edward I levied a 'tenth' in taxes off the church and among those places visited under the auspices of this taxation system was Newry, whose abbot's annual income was valued at 20 marks (£13.40; a mark was worth 67p).

At this time England was engaged in war with Scotland. The success of the Scots encouraged many of the Irish, chief among them Donal O'Neill of the Cenel Eoghain, to seek an alliance with the Scottish king, Robert the Bruce. In response, Robert's brother Edward landed at Larne in County Antrim in May 1315 with six thousand veteran soldiers. Edward soon claimed the throne of Ireland for himself, announcing he had come to liberate his fellow Gaels from foreign domination. Many, but not all, of the Gaelic Irish responded to his call, and even a few of the Hiberno-Normans joined him. Richard de Burgo, the Earl of Ulster, was imprisoned for being an ally of Bruce, largely on account of his relationship by marriage to him -de Burgo's daughter, Elizabeth, was married to Robert the Bruce. Edward Bruce's Scots captured Newry and in 1316 Edward was crowned king of Ireland at Faughart, ten miles to the south of the town. Although he often defeated the English in battle, he never conquered Ireland and like a medieval Hannibal he marched throughout the country unable to capture Dublin or win a decisive victory. Finally he was cornered at Faughart on 14 October 1318 and defeated in a bloody battle by John de Bermingham. The Scots fled from the field and Bruce himself was killed — his head later being sent to Edward II in England. On their retreat north the Scots destroyed the castle and plundered the town of Newry. Of Edward's time in Ireland the Annals commented: 'For three years and a half, falsehood and famine and homicide filled the country, and undoubtedly men ate each other in Ireland.' Despite its ultimate failure, the Bruce invasion had dealt a crippling blow to English influence and paved the way for a Gaelic resurgence that lasted until the sixteenth century. In the 1590s, Edmund Spenser, secretary to Lord Grey, the lord deputy of Ireland, wrote:

> Before Bruce's coming to Ireland the Pale extended as far as Dunluce, having in the middle Knockfergus, Armagh and Carlingford, which are now the most out of bounds, and, indeed, not counted of the Pale at all, for it now stretches no further than Dundalk towards the North.

Since a part of the abbey's territory fell outside the area of Gaelic control, it was not entirely outside English control. In 1329 the sheriff of Oriel imposed fines on the abbots of Granard in County Longford, Cashel in County Tipperary and Newry. The abbot at Newry is described in a surviving document as the 'late Rudolph'. The total amount came to £41 and was paid by the mother-house at Mellifont. In 1335 the Pipe Rolls tell us that an abbot, Roger of Newry, was accused of wrongfully seizing and detaining a horse belonging to one William Rede. Nothing much else is known about this case, except that Roger was further accused of contempt for not appearing to answer the charge. It may have been that Roger was exercising his rights to levy a toll within the abbey's territory and his refusal to appear before the court is probably the earliest written example of an accused claiming exemption under the jurisdiction of Newry and Mourne as confirmed in de Lacy's charter.

Despite the English names of these abbots, Newry remained an Irish house and was to suffer when the English attempted to undermine the Irish-controlled section of the church. In 1373, by order of Edward II, Newry was despoiled of the lands it held in the County Louth area. The reason given was that the abbey was composed of 'meere Irish conversing only with such and spending on such people their rents and profits'. The fact that such an order was given was recognition that Newry was an Irish monastery and that the king's writ could run no further than County Louth, since all to the north was beyond the Pale.

The next occasion that Newry emerges in church records is in 1378, when Maurice MacBruin, a cleric from Dromore in County Down, was promoted to the abbacy, valued, it is said, at 25 marks (£16.75). This MacBruin was not a Cistercian but a Dominican, and was succeeded as abbot by Sean O'Rooney, another outside appointment. (In 1422 another monk named Maurice MacBruin became abbot. Whether or not he was related to the first is not known.) These outside promotions indicate the unhealthy state of the Cistercian order in Ireland. In 1493 the abbot of Mellifont reported to France that the order had fallen into bad practice, due mainly to the troubled state of Ireland and the appointment of inexperienced men. Visitations from Mellifont had all but ceased because recently the provisors and commendatories, who occupied these houses, 'had manned the battlements and belfries of the churches on [the visiting abbot's] approach, threatening him with showers of javelins, stones and arrows, and expelling him violently and by force of arms'. The decline into worldliness continued into the next century, when the abbey at Newry provided an example of how far the order had sunk from its saintly ideals. It would seem that the abbot, Giolla Iosa Magennis, had taken an unpriestly interest in local politics, resulting in him being ambushed and assassinated at the hands of his nephew, Donal Óg Magennis. The place where he was killed is commemorated in the name Monk's Hill on the outskirts of Newry.

Events directly affecting the abbey took place against a background of continuing warfare between the Irish and the English. Most of Ulster was abandoned to English control after the Bruce invasion was defeated, but occasionally the government in Dublin made attempts to extend its influence or to secure the frontiers of the Pale. Sir Ralph d' Ufford, the king's deputy in Ireland, had married the widow of Richard de Burgo's successor as Earl of Ulster and so had a claim to the earldom. In 1344 he advanced northwards into Ulster by the land route and forced his way through the Moyry Gap, a mountain pass to the south-west of Newry, *cum valida manu,* by the strength of his hand. However, this expedition had little lasting effect on the area.

A pattern was being set for the next two centuries. The English never abandoned attempts to conquer Ulster but they rarely got farther north than Newry and their expeditions had little permanent effect. When thought politic, the Irish leaders might formally surrender and recognise the English king's sovereignty but would return to their own territories, still claiming their rights as Irish kings and behaving accordingly. In 1394 Richard II himself came to Ireland with an army of eight to ten thousand men, the largest yet seen in the country, and at Dundalk Niall Mór O'Neill, who claimed the kingship of Ulster, submitted to him. English advances into Ulster were halted nine years later when the O'Neills led a Gaelic alliance against them in which, the Annals relate, 'the Galls were driven from the whole province, and the North was burned. .. and the monasteries despoiled'.

The fourteenth century was to see this pattern of warfare continue. During this time Newry became increasingly important as the most secure English foothold on the frontier of Ulster, and in 1480 a second castle was built in the town to provide a larger garrison. By the end of the fifteenth century the English were at a low ebb as the resurgence of the Irish and the Wars of the Roses between Yorkists and Lancastrians seriously undermined English authority. A report written in 1515 summed up the situation by saying that the Pale was reduced to the four counties of Dublin, Kildare, Meath and Louth. Even Louth, it said, had to pay a blackmail of £40 annually to 'The Great O'Neyll' to save it from depredation.

The most significant political event of the sixteenth century was also the most significant religious one. It occurred in 1534 when Henry VIII, who had been king of England since 1509, through the Act of Supremacy became Supreme Head on Earth of the Church of England. This act posed a dilemma for all Catholics in Ireland, and was also a direct threat to the religious houses. Furthermore, the Act of Supremacy called into question the legitimacy of Henry VIII's rule in Ireland since, like all English kings, his claim to the lordship of that country rested on papal licence through the bull, *Laudabiliter.* In 1541 Henry resolved the problem by having himself declared King of Ireland, requiring authority from no one other than God.

The abbey at Newry was unaffected for the moment, but not so those Gaelic lords who lived in its vicinity. Henry VIII was determined that all of Ireland be brought under the effective control of the English Crown. Under the Tudor system of government there could be no independent lord, whether Gaelic or Hiberno-Norman, and there could be no toleration of cultural differences: the subjects of the King of England would be English. A number of measures were introduced to ensure that Irish modes of dress and the Irish language would be completely replaced by the English. The independent lords would be crushed, as was Thomas FitzGerald of Kildare, or be persuaded to give up their independence and submit to the Tudor system. Henry's policy of negotiated surrender became known as the policy of 'surrender and regrant'. It meant that any Gaelic or 'Old English'—the name given to the earliest Norman colonists — lord who agreed to surrender his lands and titles to the king would have them granted back to hold directly from the king as his liegeman under a new title. The policy began in 1542. and by 1547 over forty of the great, and not so great, independent lords had accepted it.

The lords around Newry were among the first to accept surrender and regrant. In 1542 Conn Bacach, the Great O'Neill, led a delegation of Gaelic nobles to London to meet with Henry VIII. Speaking through an interpreter, Conn swore fealty to the king and swore 'utterly to forsake' the style and title of O'Neill. In return he became the Earl of Tyrone, a peer of Henry's kingdom of Ireland. Donal Óg Magennis also swore fealty. The king reported to his Irish council: 'We have made Maguinez Knight and to him in ready money 100 marks [£67]. We have also made Arthur Mauinez knight and given him £50:00 in money.' So it seemed that without further bloodshed Ulster had been brought under royal control.

Portrait of Nicholas Bagenal,
Marshal of Ireland (courtesy
of J. Anley)

One might ask why the Gaelic lords of Ulster, who had so successfully resisted English incursions, had so easily accepted the loss of their old titles and their independence. For the minor lords there were a number of attractions. They had long resented the heavy hand of O'Neill dominance and now they could seek protection from the English king from paying tribute to O'Neill or being obliged to serve a military term in his campaigns. As Gaelic lords, they did not own the land they ruled and could not secure succession for their heirs. Now under the English system they held the land as their own property and inheritance was by primogeniture. On Conn Bacach's part, he was certainly aware of Henry's aims towards Ireland and had seen the fate of Thomas FitzGerald. The years of warfare were wearing down his resistance and making life increasingly hard for the people of Ulster. Therefore, when the opportunity came to negotiate a settlement, Conn welcomed it. To be an earl under the English system had the same attractions for him as for the other lords, and he may have genuinely believed that his real authority within the old O'Neill kingship would be unchanged.

At the time of the Ulster lords' surrender two favours were granted by Henry VIII that directly affected Newry. In a petition to the king, Sir Art Magennis requested 'that the cell of Newry as yet unsuppressed should be converted to a college of secular priests'. The second favour was asked by Conn Bacach O'Neill and it was that Henry pardon Conn's friend, Nicholas Bagenal, of the crimes he had committed in England.

The effect of the first favour on the abbey was that legally it was no longer a monastery but instead a college or seminary. The abbot, John Prowte, was to be warden of the college and the remaining monks became vicars choral. Just how many monks there were at this time is difficult to say. A later document mentions only four vicars and it may have been that the number of monks had fallen to this level. For its endowment the college was to have the entire revenue of the abbey minus 4 marks (£1.68) annually to be paid to the Crown. On the face of it, this must have seemed like the end of the abbey of Newry. However, Art Magennis had made his request so that the abbey would not fall under the scrutiny of royal officials or zealous Protestants seeking to dissolve it, as was happening throughout Ireland. The securing of Henry's favour was a ruse whereby the abbey could continue as a religious house while ostensibly being a college.

The subject of the favour requested by Conn Bacach O'Neill, Nicholas Bagenal, was to have a lasting influence on Newry and was to play an important role in the history of Ireland. Few details of his earlier life are known and even his time in Ireland before his settlement at Newry is clouded in obscurity. It is known that Bagenal came to Ireland in 1539 to escape prosecution and served for a time with the Crown forces. At some point Bagenal moved north and became involved with Conn Bacach O'Neill. It is probable that he acted as some kind of military adviser, or mercenary, to O'Neill. One may even speculate further and say that Bagenal may have been instrumental in persuading O'Neill to accept the policy of surrender and regrant. Whatever service he rendered, Bagenal gained the friendship of Conn Bacach O'Neill, and the gratitude of the English Crown, as his subsequent career shows.

Shortly after the acts of submission in London, the council in Ireland petitioned the king:

> Whereas at the repaire of the Erle of Tyrone into these parts he made humble and earnest suit unto us to bemean to your Majesty for the pardon of Nicholas Bagnalde, late your highness' servant, who by chance (as the thing is declared to us), was in company of certain lyght persones, wher ther was slayne one of your Majesty's subjects, for the whyche the sayde Nycholas hither fledde and hath sythens doon here very honest and payneful service. And therefore at the humble suete of the sayde Erle, we moste lowely beseche your Majesty to be so good and gracious lorde unto him as to grant him your most gracious pardon.

The petition was successful, for we find among the court records the king's reply: 'And of our especial grace at your like sutes and the sute of our cousin, the Erle of Tyrone, have also pardoned Nicholas Bagnal, not doubting but he will hereafter use himself as apperteyneth.' Following this pardon, Bagenal continued in Ireland and used his reputation and influence with the governors of the country to find service in the army. By the time of Henry Vlll's death in 1547 he had risen to be marshal of the king's army.

While Bagenal's career was progressing thus, the Reformation was beginning to be felt in Newry. Magennis's ruse succeeded in saving the abbey for a time but it could not succeed for ever. By 1550 the pressure on the abbot and monks was such that they had no choice but to dissolve the house. Abbot John Prowte pre-empted forced enclosure by voluntarily surrendering the abbey and its lands to the Crown. On 21 May 1550 the Chancery Rolls record the surrender by the abbot—warden, John Prowte, and the vicars choral, Art M'Gillebury, Donal M'Gillebury and Eneas O'Sheyll, of the 'College of Nivorie with the site, circuit, precincts, possessions, deeds, evidences, writings, and muniments'. As compensation for their surrender the abbot—warden received £15 and the monks received £2. each. After four centuries of existence, the long and proud history of the abbey had come to an end.

Following the surrender, two inquisitions into the abbey were conducted in August 1550. From these we know that the one-acre site of the abbey contained a church with a steeple, a chapter house, a dormitory, a hall, an orchard and a garden. The lands of the abbey consisted of forty-eight carucates (approximately 5,500 acres), with seventy-two messuages and cottages, two salmon weirs on the Clanrye and a water mill. The customs of Newry market also belonged to the abbey.

The inquisitions inform us about the precincts of the abbey but they also tell us of the town itself, since the seventy-two messuages and cottages are none other than the town that had grown up around the abbey and the castles. The town was of considerable size by contemporary Irish standards and the population must have been numbered in hundreds. We have some idea of its appearance as a messuage usually was a large type of house with more than one storey, while the cottage was the smaller single-storey building. The town, therefore, must have been a collection of houses of different sizes stretching along the ridge of the hill from the abbey to the castles at the river crossing.

The nature of warfare during the Tudor era was such that it tended to be sporadic and non-territorial. The Gaelic Irish did not attempt to secure domination through occupation. They sought to secure or dominate an area through their ability to threaten it with raids rather than by garrisoning it. They conducted war by robbing their enemies of provisions and 'slighting' their strongholds. So Newry was in little danger of being destroyed or occupied by the Irish and it should not surprise us that the town had grown in the face of the continual warfare in this part of Ireland and the uncertain nature of the English occupation, although it may seem strange that a native Irish monastery should survive alongside an English garrison. But it was probably also the case that the sanctity of the abbey did as much as the ferocity of the garrison to keep Newry safe. The town existed because it fulfilled a need. Many of the occupants of the messuages and cottages would have been tenants or servants of the abbey, and others depended on the garrison for their livelihood. Craftsmen and merchants would also have found a living, the latter by exporting livestock and hides and importing foreign or manufactured goods. The Irish warriors who attacked English incursions into their own traditional territories were the same Irish cattlemen who brought their livestock to the market to trade for imported goods and, no doubt, for weapons. Some of these Irish would also have been employed as servants or soldiers with the garrison. It is not unlikely that an Irish soldier might have been employed in the garrison in one campaigning season, and would then fight against it under his own Gaelic lord in another.

Edward VI, Henry VII's successor, intended to set down a trustworthy tenant at the abbey and its lands. Nicholas Bagenal, who already had knowledge of political conditions in the area and was settled in the town of Newry, was an obvious candidate for the tenancy. Consequently, in July 1550 the decision was made to grant Bagenal 'The Newerye' for a period of twenty-one years. The following November a document to this effect was drawn up, stating briefly that he was to occupy and possess the abbey, its lands and all civil authority previously enjoyed by the monks. The rent was set at £30 11s.8d. (£30.57). The document outlines the reasons for choosing Bagenal. It states that the abbey had been

Gaelic nobleman with Irish sword and long dagger. This style of dress prevailed until the Tudor period.

> set in a remote part far from civil order, and from its situation a place suitable for the service of the king to plant a captain with furniture of men for the reduction of those rude and savage quarters to better rule and obedience. . . for as much as the said Nicholas went there to reside amongst savages and wild people, and sithen his going thither hath been at great costs and charges, and that in all likelihood through his occasion and honest proceedings the inhabitants of those parts will the sooner incline to civillity and obedience to the king, and for that it appeareth by the survey that many of the townlands belonging to the late College be unmanured and under pasture for cattell, that there is no tithe of corne, and by reason of war clerely waste without manurance, or pasturing of cattell, and in those parts the landlords cannot procure tenants without giving great rewards, and commonly all such as become tenants are followers to one or other already, which customably will not depart from them.

Bagenal wanted to hold Newry for the duration of his own life and that of his descendants. He had long ago given up any idea of returning to England and had set his mind on securing a fortune and a patrimony in Ireland. The town of Newry and the territories of the former abbey were to provide that patrimony. To this end he used his influence among the members of the council of Ireland so that he would be granted the old abbey's lands for life. He succeeded when Edward VI issued a patent granting Newry and the associated lands as a fief to Bagenal for the fourth part of a knight's fee. Unlike the earlier contract, this patent sets out in more detail the town and lands that Bagenal was to hold. He was granted the rights held by the former abbey and permission

> to hold courtsleet [manor court where the lord or seneschal sat as judge] and view of frankpledge [review of collective tenant responsibility for payment of tithes], and all things which to view of frankpledge, appertain, assize and assage of bread, wine, and beer, tolls, customs, wrecks of the sea, chattels, waifs, estrays, chattels of felons and fugitives, felons of themselves outlawed and put in exigent.

Apart from the land, the patent also lists

> a weir and salmon fishery on the Glanry, another weir and fishery on the Glanry, the customs and tolls of the market held at the Newrie on every Thursday, a custom of six gallons of wine out of every butt of sack brought to the town for sale, three gallons and a half out of every hogshead, three gallons out of every barrel of beer, fourpence for each barrel of salt, the advowson and nomination of the vicars of the parish of Newrie, the titles of the parish and of several lands in the county Down, the walls of a chapel, and 80 riggs of land in Ean, near Carlingford, in the county of Louth, the tithes of Irish grange in Cooley, and of Newtown, the manor of Carlingford, an ancient castle, and a house called the Constable's house, the custome of herrings called 'Castlemeyse' out of every fishing boat, and the anchorage every bark or ship, the lordships and castles of Mourne and Greencastle, the entire house and site of the friar preachers called the Black Friars of Carlingford.

Nicholas Bagenal entered his lordship determined to make it prosperous and strong. He encouraged the growth of trade and the improvement of farming. He also began to extend his influence over his neighbouring lords, the Gaelic chiefs and kings, and was soon using force to drive them from the frontiers of his own domain. Even his friend and patron, Conn Bacach O'Neill, suffered at the hands of Bagenal's soldiers, who entered his territory and stole his cattle. Soon the Gaelic nobles were invoking their new liege lord and protector, the English king, Edward VI, to protect them from the incursions of the marshal. All this, however, was part of the Government's strategy to bring the Gaelic Irish into line with the English, and their petitions only resulted in them being forced to renew their loyalty and again pledge submission to the Crown if they expected to be left in peace.

The death of Edward VI in 1553, the troubled reign of Mary, and Elizabeth I's accession to the throne in 1558 were not to affect Ireland as much as the death of Conn Bacach O'Neill in 1559 and the succession of his son Shane to the headship of the O'Neills. From the outset Shane disdained the use of the title 'Earl of Tyrone' and instead styled himself 'the O'Neill Mór' (the Great O'Neill). He was not the chosen heir to Conn, who, according to Conn's patent, should have been Hugh, the Baron of Dungannon, the son of Conn's eldest son Matthew. However, Hugh, the 'English' heir, was rejected and Shane was elected according to Gaelic law. Even within the English system, Hugh ought not to have succeeded to the title, as Shane O'Neill was to argue with Elizabeth I herself. He said:

> For I as the true and legitimate son of Con, born of his lawful wife, have entered upon my father's estate. Matthew was the son of a blacksmith of Dundalk, not true born, but born after Con's marriage with his wife Alison and craftily passed off on Con by the mother as his son, so as to cheat me of the possessions and title of O'Neil.

Whatever the truth of this claim, Shane was the recognised O'Neill and soon openly claimed to be the king of Ulster. It was only a question of time before open war followed. He was an enemy such as the Tudors had never met in Ireland. Tudor determination to subdue all of Ireland was matched by his determination to resist. He marshalled all available forces to fight the Government and never let up the pressure on the English stronghold in Ulster - Newry. He dealt ruthlessly with any opposition to his over-lordship, whether among the Gaelic nobles within his territory or the increasingly powerful Scots to the north-east.

Romanticised portrait of Shane O'Neill (Linen Hall Library)

When subsequent negotiations failed, the lord deputy, the Earl of Sussex, led an expedition against Shane in July 1561. It was met by Shane's forces and defeated, the deputy retreating to Newry.

In September Sussex took a larger force against O'Neill and this time O'Neill refused to do battle. So, unopposed, the English drove five hundred cattle off to Newry. Still this did not subdue O'Neill. He refused to give up his claims and, according to Constantia Maxwell, in *The Foundations of Modern Ireland* (1921), it was said of him at the time that 'he pretended to be king of Ulster even as he said his ancestors were, and affecting the manner of the Great Turk, was continually guarded with 600 armed men, as it were his Janissaries about him, and had in readiness to bring into the field 1,000 horsemen, and 4,400 footmen'. When Shane went to London to meet Elizabeth I, he took his bodyguard with him, 'an escort of gallowglass, armed with battle-axes, bare-headed, with flowing curls, yellow shirts dyed with saffron. . . large sleeves, short tunics and rough cloaks, whom the English followed with as much wonderment as if they had come from China or America'. Unlike his father, Shane had not come to submit but to meet as one sovereign with another. The queen had decided that a protracted war in Ulster would be costly, and besides, England also had problems in its relations with Scotland and Spain to deal with, and so she agreed to negotiate. As a result Shane returned to Ireland 'with honour' and a de facto recognition of himself as the O'Neill while the queen promised that Conn's patent from Henry VIII would be reviewed. In effect Shane was left in virtually unquestioned supremacy in Ulster. A large garrison was placed in Newry which made forays into his country with little reward, while negotiations were conducted sporadically in order to achieve a settlement. The loser in all this was Nicholas Bagenal, who was removed from his office as marshal, perhaps as part of a deal with Shane.

On 21 April 1562 Bagenal complained to Secretary of State Lord Cecil that while he was marshal he had raised the value of his lands to an annual income of £1,000 and had kept the peace, and now he was stripped of office and his lands utterly wasted because of O'Neill. In what may have been a move to exert moral pressure, he offered to exchange the lands for an estate in England, if he was no longer wanted in Ireland. If his intention had been to pressurise the Government into restoring his rank and office, he was disappointed, for it was proposed that

> a marshal President, Justice and Council is to be placed in Ulster, for the governing of those parts and where Sir Nicholas Bagnal seeketh to exchange Carlingford, Newry and other of his possessions there with the Queen's Majesty for lands in England, it shall be good if that exchange take place to appoint these possessions to the use of the President.

It was then decided that an administrative change on this scale could not be implemented and so Nicholas Bagenal remained in possession of his Irish territories but still without the office of marshal.

Gallowglass (*gallóglach*) soldiers from Scotland formed the core of Irish armies from medieval times and enabled the O'Neills to hold out in Ulster.

While the English held Newry, O'Neill held the surrounding countryside. In 1563 he erected a castle at Fathom (said to be from the Irish Fiodha-Dun, the 'forest castle'), two miles south of Newry, and so cut off the land route to the town. By this stage the English seemed to have given up all hope of defeating O'Neill. Renewed negotiations dragged on but nothing came of them. By 1566 O'Neill was so strong that he was able to occupy Newry and expel the garrison there and also the one at Dundrum Castle. No attempt was made to recapture either stronghold and Bagenal was left an exile from his lordship. After this, O'Neill started a campaign to secure complete dominance in Ulster — although he claimed to be acting on the queen's behalf when attacking the Scots in County Antrim. The queen's government could not allow this situation to continue for ever, and it was only a matter of time before forces were mustered to subdue O'Neill. In October 1565 Nicholas Bagenal was restored to the office of marshal, an indication that the English were preparing to move against Shane. However, they did not act quickly enough for Bagenal; he wrote a letter to the Earl of Leicester in February 1566 complaining that the country had never been so reduced before and that while O'Neill 'had now all the countries from Sligo to Carrickfergus, and thence to Carlingford and from Carlingford to Drogheda', robbery, murder and theft were being committed throughout the Pale itself.

In his memoirs Lord Deputy Sir Henry Sidney notes:

So hopeless was the prospect of settling an English Colony in Ulster, even so far south as Carlingford, during the aggressive supremacy of Shane O'Neill, that Sir Nicholas Bagnal made proposals in the year 1562. for exchanging his Irish estates for lands in England and in

March 1565 (6) he actually sold them, together with the office of marshal, for the sum of £3,000.00 to the adventurer, Thomas Stukely, who was employed at the time to negotiate peace with O'Neill.

Bagenal may have begun negotiations to sell his estates and title to Stukely but a deal was never concluded and very shortly afterwards events in Ulster took a dramatic turn. In the summer of 1566 the Irish withdrew from Newry and the way was open for its reoccupation by Nicholas Bagenal. Shane O'Neill had attempted to extend his territory to the south but was severely defeated north of Dundalk in County Louth. His dominance in Ulster had been based not on loyalty or mutual interest but on fear and power, and his defeat led to the break-up of this hegemony. Old enemies took the opportunity to rebel and the Government could again seriously consider the occupation of Ulster. By 1567 Shane was forced to seek an alliance with the Scots under the MacDonnells of Antrim. He met with the Scots at Cushendun, accompanied by an escort of five men, 'but God blinded the eyes of Onelle that he doubted not the myschefe the Skots ment to him. Allysander Oge insteede of swyte woordes cout his throte with a skeyne and the [five] that was wyth hyme went not backe to tell no tales.' So an English official reported at the time.

The death of Shane in 1567 did not mean the defeat of the Gaelic order. The successor by primogeniture, the 'English' O'Neill, was still excluded from Tír Eóghain and Shane's Tanist, or chosen successor, Turlough Luineach, became the O'Neill. However, it did mean an end to open war, and peace - or as near to it as Ireland ever enjoyed - prevailed. Bagenal was once again secure in his possessions. He lived with his wife, a daughter of Edward Griffith of Penrhyn in Wales, in the former abbey building, which he castellated for its defence. He still regarded himself as the enemy of the Irish and when Turlough Luineach sought to marry his sister-in-law, probably to form a political alliance, Bagenal refused outright. Despite the consequent trouble with Turlough Luineach and the continuing disturbances, the Bagenal estates flourished. In 1567 Sir Henry Sidney was appointed lord deputy and visited Newry, of which he said:

> I found soche good pollecye and order in the countries where the Marshall dwelleth, his landes so well manured, his Tenants so cherished and maintained, the town so well planted with inhabitants, and increased in bewtye and buylding, as he is much to be commended as well, that he useth his tenants to lyve so welthilye under hym, as his owne bountie and large hospitalitie and housekeepinge so able and willing to give enterteinment to so maney and chiefely to all those that have occasion to travel to or froe northwardes his house lyeing in the open highway to their passage.

Sir Henry often came to Newry to meet with Turlough Luineach, as the question of who was to be the Earl of Tyrone was still unsettled.

We are fortunate in having a map of Newry that survives from this period. It was drawn about 1570 by an unknown cartographer and it gives us a good picture of the town. Each building is carefully drawn in detail, including the tree beside the church from which the bell hung that summoned the congregation. A number of the houses would appear to be of native Irish beehive construction, and are similar in appearance to many of the buildings still to be seen at the pre-Norman Irish monastery in Glendalough in County Wicklow. It would be tempting to suppose that the Irish houses were survivors from a much earlier time but it is more likely that those Irish who settled in Newry — whether drawn to the monastery or the castle — built these houses in the traditional manner. Newry is shown as a collection of houses clustered around the abbey, along the top of the hill, corresponding approximately to the present road running in front of the abbey towards North Street. In general appearance and in the number of houses it does not differ greatly from the description in the inquisitions some twenty years previously. The abbot's house can clearly be seen as a converted structure marked as 'the new castell'; nearby is a little orchard and the church, and the houses running between the two clearly form a street. Around this part of the town was a wall built for defence, with platforms for artillery at each corner. Little now remains of the wall, although a 'town ditch' was sometimes referred to in the eighteenth century. There are two gates in this wall, the North and the South.

North of this walled section, marked 'the Towne of the Newrye', is another enclosed area of similar dimensions. It is marked as 'a place for the cattell by nyghte'. Within this area, leading from the North Gate of the town proper, is a street of about thirty-five buildings - some quite large - called 'the Bayse Town'. Beyond this area are what might be called the suburbs: a street of houses — many of them of the beehive type — marked 'the way to Evaighe' and a smaller street at approximately forty-five degrees to this on 'the way to Tyron'.

Coming down from the North Gate to the river is 'the Fourde'; significantly, there is no castle or bridge here and presumably both were destroyed during an earlier epoch. We can assume that the tower beside the North Gate was originally a castle, now part of the town's walls, and the need for any other castle on or near the river was superseded by the walls, which effectively made it a fortress dominating the river. Going south from 'the Fourde', we find three boats on the river and the words, 'Into this place maye come a bark or a goye of tenne or twelfe tonne at a sprynge tyde'. This is evidence that ships came to Newry and an indication that trade was conducted there.

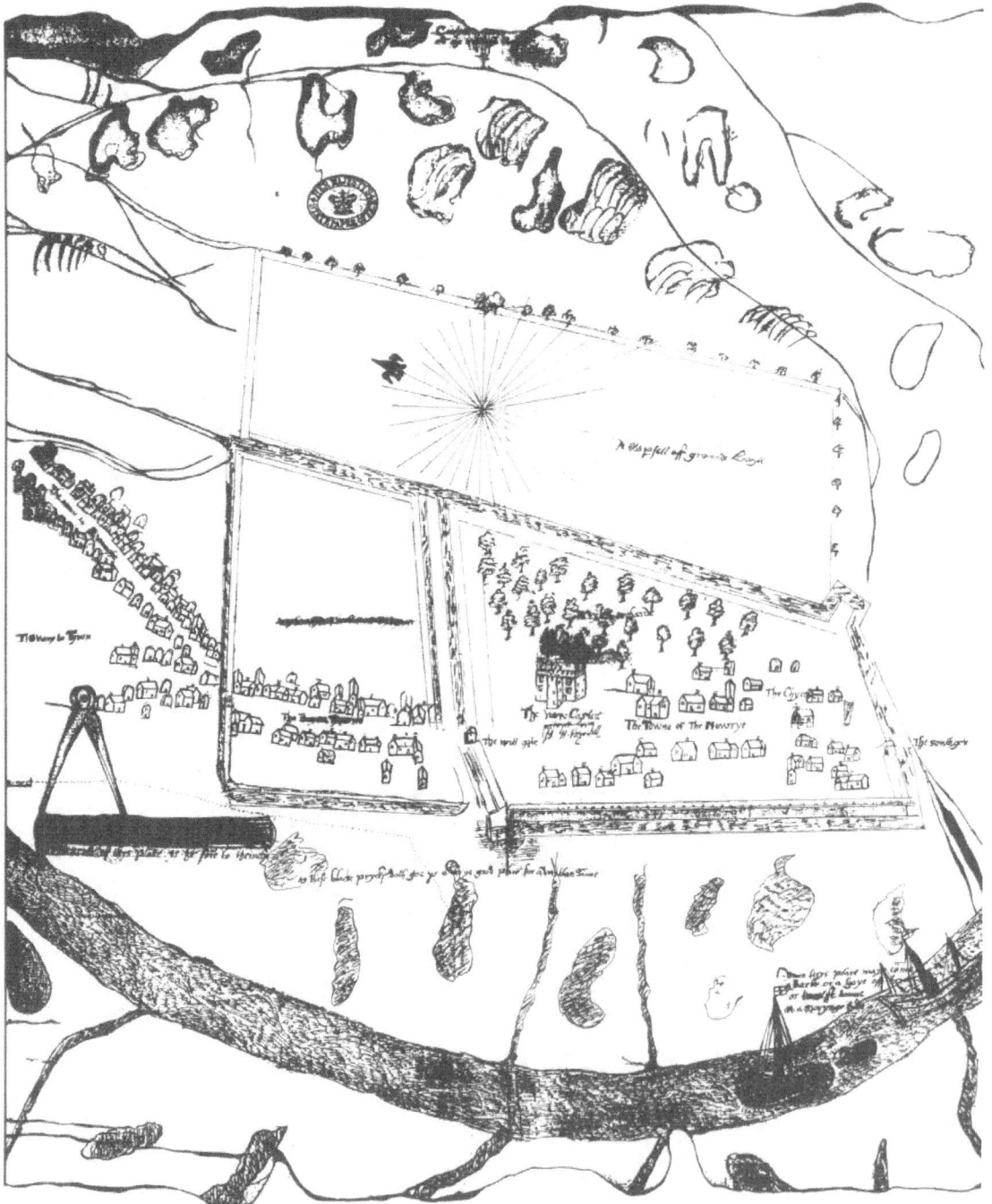

Earliest known map of Newry, c.1570. (Public Record Office of Northern Ireland

From its relationship to the other features marked on the map this place would seem to correspond more or less to the spot where the quay was built on the river in the eighteenth century and where a gasworks was to be erected in the early nineteenth century and where boats discharged their cargo until it was superseded by the ship canal in the nineteenth century.

The map indicates that despite the centuries of warfare and its recent occupation by the Irish, Newry had not only survived but had continued to grow. On his return Bagenal seems to have found the town little changed. We get an insight into Newry, and into Bagenal, in a series of proposals regarding the town that he submitted to Elizabeth I about 1570. This 'Declaration how and in what manner the Towne of the Newrie, in the Realme Irelande, may be fortified by the Queen's Majestie without her Highness' chardge by the Trayvell of Sir Nicholas Bagnal, her Highness' Marshal of Ireland, to the advancement and establishment of the peasible government of the North parts of this realme' begins by relating how Sir Nicholas had erected castles at Newry, and at Carlingford, in order to put pressure on the neighbouring Irish 'to use and govern themselves in farre more quiet and orderly sort'. The town itself has been 'trentched and fortified with a rampire of earth' but would be walled with stone so that 'merchants and others of good Habillities might persuade theyselfs to lyve there in good saefty with there shipps and goods'. Sir Nicholas's proposal was to

> wall the said Towne with stone, hable and suffcent to defend th' ennymie, and to bylde two or three churches, a jayle, a court-house for the assemblie of the people and the keeping of Lawe days, and a stone bridge over the Ryver, which by eastymacion will be ten or eleven arches, the accomplishment of which works will stand him by all judgement in £40,000 at the least.

In return for doing so much for the town, and thereby for the queen, Sir Nicholas sought certain rights and privileges. The first was that this territory could receive all criminals except those guilty of serious offences, such as treason or murder, and also 'suche persons as be broken or shall breake, cauled Banckerupts'. To request such a privilege was very much in keeping with the traditions of the abbey and would seem to be an attempt to restate, and so secure, the exempt jurisdiction within the Tudor system of government.

Bagenal asked a great deal for the town's trading position. First, that Newry should be able to trade with all nations whether at war with the queen or not, as enjoyed by the islands of Guernsey and Jersey. Second, that it should be allowed four hundred soldiers to protect the town while the wall was being erected and that some cannons be supplied for protection. Third, that Newry be incorporated with a licence to hold a market every Thursday — as was already the custom — and two fairs every year, each lasting seven days. Sir Nicholas's last demand was that his son Henry be entered into the office of marshal and that he himself should have an allowance for exercising the duties of a chief commissioner in Ulster, a post he had fulfilled so far without reimbursement. These proposals speak plainly of Nicholas Bagenal's ambition and just what he sought to achieve in Newry. Had he been given his way, Newry would have become a commercial palatinate in the British Isles, and would ultimately have enjoyed considerable wealth and power. However, the Government refused Bagenal's requests, pleading lack of adequate resources to implement the schemes. It may have been that Elizabeth I was unwilling to have a rebellious Gaelic lord in Ulster replaced by an over-haughty English one.

Bagenal did not give up his ambitions, however, and continued to improve the town with his own resources. The town was walled, English settlers were introduced and commerce was encouraged. The jewel was the building of a new church on the hill, not far from the old abbey. This was the Church of St Patrick and was the first newly built Protestant church in Ireland. Bagenal lavished much money on the church and by all accounts in its day it was a splendid building, finely furnished and with impressive carvings on the stonework. His hope was that it would become the cathedral for the diocese, but this was not to be. A church still stands on the original site.

Newry as an abbey and monastic settlement no longer existed, but this church symbolised the beginning of the new Newry; a fiefdom of the Bagenal family where trade and commerce were to be the basis of the town's existence. By an act of an Irish king in 1157 the abbey had acquired great importance and the foundation was laid for its growth; four centuries later the act of an English king dissolved the abbey but laid the foundation for Newry's growth as a town. Always on the frontier between Gaelic and English influence, Newry had not only survived but had flourished. It became a hybrid of both influences, symbolised by the English garrison and the Gaelicised abbey existing side by side. Newry was now firmly under the control of Nicholas Bagenal but it still remained on the frontier and was to be on the front line in the warfare that dominated the next hundred years.

3

THE FRONTIER TOWN

Sir Nicholas Bagenal died in October 1590, content in the knowledge that he had achieved much of what he wanted. Fleeing to Ireland as a fugitive some half a century before, he had succeeded in becoming marshal of the royal army in Ireland, possessing a huge estate and claiming for himself sole authority within his domain. He was in royal favour, his enemies, the Irish lords, were defeated, and he was able to pass all this on to his son Henry. By a royal favour granted in 1583, Henry was to succeed his father as marshal of Ireland, with 6s.8d (33 ½p) per day to himself, 12d. (5p) for a trumpeter and 9d. (4p) each to an escort of thirty horsemen. He also inherited the rights and privileges of the old abbey and could look forward to peace and prosperity in his lordships of Newry and Mourne.

The previous two decades had been good for the Bagenals. The death of Shane O'Neill was followed by a time of peace, and even the most troublesome Irish lords, including the new O'Neill Mór, Turlough Luineach, came under submission to the Crown. It seemed as though Gaelic resistance to the Tudor expansion was over and that every Gaelic lord would, like Sir Hugh Magennis in 1583, accept surrender and regrant 'to hold after the English manner for his and his heirs male'. The English supremacy was such that when Lord Deputy Perrot visited Ulster in August 1584, he entrusted the government of the province not only to Nicholas Bagenal but also to Turlough Luineach and Hugh O'Neill, Baron of Dungannon, Matthew's heir. The following year parliament met in Dublin, and County Down was represented by Bagenal and 'the civilest of all the Irishry', Sir Hugh Magennis. This parliament formally recognised Hugh O'Neill as the Earl of Tyrone and so he took his place as an Irish peer. It seemed that the O'Neills had finally been brought within the English system.

Newry had continued to grow under Nicholas and his son; the town was built up, and merchants and tradesmen were brought over from England to encourage the growth of industry and commerce. The town was beginning to be recognised as a port and ships docked at the quay on the river. The neighbouring countryside boasted farms, orchards and mills, and trade was conducted with the interior of Ulster. Politically, the future also looked good. There was no obvious 'Irish' successor to Turlough Luineach as the O'Neill Mór from among the ranks of the O'Neills in Ulster. After Turlough Luineach, the principal O'Neill was Hugh, who despite publicly voiced doubts about his parentage, was recognised as the legitimate 'English' heir to the earldom of Tyrone.

Hugh had been raised in England and was well acquainted with English customs and manners. He was far removed from the Gaelic lords, and his acceptance of the style and title Earl of Tyrone showed that he accepted the English system of inheritance and government. He sat in the parliament in Dublin and had served in the field against the Irish rebels in Munster. Indeed Hugh seemed so English that he earned for himself the name 'the Queen's O'Neill'. Neither Elizabeth I nor the Bagenals could have realised that this O'Neill was to be the greatest opponent that English rule in Ireland was yet to encounter.

From his stronghold in Newry Sir Henry Bagenal watched the rise of Hugh with resentment and anger. Sir Henry regarded the wars in Ulster between the English and the Irish as a private struggle between the Bagenals and the O'Neills. It galled him that a member of the O'Neill family should be accepted by the queen, recognised an earl, and be given possession of those lands where for generations the O'Neills had conducted war against the English. Matters were made worse when romance appeared on the scene. The youngest of Nicholas Bagenal's children was Mabel. By all accounts she was a beautiful woman and Hugh, who was a widower, fell in love with her. He succeeded in winning Mabel's heart, and despite the difference in ages — Mabel was sixteen and Hugh in his mid-forties - she agreed to marry him. For obvious reasons Sir Henry had been kept in ignorance of the relationship, and when he found out about it, he had Mabel removed and lodged with a friend, Sir Patrick Barnwell, near Dublin.

Hugh O'Neill was not to be put off so easily and he followed Mabel to Dublin, where he called on Sir Patrick Barnwell as a friend, for, as might be expected, the Queen's O'Neill had many friends among the

English of the Pale. Another English gentleman, William Warner, had accompanied O'Neill in his pursuit of Mabel, and it was he who carried the lady off to Drumcondra. O'Neill's high standing among the English is further demonstrated in that it was Thomas Jones, bishop of Meath and favourite of Elizabeth I, who married Hugh and Mabel at Drumcondra on 3 August 1591. After their marriage, O'Neill returned with his wife to his own residence at Dungannon in County Tyrone. The marriage led to a falling out between Mabel and her brother Henry. At first he refused to accept that she loved O'Neill and then he tried to prove the marriage invalid. When neither the Government nor the law officers could find any legal impediment, Sir Henry refused to pay the dowry, which had been set at £1,000, and later, it was one of O'Neill's chief demands of the Government to force Sir Henry to pay it. This tale of love amid family hate and war has a sad ending, for within a few years Mabel died. The cause of her death while still so young is not known with certainty, but she died a Catholic, and unreconciled with her family. Of her marriage to Hugh O'Neill, Henry had declared: 'I cannot but accurse myself and fortune that my bloude, which in my father and myselfe had often been spilled in repressing this rebellious race, should now be mingled with so traitorous a stocke and kindred.'

However, Henry could not allow his personal feelings to interfere with his duties as marshal. So it was that in 1593 he and Hugh O'Neill were joint leaders of an expedition against Hugh Maguire, the Gaelic leader in Fermanagh who had harboured the Catholic primate, Edmund MacGaron, and had gone to war against the queen in Connacht. Afterwards O'Neill was to complain that while he took decisive action against Maguire and was even wounded in the campaign, it was Henry Bagenal who received the credit and the reward. The grievance felt by O'Neill on this occasion was yet another factor that pushed him nearer to open rebellion. Despite his English education and his use of the title Earl of Tyrone, O'Neill was at heart a Gaelic prince. He was later to declare that he would rather be an O'Neill in Ulster than a Philip (the king) in Spain. His acceptance of the English earldom came from a belief that he could reach a compromise with the English government in Ireland. He believed that if he did not threaten the balance of power in Ulster, if he demonstrated an unquestioning loyalty to the queen, even to the extent of going to war against other Gaelic lords on her behalf, and if he used the English style and title, then he would be left to rule his own country as he wished, a Gaelic prince in all but name.

However, it was not in the nature of Tudor government to tolerate autonomies. All over Ireland the Gaelic system was being worn down and independent lords, whether Gaelic or Hiberno-Norman - Old English -were being forced to submit to the queen's writ. In O'Neill's country, too, there was increasing interference by the officers of the Dublin government. The execution of Brian MacHugh Roe MacMahon of Monaghan showed that even a Gaelic lord loyal to the queen would be sacrificed in the interests of her government. O'Neill's opposition to the encroachments on his autonomy became more hostile and open conflict had to follow. In 1595 his actions led to him formally being declared a traitor. It is said that it was largely at the instigation of Sir Henry Bagenal that the Government took this step. The story is told that O'Neill issued a formal challenge of a duel to Bagenal, but the latter declined, preferring to stay behind the walls of Newry. Cowardice has been impugned to Bagenal over this episode, but whatever his reason for declining to face O'Neill in a duel, his subsequent career showed that Bagenal was no coward.

In the autumn of 1595 the O'Neill Mór, Turlough Luineach, died. Hugh renounced his English title and was formally inaugurated as the O'Neill Mór at Tullahoge in County Tyrone, where the O'Neill kings of Ulster and high-kings of Ireland had been inaugurated for centuries. Open war followed, which was to be the longest and most hard-fought campaign between the Gaelic Irish and the English. O'Neill succeeded in forming a confederation of Gaelic and Hiberno-Norman lords to fight against the English rule. Although he had appeared indifferent to religion for most of his life - his marriage to Mabel had been a Protestant one - he now stood forth not only as the champion of ancient liberties but also of the Catholic faith. This provided a common cause among the Irish of different ancestry and enabled Hugh to negotiate with Spain for help, and throughout the nine years of war it was the expectation of the landing of a Spanish army that gave heart to the Irish and struck fear into the English.

On the English side Sir Henry Bagenal was the key commander in the field and his town, Newry, was to be the centre of operations for the English army. This was largely a war of manoeuvre and ambush with few large-scale battles and an ill-defined frontier between the opposing sides. In so far as there was a frontier in Ulster, Newry was on it, and to hold Newry was the key to English strategy.

In Ulster the war generally took the form of the English army, often under the command of Henry Bagenal, marching out from Newry in order to get supplies to a fort or to destroy an Irish stronghold, with the intention of drawing the Irish into open battle. The Irish avoided pitched battle — for most of the war they lacked proper training and suitable weapons — in favour of harassing the queen's army and attacking by ambush. Such tactics, in fact, inflicted greater losses on the English forces than open battle would have and Newry was often the last refuge for a beleaguered expeditionary force. After an expedition to relieve the siege of Monaghan town in 1595, Bagenal's forces were attacked at every opportunity on the way back to Newry and he thought himself lucky to arrive there at all. When Sir John Norris, recently appointed as lord general, led an expedition against Armagh, he found his retreat blocked by the Irish and only with difficulty fought his way through, but, as the Annals tell us, 'the Irish went in pursuit to the gate of Newry'. Even then O'Neill's army burned the mills of Newry and carried off 1,500 head of cattle.

In July 1595 Norris found the Irish prepared to do battle at Clontibret in County Monaghan. The English suffered a severe defeat, and were forced to retreat, 'leaving behind them many men, horses, arms and valuable things', the Irish Annals tell us, as they retreated to the safety of Newry. O'Neill's tactics proved so successful that the Dublin government all but abandoned the overland route to Newry, and in an attempt to secure the sea route, they tried to take over Narrow Water Castle, which belonged to the Magennises, in January 1596. It was held by the widow of one of the Magennis nobles and she was obliged to surrender her son as surety for her neutrality.

As the war was being fought on the ground, it was also being fought at a diplomatic level. With virtually the whole island in open rebellion, to a greater or lesser degree, Elizabeth I thought it wise to come to terms with O'Neill and settle the war as soon as possible. Hugh negotiated with the Dublin government, and also with Spain, in order to get its army to help him establish an independent Gaelic principality. Hugh laid claim to sovereignty within the O'Neill country, but he was prepared to leave Newry in the hands of the Bagenals. In the terms of peace that he sent to the Government in Dublin he specifically stated 'that no garrison, sheriff or other officer should remain in Tyrconnell, Tyrone, or any of the inhabitants' countries before named, excepting the Newry and Carrickfergus'.

In Newry itself conditions grew steadily worse as the forces of O'Neill ranged the countryside and all but isolated the town from contact with Dublin. The situation deteriorated to such an extent that there was a real danger of mutiny among Bagenal's soldiers, as the following report from early in 1598 from an officer in the garrison illustrates: the soldiers were complaining of receiving no wages and

> in the end James Carroll, the paymaster, [was] sent hither from the state with their leadings, the soldiers having the understanding of his entry into the town, a number of them having set themselves in the streets and in certain 'Castles' for the purpose, did so batter him with fury of snowballs, that he fell off from his horse, who they prosecuted nevertheless with that tempest and rage, that if the captains lieutenants and officers had not speedily came in to his rescue, he had died in the place and much ado they had to thrust him into a house, and to save the treasure, neither durst he, whilst he remained in the town about the issuing of the said treasure, once for his life go out of the door, but having delivered it to Mr Marshal in the night, stole away by water.

When it was discovered that there was not enough money to pay the soldiers in full,

> they fell anew into that fury against Mr Marshal himself, that I protest unto your worship, all the pursuassions that not only himself but all the captains whose friends and other could use for him, had much ado to stay them for abandoning the town at the instant.

Whether it was the threat of mutiny in Newry or a renewed determination to end the rebellion, reinforcements and supplies were sent to 'Mr Marshal' Bagenal the following summer. On 9 August 1598 Bagenal marched out of Newry at the head of an army of 3,500 foot and 300 cavalry. His destination was Armagh, which he reached safely with supplies. On 14 August he began the return journey to Newry only to find Hugh O'Neill and his soldiers waiting at a place on the Blackwater river called the Yellow Ford (in Irish, Beal-an-atha-buidhe). The battle that followed was to be the most important of the war.

A large Irish force, probably outnumbering the English by about one thousand, attacked Bagenal's men as they crossed the ford. The ensuing battle lasted most of the day, both sides fighting desperately. At one point the English advance guard broke and retreated. Charles Montague, an English officer, reported: 'Up came the Marshal, being Chief Commander, to relieve them, who was killed dead in the head with a bullet.' Slowly but surely the English force was worn down and its ranks thinned as many fell dead and wounded. Then, 'by the help of our horse, the enemy's munition being well spent, we brought off the rest into the plain and so recovered Armagh, where the captains resolved to refresh their men with victuals and munition, and so march directly to Newry'. Sir Henry's death ended his short tenure of Newry and Mourne and left the area without a lord, as his son Arthur was still a minor. He died fighting the 'rebellious race' he so hated and that he should have died at the hands of his brother-in-law lends irony to his fate. Without someone strong to watch over Newry, it was generally feared that O'Neill would soon seize the town.

For the rest of Ireland, the Battle of the Yellow Ford was seen as the greatest defeat the English had ever suffered at the hands of the Irish. Almost two thousand English soldiers were said to have been lost in the battle. It sent a wave of terror through the queen's subjects and for the first time people really believed that Ireland would be lost to the Gaelic rebels. The government in Dublin sent a pleading letter to the Great O'Neill, saying that the war had been Sir Henry Bagenal's fault and promising to support O'Neill's demands. In fact he never received the letter sent to him by the Government, but Elizabeth I heard of the letter and sent a stinging rebuke to her Irish ministers for not only allowing O'Neill to 'range where else he pleased, but provincial rebels in every province, by such as he can spare enabled to give law to our provincial governors, besides that the Pale is not only wasted, but the walls of Dublin (where our State is seated) esteemed unsafe'. In any case their fears were largely unfounded. Even if O'Neill had wished to follow his victory at the Yellow Ford by seizing the royal garrisons and sweeping into the Pale to capture Dublin, he would have been unable to do so. He lacked the means of keeping an army in the field and he had no artillery with which to threaten even a small castle.

Meanwhile O'Neill returned to his former tactics and once again the garrison at Newry found itself caught off guard and out of supplies. In 1599 Sir Samuel Bagenal, the new governor of the town and a nephew of Henry's, reported to the privy council in Dublin:

> I made one journey into Magennis his country, where I took from him (Tyrone himself being insight) a thousand cows which I brought to the Newry with 60 horses and 120 foot, and these left them to relieve that place which before was so distressed that myself saw some of the soldiers of that garrison (drawn out for that service) fall dead in marching with very poverty and want of victuals.

The situation had not improved much in 1600 when a disaster occurred in the town. Lord Deputy Mountjoy had been in Newry and

> within three days after the Lord Deputy's departure of Saturday the 31st of May the town of Newry was in great part burnt by mischance, as it is said of a woman who was brewing aquae vitae. The fire took hold of her house, and by reason of a great wind burnt many houses thereabouts, to the impoverishing of the poor inhabitants.

It was Lord Mountjoy's policy of destruction that eventually broke O'Neill's rebellion (16th century, after painting by Juan Pantoja)

This is the first reference we have of whiskey, *aqua vitae,* in relation to Newry and shows that excessive intoxication was not the only danger from the 'water of life'.

O'Neill and his allies had the upper hand, and it appeared to be only a matter of time before peace would be agreed on their terms. However, the course of the war had changed with the appointment of Lord Mountjoy as the lord deputy. He was a man of intelligence and tenacity who adopted a strategy that was designed to wear down the Irish and limit their freedom to manoeuvre. From February 1600, the time of his appointment, the war began to turn in England's favour. Initially Mountjoy's operations centred on the Moyry Pass. He was determined that the Irish would not dominate the land route to Newry. Despite setbacks and defeat in a battle at the pass, Mountjoy returned to it again and again until he succeeded in erecting a castle there in 1601. This was to be his policy: the erection of castles and forts throughout Ulster in order to hinder the movement of the Irish.

He also conducted a deliberate campaign of spoilation and destruction; crops were systematically destroyed, cattle were driven off and any building that might give shelter to O'Neill's forces was demolished. Like O'Neill, Mountjoy avoided open battle and instead sought to bring the Irish into submission by starving them. From Newry there extended a network of forts that cut across O'Neill's country, and from Newry expeditions set out to lay waste the countryside. Such tactics were repeated throughout Ireland wherever there was rebellion. The hardships brought about by Mountjoy's policy and his skilful exploitation of divisions within the Irish ranks led to the break-up of the alliance that O'Neill had built up. Its cohesion depended on success and with failure came instability. Writing from Newry in August 1601, Mountjoy could report to Dublin:

> The Lords hereabouts, namely Mac Gennis, Tirlogh Mac Henrie, Eiver Mac Cooley, and O'Hanlon keepe with us notwithstanding that Tyrone hath sent them word that hereafter it will be too late for them to make their peace with him, if they doe not now upon this occasion, and they assure us as much as men can doe, that they will not fall againe from their obedience, though thereby their state bee no better than horseboyes. But of this wee can give our Lordships no assurance, neither in them have wee any extraordinarie confidence.

Now more than ever O'Neill needed a Spanish landing if he were not to lose everything, and the long-awaited Spanish army did come — but at the wrong time and to the wrong place. In September 1601 an expeditionary force commanded by Don Juan del Aguila landed in Kinsale in Munster, on the south coast of Ireland, at the opposite end of the country. O'Neill had no choice but to travel down to meet them. He and Hugh O'Donnell of Tyrconnell marched their army across Ireland in a remarkably short length of time to go to the assistance of their allies, now besieged in Kinsale. Along the way they were joined by the Gaelic of Connacht and Munster.

The subsequent battle fought on Christmas Eve 1601, so far away from Newry, decided the fate of the town and of Ireland. For the first time the Irish troops had to fight on a battlefield in regular European fashion. The seasoned soldiers of Lord Mountjoy inflicted a crushing defeat on them, and the Spanish surrendered on terms. O'Donnell took the opportunity to travel to Spain, promising to return at the head of a new expedition, but he died shortly after arriving there. O'Neill and what remained of his army retreated to Ulster, and this was really the end of the war. O'Neill continued to hold on but was simply delaying his inevitable defeat. So confident was Mountjoy of his success that the garrison at Newry was reduced to two hundred infantry and fifty horse, and Irish prisoners were soon being sent there. O'Neill was being held at bay in his final stronghold of Killultagh and was no longer a threat.

As a result of Mountjoy's policy, parts of Ulster were reduced to wasteland. Famine and disease were everywhere, and the ordinary people driven to desperation. The state of the country can be judged in this story related by Mountjoy's secretary, Fynes Moryson:

Captain Trevor, and many honest gentlemen lying in the Newry, can witness that some old women of those parts used to make a fire in the fields and divers little children, driving out the cattel in the cold mornings and coming thither to warme them, were by them surprised, killed and eaten, which at last was discovered by a great girle breaking from them by strength of her body, and Captain Trevor, sending out soldiers to know the truth, they found the children's skulles and bones, and apprehended the old women who were executed for the facts.

According to Moryson, these conditions prevailed because 'of our destroying the rebels' corn and using all means to famish them'.

Newry was also feeling the effects of Mountjoy's campaign. A visitor there shortly before O'Neill's surrender recorded: 'For that town produces nothing but lean beef, and very rarely mutton, very bad wine indeed, nor was there any bread except biscuits even in the house of the Governor.' After nine years of war the whole country was in a pitiable state. Under conditions such as these and following the surrender of his allies, Hugh O'Neill could hold out no longer and on 30 March 1603 he met Mountjoy at Mellifont in County Louth and 'made a most humble submission'. He renounced the title of O'Neill Mór and his pretensions to be a prince in Ulster. He once again took on the title of Earl of Tyrone and swore to be the queen's loyal subject. The irony was that Elizabeth I had died some days earlier and had he only held out for a few weeks more, O'Neill could probably have got favourable terms of surrender from the new king, James VI of Scotland, now James I of England.

This is an English view of negotiations in which O'Neill offers a 'false submission'. (The Hulton Picture Company)

Conscientia mille testes

Tyrones false Submission afterwards rebelling.

The English continued to make incursions into O'Neill's territory and continually accused him of disloyalty to the Crown, and when he was eventually openly charged with plotting a second rebellion, he and a few close companions sailed for Spain on 4 September 1607 — the Flight of the Earls — rather than be arrested and tried for treason. This truly marked the end of the Gaelic order in Ireland. Whatever form Irish resistance to English rule was to take in the future, it could no longer seek to re-establish the Gaelic system or the rule of a Gaelic prince in Ireland.

Newry, of course, had been lost to the Gaelic order some time before this and now found itself a stable haven in the turmoil of Ulster. James I of England had decided that the best way of ensuring that Ulster would not rebel again was to colonise it with Scottish and English settlers. Lands were confiscated and given to these settlers in what is known as the Plantation of Ulster. Much of the land around Newry was affected by the plantation but the lordships of Newry and Mourne, being the Bagenal domain, were exempt from it.

Arthur Bagenal had come of age in 1603. He married Magdalen, a daughter of Governor Sir Richard Trevor, and formally took possession of his inheritance. He spent the following decade rebuilding Newry. The work of his grandfather, Nicholas, had been set back because of the Nine Years War against O'Neill, and now that peace had come, Arthur sought to restore the town, encouraging merchants and tradesmen to settle there. An inquisition in 1612 records that Newry consisted of three hundred buildings, two water mills, two weirs on the river — one for salmon, the other for eels — a weekly market and an annual fair. There was also a jail.

It was considered time for the new king to summon a parliament in his Irish kingdom, where parliament had not met since 1586. James I wanted a pliant parliament that would cause little trouble, and to this end he had to ensure that the Old English — the pre-plantation colonists — and the native Irish would not dominate the assembly. The best way of guaranteeing this was to create a number of new boroughs from which 'reliable' representatives would be sent to Dublin. So it was that on 27 February 1613 Newry received its charter from James I.

After the usual introductory formalities, the charter grandly states:

> The aforesaid Town of Newry, and all and singular the Castles, Messuages, Tofts, Mills, Houses, Edifices, Structures, Curtileges, Orchards, Gardens, Wastes, Farms, Lands, Tenements and Hereditaments whats so ever lying or being in or within the said town of Newry, or within the precincts of the same in the county aforesaid, from hence forth may be and in all future times shall be one entire and free Borough of Newry.

It goes on to lay out the constitution of the borough:

> One Body Corporate and Politic and consisting of one Provost, twelve Free Burgesses and of the Commons, and ... all the inhabitants within the aforesaid town and the lands aforesaid, from hence forth are and shall be forever one Body Corporate and Politic in deed, fact, and name by the name of the Provost, Free Burgesses and Commons.

The crux of the charter states that the borough 'may have the power and authority of electing, sending and returning two disenset and fit men to serve and attend in any Parliament in our said Kingdom of Ireland'. The charter goes on to appoint Anthony Homes as the first provost of the borough and names twelve burgesses who were chosen primarily because of their known loyalty to the Crown.

The charter regulates the meetings of the burgesses, the procedure for appointing a burgess, and similar matters. It also grants to the borough the right to

> hold one court in some fit and convenient place within the Borough aforesaid, to be held before the Provost of the same Borough for the time being, and in the same court to hold pleas on every Monday, from week to week, of all and singular actions, debts, agreements, trespasses, detentions, contracts, and special demands whatsoever not exceeding five marks sterling [£2.01] which may happen or emerge in or within the aforesaid Borough.

The responsibility also lay with the provost, free burgesses and commons to enact regulations and statutes which 'may seem necessary for the good management and safe government of the aforesaid Borough' and to enforce them 'that they may have power and authority by fines and Pecuniary malucts to punish, correct, and chastise any persons transgressing'. Finally, it is laid out in the charter that Newry may have a guild of merchants and that two sergeants-at-mace and any other officers deemed necessary may be appointed to better carry out the business of the borough. Under the auspices of the charter Newry sent Arthur

Bassett and John Leigh to sit in the 1613—15 Irish parliament. Bassett was a captain in the army and Leigh was favourable to the Crown's interests.

About this time — probably shortly before the borough charter - Arthur Bagenal received his own charter, or grant of a patent, from James I. The patent begins by recording that it was granted in consideration of £40 being paid by Bagenal into the Hanaper, a department of the treasury. Bagenal was to have jurisdiction within Newry and in the surrounding districts, which constituted a considerable tract of land, corresponding to the property of the former abbey, in modern-day counties Armagh, Down and Louth, with Newry at the centre. Newry itself was to be a manor with Arthur Bagenal as its lord, on condition that he 'directly possess' one thousand acres of the land, but that he 'may lease out the remainder'. The patent also specifies the officials and officers that the lord of the manor should appoint, such as his seneschal and bailiffs. The town court was to be held before the seneschal, 'with power to hold pleas of all and singular actions and trespasses, covenants, accounts, contracts, detinues, debts, and demands whatsoever, not exceeding the value of 100 marks Irish [£67]'. The lord of the manor could also hold under his jurisdiction a court 'barron' - that is, an assembly of freehold tenants of a manor — every three weeks, and a court 'leet', or 'view of frankpledge', twice a year. Of the bailiffs, the patent says that they

> shall have return and execution of all manner of writs, executions, precepts, warrants, etc, and the summons, attachments and distringuas of the Exchequer returnable either before [the king] or before any of the Justices or Commissioners, so as no sheriff, bailiff, or other minister may enter into the said Manor at any time or by any means to execute, prosecute, or serve any such like writs, precepts warrants etc.

In effect this clause confirms the exempt nature of Bagenal's jurisdiction within his manors of Newry, Mourne and Carlingford, and relate directly to the status previously enjoyed by the abbot. The patent specifically says that Bagenal would have the authority to appoint the rector of Newry and by his vicar-general could grant probates of wills, marriage licences, and transact all business pertaining to an ecclesiastical court. Although not entered into holy orders, Bagenal was to have the rights and privileges of an abbot, hence the term lay-abbot that came to be applied to him and his successors.

The seal of the abbey — the abbot enthroned between two yew trees - became the seal of Arthur Bagenal. To make sure nothing was excluded there is a catch-all clause in the patent which states:

> And we do give grant, bargain and confirm unto the said Arthur Bagnal, his heirs and assigns, all and singular and so many and the like court leets, frank pledge, law days, rights, jurisdictions, liberties, privileges. . . in as large, ample and beneficial manner as any Abbot, Prior, or Convent, or other chief head or Governor of the late dissolved monastery heretofore seized, held or enjoyed.

Oliver Cromwell's New Model Army crushed all resistance after his arrival in Ireland in 1649 (painting by Peter Lely, 1653)

These privileges, the exempt jurisdiction, survived the troubles and changes of succeeding centuries and the situation remained unchanged until the nineteenth century.

It is interesting to note that the patent includes a provision regarding one Patrick Creely, or Crilly. The patent specifies a rent of £3 6.s. 8d. (£3.33 ½) for a castle and certain lands in the town, to be paid to Arthur Bagenal. This is the first mention we have of another holder of land within the precincts of Newry. It would appear that Creely had built the castle some time during the reign of Elizabeth I and had held it ever since. Later the castle was sold to Thomas Hill, an ancestor of the Marquis of Downshire.

The years 1601 to 1640 were a period of peace but of little prosperity for Ireland, and Newry was no exception. It was still largely a garrison town centred around the abbey, now the Bagenals' castle, and was important as a place of commerce through markets and fairs rather than as a port. In 1635 Sir William Brereton, an English gentleman who was making a tour through Ireland, and was not favourably impressed by it, left this description of his visit to Newry:

> July 7th wee left Dromore and went to the Newrie, which is sixteen miles. This is a most difficult way for a stranger to find out. Herein wee wandered and being lost, fell amongst the Irish townes. The Irish houses are the poorest cabins I have seen, erected in the middle of the fields and ground which they farm and rent. This is a wild countrie, nott inhabited, planted nor inclosed yett it would see corn if it was husbanded. I gave an Irishman, to bring us into the way, a groate, who led us, like a villain, directly out of the way, and soe left us, soe as by this devitation it was 3 hours before we came to the Newrie. Much

land there is about this towne, belonging to Mr Bagnal, nothing well planted. Hee hath a castle in this towne, but is for the most part resident at Green Castle. A great part of this towne is his, and it is reported he hath £1000 or £1500 per annum in the countrie. This is but a poore town, and is much Irish, and is navigable for boates to come up with the tiede. Here wee hailed at a good inn, the signe of the Princess's Arms.

Charles I acceded to the throne in March 1625. From the outset his reign was marked by trouble and dissent. Discontent and opposition to his government increased steadily and even led to open war with his Scottish subjects. During this time Ireland was quiet but not peaceful. Grievance was never far from the surface as the issues of land and religion caused fear and hatred, fragmenting the country between Catholic and Protestant, between those for and those against the king. Sir Thomas Wentworth, Charles I's lord deputy in Ireland, had overhauled the royal government in the country, creating widespread resentment. The measures had brought the country closer to open rebellion and Wentworth's successors could not contain the problem. The 1630s closed with the government of Ireland in a fragile state, and Charles I's position in relation to all his kingdoms becoming more precarious.

Rebellion came on 23 September 1641, when the remnants of the old Gaelic order in Ulster attempted to reclaim the province for themselves. On the first day of the rebellion Newry was taken for the rebels by Sir Con Magennis. This rebellion soon became merged in the wider conflict of the English Civil War. In England the conflict took on the character of a struggle between the king and parliament, but in Ireland the situation was more complex. Although most of the Irish were ostensibly united in the Confederation of Kilkenny, they were divided into two factions, sometimes at odds with each other; those, mainly of Gaelic stock, who sought to establish an independent Ireland; and those, mainly of Old English stock, who sought to defend their Catholicism and the king. The Ulster-Scots plantation settlers fought to defend their Protestantism and their land, aided by their allies, soldiers sent over by the Scottish parliament under the command of Major General Robert Monro; at times they were supporters of the king and at times his opponents. After the execution of Charles I in 1649, Oliver Cromwell arrived in Ireland with his army to impose the rule of parliament on all Ireland, irrespective of the religion or loyalties of its people.

Once again Newry found itself on the front line of the battle and as war spread through the whole island the town was fought over by the opposing armies. The English commander of the garrison at Newry, Sir Arthur Terringham, effected an escape from the occupying force but his officers and men were taken prisoner. Among those taken under escort to Newcastle in County Down were Sir Charles Poyntz and his son, a Mr Reading, Lieutenant Hugh Trevor and a Mr Weston. Nicholas Bagenal, who had succeeded his father Arthur, was not in town.

The Irish — that is the Gaelic nobility and its followers — held a great part of the north of Ireland, with Newry being on the frontier with those parts of County Down being held by the Ulster-Scots and English. Shortly after his occupation of Newry, Sir Con Magennis sent the following message to the English commanders at Downpatrick and Dromore:

> To my loving friends, Captain Vaughan, Marcus Trevor, and other commanders of Down there be. Deare friends — My love to you all, although you think it is yet otherwise. Sure it is, I have broken Sir Edward Trevor's letter, fearing that anything should be written against us. We are for our lives and our liberties, as you may understand out of that letter. We desire no blood to be shed but if you meane to shed our blood, be sure we will be ready as you for the purpose. I rest your assured friend, Connor Magenisse.

The accounts of some of those who were in Newry at the time of the outbreak of rebellion still survive. 'Thomas Richardson, late of Newry in the Countrie of Downe, saylor and English protestant', told how he was 'expelled from the dispoyled of his houses and farmes in Newry. . . and was by the same rebells then robbed of £10.00 in ready money of beasts and cattle'. Richardson tells us that the rebels appointed Michael Carrie - a gentleman and a sub-sheriff of the county - the provost of Newry. The fears aroused by the rebellion are clearly stated in the claim by 'James Verden of the Newry, gent captain of the rebels, who said that the protestants were all blynd for that thousands of years the papists' religion which was true hadd contynued and that it was then in [the papists'] power to bring the protestants to god'. Richardson's account ends with a description of how he and his family were driven from Newry after he was

> pillaged and robbed of his goodes and after that he and his wife and children had gathered or regained some poor clothes as other Poore English had done, the rebells made a proclamacion for all English to depart or suffer perpetual imprisonment. [Richardson] and his wife and five smalle children goeing away were stript of all their clothes and meanes left and flying away for saftie naked in the frost one poore daughter of his seeing him and his mother greeve for their generall misery in way of comforting said she was not cold nor would crye although presently after she died by that cold and want and the first night this deponent and his wife creepeing for shelter into a poor crate were glad to ly upon their children to keepe in them heate and save them a live.

The English in Newry were undoubtedly treated harshly by the common soldiers, although most accounts agree that their officers prevented cruelty when they could. It was made plain to one person, Elizabeth Pearce of Newry, that the Irish saw themselves as taking revenge for their past treatment at the hands of the English and their loss of land to the colonists. She reports that the Irish

> did confidently averr that they and the other Irish soe much hated the English and their very fashions in cloths that they resolved after the

John Speede's 1610 map of Ulster is an invaluable record of the province before the Plantation. Note Newry is drawn as a fortified town belonging to 'Bagnall'.

Irishe had gotten the victory, all the women in Ireland should as formerly goe only in smocks, mantles and brouges as well ladies as others and the English fashions to be quite abolished.

Although there were no executions or any massacre of prisoners in Newry, a number of those who had been sent under escort to Newcastle in County Down were hanged. One report states that 'Mr Tudge, minister of Newry and chaplaine to Sir Arthure Terringham nere Newcastle, and Lieutenant Trevor and his wiffe, one Mr Weston, and others to the number of 24 protestants more' were hanged by George Russel of Rathmullan and one of the Magennises. The reason given for these deaths was 'because some of the papist priests were putt to death in England'. It was shortly after this incident in 1642 that Sir Con Magennis, one of the most able of the rebel leaders, died and on his death bed 'he left directions that noe more protestants from that time should bee slaine but should be killed in battayle'.

About this time the tide of the war in Ulster began to turn. Marching from Drogheda in County Louth, a force of English troops under Sir Henry Tichbourne took Dundalk, driving out the rebel commander-in-chief, Sir Phelim O'Neill, and so isolating Newry to the south. Three weeks later a force of 2,500 Scottish troops landed at Carrickfergus in County Antrim, under the command of General Monro. They had been dispatched by the Scottish parliament to help suppress the rebellion.

Monro was joined by Lord Conway, the marshal of the king's army, with just under two thousand troops and together they marched southwards, dealing harshly with any resistance. On 31 April 1642 the Anglo-Scottish force arrived in Newry to find that the civilians had all but deserted the town and that the garrison had retired to the castle. The town's defences, which had been in disrepair since the defeat of Hugh O'Neill in 1603, were in such a bad state as to be virtually useless. Monro and Conway stationed their troops a short distance away and while this was happening someone rode out to meet them under a flag of truce. It transpired that it was one of the prisoners, Mr Reading, who, according to a contemporary eyewitness report, 'informed them that the people had fled, except some of the ancient town dwellers, and that they willingly gave up the town'. So Colonel Chichester's regiment was sent forward to occupy the town, where, it is said, they ransacked almost every home.

The castle was still in rebel hands. It was not until the second day that Monro called on the garrison to surrender. The Scottish and English were hesitant to make an attack as there were a number of prisoners, including Sir Edward Trevor, in the castle and so they were willing to negotiate. Monro's patience did not last long, for the following morning he approached the castle and threatened to blow it up if the Irish did not surrender at once. The Irish commander gamely replied that if he wanted to blow up the castle, Monro would need to borrow some of the Irish gunpowder. But realising that the situation was hopeless, the castle commander agreed to a surrender on terms. When the besiegers entered, they found that the Irish had only sixty muskets and half a barrel of powder with which to defend the whole place.

Monro stated that he had granted quarter — the right to leave without arms — to the soldiers of the garrison but not to the town. The official report relates that on the day following the surrender of the castle, 'the townsmen were detained until trial should be made of their behaviour. We entered into examination of the townsmen if all were papists, and the indifferent being severed from the bad, whereof 60, with two priests, were shot and hanged, and the indifferent were banished'. An eyewitness from Monro's army reported that

> the town came immediately into our hands, and the rebels in two days, when most of them, with many merchants and tradesmen, of the town, who had not been in the castle, were carried to the bridge, and butchered to death, some by shooting, some by hanging, and some by drowning, without legal process, and several innocent people suffered. Monro could not purge himself of this cruelty, nor can Lord Conway, as Marshal of Ireland, be exempt from his sense of blame.

The killing did not stop there, however, for some of the common soldiers 'stripped about eighteen women naked, and threw them into the water, where they perished by drowning or being shot'. More would have been killed had not an officer, Sir James Turner, intervened. Having thus purged Newry, Monro and Conway proceeded on their march, but not before Conway had conscripted most of the surviving townspeople under his banner. Major Turner and his regiment of Orkney and Caithness men, about three hundred strong, were left as a garrison.

In June a further five hundred soldiers sailed from Carrickfergus in County Antrim. Landing at Carlingford they marched to Newry and so reinforced Major Turner's garrison. Most of Ulster was now held by the Scots and English. Newry was a pivotal point for the English and Scottish forces, as they would have to hold the town if they were to march south to oppose the forces of the Confederation of Kilkenny, the alliance brought about between the Gaelic Irish and the Old English to protect their Catholic religion and their independence, although claiming to act in the name of the king. The confederate forces received a morale boost when Owen Roe O'Neill, a nephew of the great Hugh and a celebrated soldier on the Continent, landed in Ireland to offer his services to their cause. This was to have no immediate effect on Newry. Nevertheless, though not subject to attack or siege, Turner's garrison was finding conditions at Newry unfavourable. Turner reported:

> We had not homes for the hafe of them, for we were necessitated to take down a great many houses to make the circumference of our walls the lesse. Our own preservation taught us to work almost day and night still we had finished the irregular fortification begunne by the rebells. This great fatigue and toile, a very sparse dyet, lying on the ground, little sleep, constant watching - Sir Phelemy being for the most part always within a day's march of us — all these, I added to the change of the aire made most, or rather, indeed all our officers and sojurs fell sicke with Irish agues, fluxes, and other diseases, of which very many dyed.

The sickness, caused by Newry's proximity to the marsh, and the lack of supplies greatly weakened the garrison. Turner was forced into trying to come to terms with his opponents so that a truce might be arranged under which supplies and medicines could be brought to Newry. However, this was superseded by a more general treaty negotiated by the Marquis of Ormond, Charles I's representative in Ireland, under which the Scots surrendered Newry to a royalist garrison in December 1643.

On 12 July 1644 the garrison found itself threatened by none other than General Robert Monro, leading his Scottish forces. As a result of the threat posed to the Ulster-Scots by the Confederation of Kilkenny, Monro and the Scots had come over to the side of parliament against the king. Consequently, when they were marching north from Dundalk back into the heartland of Ulster, they found the royalist garrison of Newry blocking their path. Unlike the previous occasion, Newry was now well fortified and could not be overawed by larger numbers alone. Ironically, this was due to the efforts of Monro's own men, when Major Turner had rebuilt the town's defences during his period of occupation. Colonel Matthews, the royalist commander, denied Monro passage and the following day Monro assembled his forces and sent a messenger to demand entry. Matthews again refused and ordered their royal standard to be raised and the garrison to stand ready for battle. In response Monro sent Lord Blaney forward to plead with Matthews, arguing that the town could never withstand Monro's artillery. Matthews called his bluff and Monro was forced to withdraw.

The critical battleground of the war in Ireland now moved away from Newry and for almost two years the town was ignored. Meanwhile, Owen Roe O'Neill was conducting his celebrated campaign against the Scots, culminating in the defeat of Monro at the Battle of Benburb in June 1646. This victory did little to alter the overall situation and the following year the parliamentary forces had recovered so well that they began to assert their dominance throughout Ulster. In the summer of 1647 they seized Newry and expelled the royalist garrison.

Owen Roe O'Neill, nephew of the
legendary Hugh, was the greatest general
to support the Confederation of Kilkenny
(Armagh County Museum)

Newry comes into the story of this rebellion again in 1648 when there is mention in the records that the Supreme Council of the Confederation of Kilkenny sent as an envoy to the Pope in Rome one Patrick Crelly, abbot of the Cistercian Abbey in Newry. This is particularly significant in that it is an indication that the abbey had survived in some form after its official dissolution. We should not be far off the mark in speculating that this Patrick Crilly is one and the same as the Patrick Creely or Crilly who leased a castle and some land from Arthur Bagenal in the reign of James I. If so this raises interesting questions about the implementation of the Reformation in Ireland and its effect on Catholic institutions.

The year 1649 was an important one both for Ireland in general and for Newry in particular. The execution of Charles I caused many to desert the side of parliament and declare for the monarchy. In Ulster the Scots proclaimed the Prince of Wales as Charles II, and by July the royalist cause was so strong that Lord Inchiquin could march into Ulster at the head of 3,500 troops. He reclaimed Dundalk, Carlingford, Greencastle, Narrow Water and Newry for the king. All this was overshadowed by Oliver Cromwell's arrival in Ireland on 15 August 1649. He had come to establish the authority of parliament over all the

Irish, irrespective of whether they were Gaelic Irish, Old English or Ulster-Scots. Shortly after the siege and capture of Drogheda, Cromwell sent Colonel Venables to Carlingford to conquer it for parliament. In a combined naval and land operation, Venables took Carlingford and then advanced on Newry. The royalist commander negotiated a surrender and the town was thus spared further bloodshed. For Newry, this was the end of the fighting, and for Ireland, too, it was soon to end. Cromwell crushed the last of Irish resistance and imposed his settlement. Many of the inhabitants of counties Armagh and Down were transported to Connacht but Newry itself was left largely unmolested.

The war formally came to an end for Newry on 15 February 1656. On that day Oliver Cromwell confirmed Nicholas Bagenal's possession of Newry as Bagenal had done nothing to oppose the cause of parliament in Ireland. Nicholas had played no great part in the events of the preceding fifteen years and seems to have been able to convince the parliamentary authorities that he was no threat.

Within a few years Cromwell was dead and Charles II sat upon the throne. Peace seemed to have finally come to the troubled land of Ireland and the task of rebuilding the economy could begin in earnest. The new king summoned his first Irish parliament in May 1661. In this parliament Newry was represented by Trevor Lloyd, and Nicholas Bayley, who was a nephew of Nicholas Bagenal's and is reported to have been the person who carried word to Charles II in Brussels of his restoration to the throne.

These were relatively prosperous years for Newry as for most of Ireland. Much of the town was rebuilt, including the Church of St Patrick, which was, as Dr John O'Donovan says in his *Letters of the County Down* (1909), 'demolished in 1641, the wall and steeple however having been suffered to remain. It continued in this ruins state till after the restoration, when one half of the church together with the vestry was covered.' Many of those who had fled or were driven from Newry by the troubles of the previous years began to return, and the town escaped the effects and consequences of Charles II's Act of Settlement, which did much to sow the seeds of future trouble. Despite legislation which restricted Irish trade where it competed with the English, Newry began to grow as a port.

The reign of Charles II came to an end in 1685 and he was succeeded by his brother, James II. His reign was short but troubled and Newry was to suffer severely during it. In Ireland, James II was intent upon redressing the balance of power to the disadvantage of those who currently controlled government and property — a great many of whom were Cromwellian colonists — in favour of the Old English and the Gaelic Irish. This meant threatening the political and property settlement of his brother's reign and bringing to the fore the political and religious divisions that had led to war in the 1640s. Municipal government was among the first areas that James II and his lord lieutenant, Richard Talbot, the Earl of Tyrconnell, sought to reform. Most towns and cities were induced, or forced, to accept new charters. In Newry the corporation, the 'Provost, Free Burgesses and Commons', refused to surrender its charter and in September 1688 James I's charter was annulled and replaced by a new one. The terms of the new charter were not much different from those of the old one, except that Tuesday was now the market day, fairs were to be held on 9 June and 9 September and a court of 'Pie Poudre and Tolls' was to be held annually. The important change was in the number and constitution of the burgesses. There were now twenty-two burgesses named in the charter, and Richard White was appointed the town clerk. Unlike the appointees under the charter of James I, the majority of these burgesses were not landowners or gentlemen but merchants of the town. They were representatives of the pre-plantation stock and mostly Catholics - that is, in Protestant eyes, those same people who had been the rebels forty years earlier. While this was in keeping with Newry's own population, which remained in Sir William Brereton's words 'much Irish', such appointments caused alarm in other parts of the country, especially in Ulster.

William of Orange landed in England in 1688 at the invitation of the English parliament and the following year he dispatched an army against his father-in-law, James II, who sought refuge in Ireland where the majority of people and the parliament still recognised James as king. In the war that followed Newry was again at the centre of hostilities.

The Duke of Berwick, James II's illegitimate son, ordered that Newry be put to the torch rather fall into Williamite hands.

In March 1689 the Jacobite army, under Lieutenant General Richard Hamilton, occupied Ulster for James. Shortly after the king had arrived in Ireland and as part of a tour of inspection, he stopped at Newry on 23 April. The Irish parliament that James summoned in May passed an act of attainder in which Nicholas Bagenal was named and his lands given to a cousin, Dudley Bagenal, who was to raise a regiment to fight for James II. Also named under this act was Henry Gardiner, a burgess under the new charter. At this parliament Newry was represented by Richard White and Rowland Savage. Two months later the Duke of Schomberg landed in Ulster with ten thousand men and after the surrender of Carrickfergus, only Newry remained as a Jacobite garrison, with some two thousand men under the Duke of Berwick, an illegitimate son of James II's. On 4 September, Schomberg occupied Loughbrickland and the following day marched towards Newry, where he expected to meet stiff opposition. However, he had not gone far when a reconnaissance party returned with the news that Newry was ablaze.

Berwick had taken the decision that his force alone could not keep the larger Williamite force at bay. He considered it more prudent to retreat south with the long-term aim of consolidating the Jacobite forces for a decisive blow against Schomberg's army. A corollary of this plan was to deprive the enemy army of food and shelter on its march so that it would be out of supplies by the time the Jacobites struck; so it was that he ordered Newry to be burned to the ground. From a military point of view the plan had little to recommend it, and politically it showed a lack of sensitivity to Irish concerns that could only undermine the morale of the Jacobite army. Nevertheless, Newry — and subsequently Carlingford — were put to the torch. Nowhere else was burned in this manner, because Schomberg issued a threat of such severe retaliation that Berwick's strategy was abandoned.

A chaplain with Schomberg's army, George Storey, describes their arrival at Newry:

> I went abroad into the country, where I found all the houses deserted for several miles. Here the corn also was either lying and rotting on the ground or else was shaken by the violent winds, for the people were all gone, the Protestants the March before, and the Irish now at the retreating of their Army.

Of Newry he says: 'The town itself had been a pretty place and well built.'

All that remained from Berwick's conflagration were the castle and five or six houses. Schomberg left a garrison there that consisted of fifty men under a Captain Palliser. This was to become the southern strongpoint of the Williamites after Dundalk was abandoned, as Schomberg decided to await the arrival of William before making any further advances.

In September 1689 the Jacobites launched an assault against Newry but were driven off. In October sickness forced the Williamites to abandon Dundalk. Several men had already died, and Storey tells us that 'the rest were put upon waggons, which was the most lamentable sight in the world'. All the roads from Dundalk to Newry and Carlingford were 'next day full of nothing but dead men'. Many of the sick and able-bodied from the Dundalk garrison were lodged 'amongst the ruins of the old houses at Newry'. Command of the Newry garrison was given to Sir Harry Inglesby and he now found himself on the front line against the Jacobites. Towards the end of November a large force of Jacobites under the command of Major General Boiseleau advanced on the town. In the confused fight that followed, the garrison held out and the

Jacobites retreated, having lost a lieutenant colonel and six men, while two were taken prisoner.

Events in Ireland dragged on, with sporadic fighting and no decisive action, until the landing of William of Orange at Carrickfergus on 14 June 1690, accompanied by a large army. William quickly marshalled the troops available to him and marched south in order to force the issue with James. On 25 June, William and his army entered the ruins of Newry. They camped on the hills to the west of the town and the following day began the march that ultimately led to the Battle of the Boyne and the securing of the Irish Crown for William. William rode through Newry but the town had no involvement in the subsequent events of his reign, except in so far as the Jacobite charter was abolished and Nicholas Bagenal was restored to the lordship of Newry and Mourne.

Whatever hopes Bagenal and the people of Newry had that the defeat of Hugh O'Neill would bring prosperity were short lived. The period of peace only lasted from 1603 to 1641, and the later seventeenth century was characterised by warfare, beginning with the rebellion of 1641 and ending with William of Orange's war against James II. In all of these conflicts Newry had been on the front line, experiencing military occupation and massacre. Far from developing as a commercial centre under the lordship of the Bagenals, the town reeled from one disaster to another, culminating in its almost total destruction at the hands of the Duke of Berwick. The seventeenth century began with Newry being of some size and importance and ended with the town in ruins.

William of Orange's victory meant that James II's charter to Newry became null and void leaving the town with no proper municipal government until the 19th century. (Public Record Office of Northern Ireland)

4

'DIRTY STREETS AND PROUD PEOPLE'

The closing decade of the seventeenth century had seen Newry dealt a blow from which it seemed the town might never recover. Almost all its buildings had been destroyed and the inhabitants had fled. What had once been 'a pretty place and well built' was left a collection of ruins, destroyed by fire and cannon. Yet within a few decades Newry was not only rebuilt but was the busiest port in Ulster and owned the first canal ever constructed in the British Isles.

The geographic and strategic factors that had brought Newry into being, first as a monastic settlement and then as a medieval town, meant that it would not and could not be left an abandoned derelict. Its location at the end of Carlingford Lough and its position on the important route into and out of Ulster meant that for economic — and governmental — reasons it was too important not to be built on. Emotion too must have played its part. Those families who were uprooted by the armies of William III and James II and forced to seek refuge in the neighbouring towns wanted to return to the place where they had been born and where their forefathers were buried. To them Newry was the only home they had, and their fortunes and those of their children were with the yew tree at the head of the strand.

The final defeat of the Jacobite armies and the signing of the Treaty of Limerick in 1691 were not followed by a period of reconciliation. The fears and hatreds on both sides were too deep-seated for that. Within a short time the Irish parliament introduced legislation that was intended not only to prevent Catholics, and to a lesser degree dissenters, from practising their religion but also to exclude them from politics and property ownership. Historians have argued over the extent to which the penal laws, as they are called, were enforced, but it cannot be denied that they excluded the vast majority of the Irish population from enjoying full privileges as the king's subjects. In Newry, where the majority was Catholic, this was particularly relevant.

The victory of William of Orange had brought peace to Ireland — many may not have seen it as just, but it was peace—and in its wake commerce and industry could be rebuilt. In a surprisingly short time Newry had streets, shops and houses. By 1700 Mill Street contained six or seven slated houses and there were more in Market Street. The destruction of 1689 had in reality provided the opportunity to plan the rebuilding of Newry. The town was given a chance to escape from the narrow steep streets of the medieval period. The topography dictated much of the layout and so prevented Newry from being planned as a concept in the manner of plantation towns such as Banbridge and

The opening stretch of the ship canal south of Newry. The tall building on the left is the Collector's House near which the gasworks was built in 1822 (*The Collector's House and canal near Newry* by John Nixon, Armagh County Museum)

Hillsborough in County Down or Draperstown in County Derry, but the new streets were broader and the houses more elegant than they had been. It provided the opportunity, also, to reorientate the town away from the hilltop on which the abbey had stood down to the quays, where the great families of the town — the Bagenals, Nedhams, Hills, Corrys and so on — knew their future prosperity lay.

It was this, what we may regard as the second foundation of Newry, that created the town as we know it today. The town boundary, the layout of the streets, and the majority of the best buildings owe their character to this period of rebirth. Once William III's succession to the British throne had been settled, Nicholas Bagenal devoted his energy and resources to this renaissance. He encouraged resettlement and the establishment of commercial enterprise. The ruined walls of the town were not rebuilt and in some instances provided the materials for the new constructions. The bridge over the Clanrye river into County Armagh was restored and the little mud cabins that were once the town's suburbs were rebuilt in stone.

The death of Nicholas Bagenal in 1712 marked the end of an era and brought an end to the Bagenal line. For over one hundred and fifty years the family had fought for and ruled over Newry. Its existence as a town of importance, its development as a port and the subsequent wealth enjoyed by its citizens were all based on the foundations laid down by three generations of Bagenals, from the first Nicholas who came to Ireland to escape prosecution, to the last Nicholas who returned to rebuild the town from the ruins of 1689. In expectation of his death, Nicholas Bagenal had his will drawn up in 1708. Unfortunately the revelant papers do not survive and we are left to piece together as best we can the story of the succession. What is certain is that he left his estates and wealth jointly to Edward Bayley (or Baylie) and to Robert Nedham. Their exact relationship to the last of the Bagenals is uncertain. It would appear that they were either his cousins or his sons-in-law. Given the nature of family allegiances at this period, it is not impossible that they were both.

Edward Bayley had been elected as a Member of Parliament (MP) for Newry in 1704, and he originally came from Gorsenon in the county of Caernarvon in Wales. His descendants became an important family, later coming into the Marquisate of Anglesey. Robert Nedham was the scion of a landed Shropshire family. At the time of Nicholas Bagenal's death Nedham was in Jamaica. This is significant in view of Newry's later association with Jamaica and the importation of sugar. Whatever the relations between these two successors to the Bagenal estates, it was decided that their affairs could be better managed if the properly was divided between them. Consequently, Edward Bayley was given those lands on the western side of Carlingford Lough, that is in County Louth, and to all intents and purposes passes out of the history of Newry. Robert Nedham retained the other lands, that is those comprising the old lordships of Newry and Mourne, which not only gave him a huge estate but also the ownership of Newry.

Newry was lucky to become the property of Robert Nedham. It was his granting of leases in perpetuity that directly encouraged men of capital to settle in the town. For example, in 1730 he leased building land in Boat Street to Edward Corry, where he built many fine houses. The Corry family had originally lived in Rockcorry in County Armagh, but moved to Newry where Isaac Corry, Edward's father, came to establish himself as a merchant. For the next one hundred years the fortunes of the Corry family and of Newry - in fact of Ireland - were closely linked.

Robert Nedham and his successors were a benevolent influence. They encouraged commerce and industry and were sympathetic to the religious sensibilities of the inhabitants. In 1720 St Patrick's Church was restored as a place of worship. In 1722, when the Presbyterians of the town were seeking land on which to build their meeting house, Robert Nedham leased a site on High Street to them, then the busiest street in town, for a nominal rent of 6d. (2½p). Later, similarly generous terms were offered to the Catholics for the building of a new chapel in the street that was to be called after it, Chapel Street.

Such was the success of Newry's commercial enterprise that in 1726 the Government decided that Carlingford could no longer be regarded as the principal port on the lough and so transferred the customs office to Newry, where it was housed in a spacious building on the quays. The customs duties collected for 1726 amounted to £1,069 12s. (£1,069.60). At this time there were only four ships registered in Newry, so its trade was developing steadily rather than blossoming overnight.

The transference of the customs marked the beginning of a new era and the prosperity fostered by Robert Nedham resulted in the building of new warehouses along the quays and in 1730 the increased traffic travelling through the town necessitated the expansion of the Dublin Bridge and the building of a new bridge across the Clanrye, at what is now Sugar Island. Thomas Bradshaw's 1820 directory informs us that the bridge was built

> for the accommodation of foot passengers, by a person named Murphy. In consequence of this, the stone bridge afterwards built over the river, at this place, bore the name of MUDDA, MURPHY BRIDGE, or the Bridge of Murphy's Stick. It is a good bridge of five arches. Formerly these were ten arches, but five of them being of no use for venting the water it was thought unnecessary to retain them.

Newry was a busy and expanding town. We know that at this time it contained four hundred households. Not only had the town been rebuilt but within three decades it had extended beyond its previous limits. We can make a fairly accurate assessment of the number of households because of the nature of the electoral franchise in Newry. In John F. Small's *An Historical Sketch of Newry* (1876) we are informed that the borough returned two MPS on the basis that 'all the inhabitants of the town who had a separate fire in their own property, and paid Cess and Press, or Scot and Lot [forms of tax], should be allowed to vote'. In effect this meant that almost all male householders - excluding Catholics, of course - had the right to vote. This was popularly known as a 'potwalloper' constituency; *wallop,* apparently, was an Anglo-Saxon word meaning 'to boil' and hence the principle that any man who could boil a pot over his own fire had the right to have a say in who represented him in parliament.

The Fortescue Lock terminus of the early ship canal enabled large vessels to dock at Newry. The ship canal was replaced in 1850, by a new one incorporating the Victoria Locks and Albert Basin. (*Fathom near Newry* by John Nixon, Armagh County Museum)

The outcome of any election, therefore, could not be guaranteed, unlike a 'pocket borough' where the electorate was so small that a local magnate could dictate the way of the vote. There was greater freedom of debate, therefore, and a more lively interest in politics in Newry than in other constituencies. It accounts in some measure for the strength given to opposing opinions within Newry and for the influence that Newry-reared politicians, from Isaac Corry to John Mitchel, were to have on Ireland as a whole. Elections in Newry were rarely dull affairs and candidates had to take serious steps in order to gain votes: oration, intimidation, bribery and intoxication.

One election that was more lively than most and reached almost legendary status in the folklore of the town occurred on 4 November 1715, on the occasion of the accession to the throne of George I. Three candidates stood for the two seats, and subsequently the losing candidate petitioned parliament to overturn the result. It is from this petition that we get the full — if not the unbiased — story. The candidates were: Hans Hamilton, who resigned as seneschal of Newry in order to run for parliament; Robert Clements, a gentleman from County Cavan; and Sir William Johnston, a member of a landed family from Gilford, County Armagh. In accordance with the practice at Newry, the election was supervised by the seneschal of the manor court, William Workman, who had succeeded Hamilton, and his deputy was Henry Gardiner. Gardiner had been named as a free burgess in the corporation established by James II in 1689 that became defunct at the accession of William of Orange to the throne.

Voting was conducted not by secret ballot, but openly before the candidates. Hence it was known who had voted for whom and so who was to receive rewards or punishment from the successful candidates. Workman, the seneschal, set up the polling booth in an apothecary's shop, it being 'the most convenient in the town, being a large room, with a door and a large shop window on one side, fronting to the big street, and another side door that opened to another street'. The 'big street' was either Mill Street or Market Street, these being the two most important at that time. The seneschal and the three candidates sat opposite the window.

At the booth itself a sizeable crowd had gathered, cheering or jeering candidates and voters alike. As each voter arrived to cast his lot, attempts were made to influence his decision. One voter was offered 5s (25p) to vote a particular way, while the agent of one candidate offered another citizen a horse if he voted for his patron. Other means of persuasion were not so pleasant. When one of Sir William Johnston's supporters approached the steps to the apothecary's shop, he 'was hindered from going up stairs, and went to the window to complain, where he was threatened to be kicked by Oliver Gardiner'. This was the seventeen-year-old son of the deputy seneschal, Henry Gardiner. A friend of Oliver's then knocked down this anonymous supporter of Sir William.

By mid-afternoon tempers on all sides were becoming heated. The crowd about the polling booth was getting unmanageable and became progressively more rowdy. The constable feared that a riot would ensue if action were not taken soon, so he, with the Town Guard,

> came to Mr Stannus and told him they could not secure the peace of the town by reason of the insolence of the mob who cried about the street 'Down with the Whigs'. Mr Stannus ordered them all to get clubs and knock every person down that dared to distinguish himself by that rebellious expression.

Mr Stannus was the MP for Carlingford and as such carried a certain authority.

By six o'clock Sir William thought it best to call it a day and resume voting the following morning, when he could round up more of his supporters. He approached William Workman with the request for an adjournment on the grounds that it was getting too dark to continue with the election and that the people could not be asked to wait in the street any longer. Workman, who clearly had little sympathy for Sir William, said that as almost everyone eligible had voted, he would keep the booth open for a little while longer and then close the voting for good. Sir William replied that by his reckoning there were still forty voters who had not come forward, and they would not do so unless the polling booth reopened in the morning. Workman stood his ground and Sir William stormed off in a fury. Workman summoned the town sergeant, who was ordered to make the proclamation that all those who had not yet voted should do so at once. Shortly afterwards the election was declared over and the votes were counted.

Robert Clements came top of the poll and was declared returned without further opposition. However, Sir William Johnston polled 113 votes, which put him 26 votes behind Hans Hamilton, who was duly declared the second elected member. The forty outstanding votes would have swung the election in Sir William's favour and he duly appealed the result. He complained that the polling booth had closed too early, that voters had been bribed and threatened, and that among Hamilton's friends who sat with him in the apothecary's shop, 'there was a Papist there'. It seemed to be his opinion that the presence of a Catholic at the polling booth, even though he had no right to vote, was reason enough to nullify any election. While unimportant in itself, this accusation does give us an insight into the deeper divisions that fractured Irish society at this time, and which would again and again result in violence.

As it turned out, parliament found in favour of Hamilton and so he retained his seat. Hamilton had also been elected as the MP for Bangor in County Down — as an insurance against defeat in Newry — and on confirmation of the result in Newry he renounced his seat in the other borough. Such was the importance attached to representing Newry in parliament.

An important outcome of this particular election for Newry was that the inhabitants of Ballybot who were eligible to vote were now recognised as voters in the borough of Newry. Sir William had claimed that they had no rights in a Newry election but parliament denied this and so in effect declared Ballybot to be a part of the town. Ballybot lay on the County Armagh side of the Clanrye river, well beyond Newry's traditional boundary. As the town grew in wealth it attracted many people to it from the neighbouring countryside, and because there was little or no room in the town proper for these newcomers, they established themselves as a suburb on the western side of the river. Initially they were a poorer class of people, seeking employment as labourers in the rebuilding of Newry, or down on the quays, or as servants in the houses of the richer townspeople. The place became known as the 'Ballybought', from the Irish *baile bocht,* meaning the 'poor town', and for many years was recognised as a separate community. As Newry grew, it spread down from the hill on the County Down side, crossed the river and merged with Ballybot, where warehouses and factories were established on the open ground west of the Clanrye. However, it was not until the 1715 election that Ballybot, which now contained citizens eligible to vote, was deemed to be an integral part of Newry.

ANNO QUADRAGESIMO SEPTIMO

GEORGII III. REGIS.

C A P. XLV

An Aft to continue an Aft made in the Parliament of *Ireland^* in the Thirty-firfi. Year of the Reign of His late Majefty King *George* the Second, for the better fupplying the City of *Dublin* with Coals, and for the better Encouragement of the Collierie* of *Ireland,*   [2 5 th *April* 1807.]

Whereas it is expedient that an Ad made in the Parliament of *Ireland* in the Thirty.fiiil Year of the Reign of His late Majefty King Gwrg* the Second, intituled, *An Aft for the better fupply. ¡ ing the City c/~Dublin with Caals, and for the better Encouragement of the • Collieries oj this Kingdom,* and which hdS been continued by feveral Acts of the Parliament or. *Ireland* to the Firil Day of *Aitgvft* One thoufand eight hundred and feven, mould be further continued ; be it therefore enacted by the King's molt Excellent Majefty, by and with ihe Advice and Con-fent of the Lords Spiiitual and Temporal, and Commons, in this prefent
                                                                  5 B
Parliament

The discovery of coal in Co. Tyrone prompted the digging of the Newry Canal

Newry would have remained a busy, but small, port had it not been for the discovery of coal in County Tyrone. Initial explorations indicated a substantial coal deposit centring on Coalisland. The Irish government - and in particular the MPS for Dublin - had a grand vision of the nation's capital being self-sufficient in coal, no longer having to import it expensively from Newcastle upon Tyne, and so fulfilling Jonathan Swift's maxim 'to burn everything English but their coal'. It was calculated that coal could be sold in Dublin at 12s.6d. (62 ½p) per ton and so reduce the capital's fuel bill considerably, where, according to W. Harris in *The Antient and Present State of the County of Down* (1744), 'the consumption of that sort of fuel is computed to cost £70,000 per annum'. The main problem was to devise the most efficient and economic means of transporting the coal to Dublin. Transporting it by road was seen to be completely impractical. Roads in Ireland were notoriously bad; their upkeep was in the hands of local grand juries who relied on local tolls and enforced labour, and in consequence the roads were unevenly maintained. Most roads were unpaved tracks of varying dimensions, following circuitous routes to avoid any natural obstacles, pitted with potholes, and at best were passable in summer and usually reduced to rivers of mud in winter. The roads did improve in the late eighteenth century but in the 1720s they were in a very bad state. Outlaws of various sorts — from 'rebellious' peasants to rapparees — made travelling by road a hazardous business. Even if the roads in Ireland had been perfect, it would have been impractical to rely on horse-drawn wagons to transport coal in the quantities demanded by Dublin. The only logical solution, therefore, was to carry the coal to Lough Neagh, from where it could be carried by ship to Carlingford Lough, and so down the coast to the capital. To get a ship from Lough Neagh to Carlingford Lough it would be necessary to build a 'navigable trench'.

The proposal to dig a canal from Lough Neagh to Carlingford Lough had first been suggested in the 1640s by Colonel George Monck, an officer in Oliver Cromwell's army, who, no doubt, saw the potential military as well as commercial use that such a passage might be put to. Nothing was done about a trench at that time, although Colonel Monck went on to make a name for himself in the history of these islands by engineering the restoration of the monarchy in 1660.

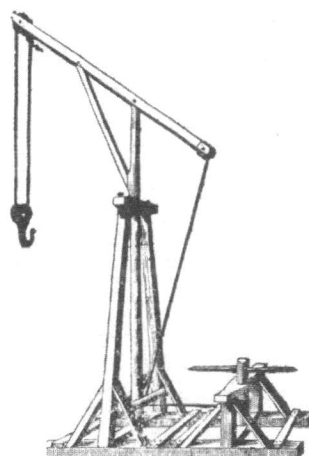

Rubble from digging the canal was winched out of the trench by manually operated cranes similar to this.

A more serious proposal was made in 1703, when Francis Nevil, Collector of Her Majesty's Revenues in Ireland, presented to parliament a survey of the land 'between Lough Neagh and Newry. . . with a design of drawing a canal or making a passage for boats from the said Lough to the Sea'. Nevil was paid £200 for his trouble, but nothing was done to implement his proposals. However, in 1715 parliament did pass an act to encourage inland navigation, with the intention of benefiting the River Liffey, entitled 'An Act passed for the Encouragement of Tillage, and the better employment of the poor; and also for the more effectual putting in execution an Act to encourage the draining of bogs and unprofitable low grounds & C.' It was this act that was later used to raise revenue to cover the expenditure of digging the Newry inland navigation.

The expectation of great quantities of cheap coal from County Tyrone prompted parliament to take direct action in constructing a canal that would link Lough Neagh to the sea. In 1729 it established the Commissioners of Inland Navigation for Ireland, consisting of the lord lieutenant of Ireland, the lord chancellor, the four archbishops of the Church of Ireland, the speaker of the House of Commons and eighty other 'responsible persons'. As a result of Lord Lieutenant Duke of Dorset's absence from Ireland, executive responsibility lay with the lord justices — the archbishop of Armagh, John Boulter, Lord Wyndham, and Sir Ralph Gore — and it was they who took direct responsibility for the canal. The actual construction of the canal and the day-to-day running of the operation were the responsibility of Sir Edward Lovett Pearce, His Majesty's Engineer and Surveyor General, an eminent architect who had been appointed in 1730. His deputy was Richard Castle. The money to pay wages and buy the materials needed for the excavation and construction of the waterway was raised under the auspices of the 1715 act, 'by virtue of which, and out of the Duties arising from Coaches, Berlins, Calashes, Chaises and Chains, as also from Cards and Dice, and manufactured gold and silver plate imported into or made in this Kingdom' revenue was raised to be used by the Commissioners of Inland Navigation. In the early part of 1731 work began on the Newry Canal.

Perhaps we should pause and consider the magnitude of the task that was about to be undertaken. The proposal was to build a channel of some eighteen miles in length that would be large enough to take vessels capable of carrying a load of coal and sailing upon the open sea. The channel itself would have to climb to a height of seventy-eight feet above sea level and, of course, retain an even depth of water along its whole length. This would be a daunting task by any standards but when we remember that this was the period before the Industrial Revolution, when engineering was still at the 'pick and shovel' stage, with no mechanical or steam-powered drills or excavators to assist in the digging of the canal, we can perhaps appreciate the enormity of the challenge. No undertaking of this size had been carried out in the British Isles before, so the engineers and labourers involved had to learn as they went along. If the canal was successful, then they would be taming one of the great elemental forces. A comparable engineering feat in today's terms would be the digging of the Channel Tunnel.

The first difficulty encountered by Pearce in constructing the canal was not an engineering one but a personnel one: how was he to assemble sufficient manpower for the task? Local labour was employed as much as possible and attempts were made to attract men from other parts of Ireland. These early navvies were engaged on a seasonal basis, as little or no work was done during the winter months. The problem of labour was so acute that Pearce was forced to turn elsewhere to get enough men to work on the canal. The following letter was sent from the lord justice to the lord lieutenant on 10 May 1732.:

> My Lord
> A memorial and scheme have been laid before us, by Sir Edward Pearce, His Majesty's Engineer and Surveyor General, for employing part of the Foot Forces in making a navigable canal between Lough Neagh and Newry. Such a proposal being entirely new in this Kingdom, and there being no opportunity of learning here, whether the Colonels of Foot, who are almost all in England, have any objections to it. And though the Colonels should agree to it, the General Officers, who are here, seeming desirous to know, whether it would be agreeable to His Majesty to have his troops employed in such a Service, before they take upon them to consider any Scheme for it: We herewith transmit the said Memorial and Scheme, and submit this matter to your Grace's consideration.
>
> > We are with great respect,
> > My Lord your Grace's most
> > obedient, humble servants,
> >   Jhn., Armagh
> > Wyndham
> > Ralph Gore

Like so many of the landlords in Ireland, the colonels of the army were, by and large, absentees.

For those who volunteered to work on the canal - that is the civilians employed - the conditions of work were better than those of labourers elsewhere. The work was hard, and could be dangerous, but the pay was good. In the *Dublin Journal* of 4-7 May 1734, the following advertisement appeared:

> Whereas the Rt. Hon. and Hon. the Trustees of the Tillage Act have given me Directions to proceed this Summer upon the work of perfecting a navigable canal, between Lough Neagh and Newry, and have found it necessary to give the following encouragement to such labourers who shall offer themselves for that service. This is therefore to give Notice, that all such diligent and sufficient working men who shall present themselves at the Village of Acton in the County of Ardmagh, on Monday the 20th of May, inst, provided with one good working tool, such as spade, pick, stubbing axe or shovel, will be there employed and received into pay at the rate of seven pence per Diem [3p] provided they enrol themselves to continue at said work till the 10th of August next, if so long required, and submit to such other Regulations as shall be directed for the better carrying out on the

same; then to be at liberty to return to their respective homes, except such labourers shall choose rather to be employed till the season is over. Note, that care will be taken to procure a cheap market at Acton.

Richard Castle.

The advertisement is signed by Richard Castle, for he had taken over as supervisor of the work on the canal when Pearce died in 1733. Castle was not Irish but a French Huguenot. Like many of his co-religionists, he had been forced to leave his native France because of the injustices suffered there after the revocation of the Edict of Nantes by Louis xiv in 1685. Many Huguenots had come to Ireland — such as Louis Crommelin, the linen manufacturer — but Castle had initially travelled the Continent, learning the skills of an engineer and earning his living as such. For a time he lived in Hesse-Cassel in Germany. He learned much about the building of inland navigation works on the Continent, a field in which they were much more advanced than Britain and Ireland. Castle came to Ireland in 1728 at the invitation of Sir Gustavus Hume, who wanted him to design a country house on his estate at Lower Lough Erne in County Fermanagh. When the Commissioners of Inland Navigation were established in 1729, Sir Gustavus was named as one of their number. It was probably in his capacity as a commissioner that he found employment for Castle under Sir Edward Lovett Pearce. Due to his previous experience on the Continent, Castle had had some influence on the digging of the Newry Canal from the very beginning and was the obvious successor to Sir Edward. He was in charge of the canal for the following three seasons and responsible for what was probably the first stone lock chamber to be made in Ireland.

We know much about the men who were responsible to parliament for the construction of the canal and also of the engineers who oversaw the work, but of the ordinary men, the original Irish navvies, we know very little. We know they were men who had to be strong enough to do back-breaking work without complaint. They were poor men who were willing to travel far to earn their 7d. per day. They were forced to leave their families behind — whether they were husbands leaving wives and children or sons going off to support parents and younger brothers and sisters — for months at a time, so setting a pattern of seasonal migration in construction work that was to survive until the twentieth century. They lived in makeshift camps along the route of the canal, buying their provisions at the nearest market, and not always at the cheapest prices. The intention was to bring back enough money to last the family through another hard winter, but with temptations such as drink and gaming the money brought back rarely lived up to the initial hopes.

'Spade, pick, stubbing axe or shovel' — this tells us the nature of the work in which the navvies were employed. Without the help of machinery and using only the strength of their own muscles, or of draught animals, they had to dig a trench over forty feet wide and six feet deep, and then carry away the soil, rocks and other debris they had dug up. As they went along, the trench had to be shored up lest it caved in or became flooded when going through boggy ground. The men worked in teams: one team on the face, digging into the bank of earth and moving the trench forward inch by inch; behind them another team shovelled the loose earth into baskets or manhandled rocks out of the way; a third team hauled the baskets and rocks out of the trench; and behind it, working further down the trench, other men shored up the sides and packed in the earth, making sure it was firm. A working day lasted from first light to dusk, with little time allotted for rest— 'spade, pick, stubbing axe or shovel'.

The course of the canal generally followed the line of least resistance. For the first few miles from Newry it followed the route of the Clanrye valley, and from there it twisted northwards around hills and through bogs. Where possible it took a straight route and where unavoidable it went up an incline or over a hill. However, there was no attempt to cut a level line through hills or to take the canal over depressions via an aquaduct. Along the route the canal encountered various soils, such as gravel, clay and peat, and each soil presented its own problem. Gravel, for example, was difficult to work with as it was not firm enough, while cutting through a bog could result in water seepage and even flooding.

The bogs, in particular, yielded some unusual finds. As W. Harris relates:

> A forest was discovered, or a great multitude of fallen trees of oak ,in some places six in others eight feet deep; many of them of large bulk, tumbled down one over another, some lying in straight lines, and others in an oblique or transverse position.

Discoveries of trees like these were quite common and the popular belief was that they had lain there since the Universal Deluge spoken of in the Bible. In this age of science, sensible people dismissed this 'vulgar opinion' and reasoned that

> if trees thus found were felled by the Deluge, they would all lie in one position; whereas in the instance before us the contrary appears, none of them would be found with the mark of an axe on them, or in part burned, as is often the case.

Educated people argued that the bog grew up after the trees had been felled or burned, and developed theories to explain the growth of bogland. Harris tells us: 'We are told of bogs lately formed in Ireland. . . and that there is a great tract of ground, now a bog, which was then plowed land, and that a mansion house of a Nobleman is to be seen in the midst of it.'

However, many problems encountered by the canal builders stemmed not from natural obstacles but from human interaction. Castle had an uneasy relationship with the commissioners and although he was to remain in charge of the canal until the end of the 1736 season, they were already looking for a replacement. Castle was dismissed from his position as supervisor and returned to Dublin to live with his wife Jeanne Trufer, a Huguenot from Lisburn in County Antrim, where he lived and worked until his death in 1751.

While Castle was still in charge of the canal, the commissioners had made an approach to Thomas Steer, an English engineer. In the spring of 1736 Steer was paid fifty guineas (£52.50) to conduct a survey of a route that would bring the canal to completion. This he did, and in the belief that it would be a straightforward job, undertook to complete the canal. His contract stipulated that he work for three seasons: four months in 1737, and two months in the following two years, for an overall fee of eight hundred guineas (£840). Steer was so optimistic that he accepted two other commissions at the same time. One was the building of a new dock at Liverpool and the other was the building of a new harbour at Ballycastle, County Antrim. But the construction of the canal ran into so many problems that Steer was forced to spend twice as long working on it as he had intended. When Steer left, another engineer by the name of Gilbert was appointed in 1741 to put the finishing touches to the canal.

There were further delays, again caused by people rather than by nature, so the first vessels did not sail through the canal until March 1742. A small ship, the *Cope,* was loaded with coal on the western shore of Lough Neagh, sailed across the lough to the inland navigation, through it to the sea and so down the coast to Dublin. The *Dublin Newsletter* of 28 March 1742 reports:

> On Sunday last the 'Cope' of Lough Neagh, William Simple Commander, came into [Dublin] Harbour laden with coals, and being the first vessel that has come through the canal, had a flag in her topmast head, and fired guns as she came up the channel.

On the stern of the *Cope* was the motto *Vincet Amor Patriae* (love of country prevails). A second vessel, the *Boulter,* arrived shortly afterwards and so the canal could really be regarded as open for business.

The canal was eighteen miles long, forming a channel forty-five feet broad and five to six feet deep. It originally followed a route that took it out of Newry via Damolly, Poyntzpass, Scarva, Madden Bridge, Knockbridge, and so on, to Whitecoat Point, near Portadown, from where the River Bann was navigable to Lough Neagh. The summit was reached at the stretch between Poyntzpass and Terryhoogan, seventy-eight feet above sea level. Locks were used for the ascent to and descent from the summit level. In all, the canal had fourteen locks, nine of them south of the summit. Shortly after the canal was completed, Harris's survey was published in which the locks are described:

> The Locks are 15 feet 6 inches wide, 44 feet long, except three, which vary a little from these dimensions, but they are of an unequal depth according to the Situation of the Ground, some being 12., and others 13 feet deep.. . faced with a hard gritty stone conveyed by water from Benburb, in the County of Armagh, down the River Black-water to Lough Neagh, and so through a part of that Lake, and from thence by Portadown into the Canal. They are all boarded at the bottom with Deal Planks two inches thick. Some of them next to Newry are already pitched to render them stanch; and the rest intended to be so done.

Much was expected of the canal. After all, a huge amount of public money had been invested in the project — and would continue to be invested for the next two hundred years — and a great deal depended on its success. Confidence in the canal was high:

> The Benefit arising to the Kingdom from the Execution of this Scheme will be very considerable, as a thorough Trade will be carried on by inland Navigation between Dublin and the Counties of Armagh, Down, Antrim and Tyrone, for all kinds of Goods and Manufactures, besides that Dublin and all other parts of the Eastern and Southern Coasts will be supplied with firing at a very easy rate, while other parts can be easily served from the Colleries at Ballycastle. . . Both these Colleries will save a predigious sum of money yearly to the Nation in a single Article of firing.. . One advantage more from this inland Navigation we ought not to pass over, which is, that by the broad and deep Channels which are cut for this end through the moist and low grounds, great quantities of land will be hereby effectually reclaimed and recovered to the Nation; the Benefit of which would otherwise be lost.

Plans were already in preparation to excavate other canals throughout Ireland, paid for by the tax on luxury goods, 'the Duties being only paid by the Rich who are well able to spare them'. By the end of the eighteenth century there was a network of canals throughout the island, and all parts of Ulster could be reached from Newry by water. However, the promise of plentiful supplies of cheap coal from County Tyrone was never fulfilled, and ironically, the Newry Canal was to become the chief means of importing coal into the north of Ireland.

St Patrick's church was first erected on this site by Nicholas Bagenal in 1573 and was completely rebuilt in 1866 (Lawrence Collection)

The canal may not have become the main channel for transporting coal from Tyrone, but it very quickly found itself the chief artery for commercial traffic in Ulster. Trade had been growing steadily in Newry but with the completion of the canal it increased dramatically. Within a decade Newry had become the busiest port in the north of Ireland and the local merchants became very wealthy. In the canal's first twenty years of operation, 1,750 vessels, some as big as fifty tons, plied their trade there, bringing an average of £1,850 per annum in tolls.

By 1740 the Catholic population of Newry had become large enough, and some of its members wealthy enough, to build a chapel for themselves at Boat Street, which, as the name implies, was close to the quay, near where the canal joined the river. When this part of the town became overcrowded, a new chapel was built in the 1790s, just outside town, which is the present St Mary's in Chapel Street.

Newry was by now a bustling and important town, an essential stopoff for anyone touring the north of Ireland. In 1742 the composer George Frederick Handel came to Newry to perform his work *Alexander's Feast.* Jonathan Swift was a frequent visitor as he travelled on his way to Loughry House and Gosford, and it is his much-quoted couplet that describes Newry at this time:

High Church, Low steeple,
Dirty streets and Proud people.

The 'High Church' was St Patrick's, on the hill overlooking Newry, where Swift himself had occasion to preach. Of the 'Dirty streets', more shall be told later.

This 1838 painting by William Greenlees shows how Newry grew thanks to the canals. Tall chimneys bear witness to burgeoning industry and international trading ships dock in the basin. (Ulster Museum)

Another well-known clergyman who often visited Newry was John Wesley, the English founder of Methodism. He travelled a great deal, spreading his interpretation of the Word of God, and fortunately for historians, kept a journal of his travels. He had a kinder opinion of Newry than Swift, for he says that 'allowing for size, [it] is built much after the manner of Liverpool'. In 1756 Wesley was invited by the local Presbyterian congregation to preach to them. The meeting house in High Street must have been filled to capacity on this occasion as all those interested gathered to hear him speak. Wesley revisited Newry on several occasions.

The construction of the Newry Canal had been accompanied by work to contain and direct the flow of the Clanrye river. Previously, the fact that the low ground on the glen floor had been marshy and subject to flooding was not a problem — and had, in fact, contributed to the town's defences — but with the growth in trade the citizens of Newry wanted to ensure that there would always be enough water at the quayside for large vessels. When the town's commercial orientation moved towards the canal, the availability of land alongside it and the river became increasingly important. The banks of the river were built up and in parts it was 'canalised' down by the harbour. This work resulted in the drainage and drying out of the low ground. When Thomas Bradshaw was compiling his directory in 1820, he met Charles Havern, 'a man of one hundred and eleven years of age, [who] remembered when the Low Ground was altogether a marsh; and afterwards when there were two bleach-greens where the coffee-room now stands'. This area was traditionally known as Seymour's Green, presumably after the linen manufacturer who used it for bleach-greens.

William Greenlees's 1838 painting shows how Newry had spread from its original hill site down to the canal and beyond (Ulster Museum)

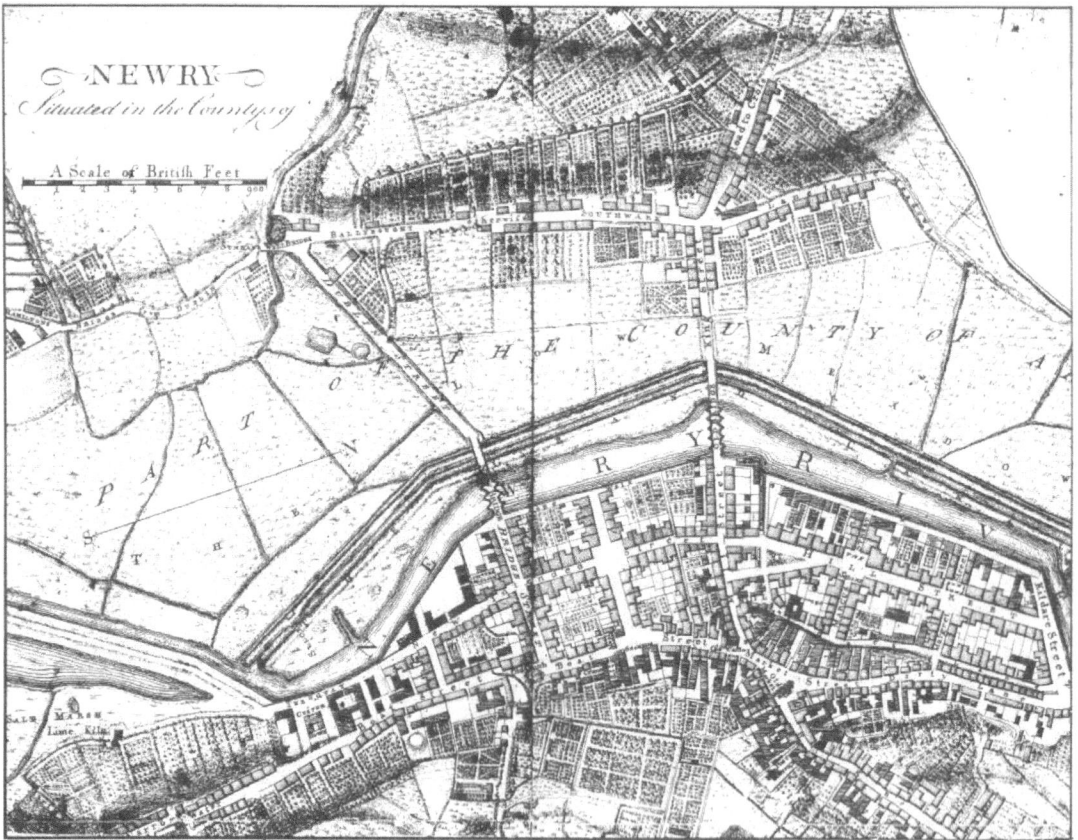

The middle decades of the eighteenth century were to see the building
of houses and places of business on this newly reclaimed land alongside
the canal, initially on the County Down side but soon spreading to
Ballybot on the Armagh side. This expansion was far from haphazard
and uncoordinated but rather a result of foresight and planning by the
merchants and wealthier men of the town. The work of channelling the
river and reclaiming the land had been undertaken by Robert Nedham
himself. Although he received a grant from parliament of £4,000 in
1755, he went on to spend over £6,000 of his own money on the
project. He in turn leased land to other wealthy men, who contributed
to the improvement of the town. In 1746 Isaac Corry rented a large area
at the bottom of Canal Street, where he built houses and stores. Other
merchants followed him there, leading to the establishment of
Merchants' Quay. Corry further developed Abbey Yard, at the other end
of town, where he also built his own home. The Earl of Hillsborough
laid out two squares, Marcus Square and Margaret Square, through
which ran Hill Street, named after the earl's family. We know from
John Rocque's 1760 map that the earl's original intention had been to
add another street and a third square. However, for reasons lost to us,
this objective was never fulfilled. The earl also built a market house in
1752. The final project in this period of Newry's expansion came in 1783
when Corry's grandson, 'Young Isaac Corry', as Dr William Drennan, a

doctor in the town, tells us, was 'laying out a new town here consisting of two fine streets and a square which will, I doubt not, to be taken in a few years'.

By 1770 Newry possessed 1,600 houses and more were being added every year. These new houses were in the current popular style and presented an elegant appearance, as Myles Gilligan remarks in *Newry* (1950), 'displaying all the good manner of this period. . . Pediment Tuscan and Ionic columns and elaborate fanlights with a careful proportioning of windows to walls'. Many of the richer homes contained impressive interior decoration. Rooms were panelled in wood, carved arches framed the entrance halls and pillars and ornate frames highlighted the windows. The terrace at Trevor Hill and the Corry residence known locally as the 'Abbey' belong to this period. Along the canal, tall and narrow warehouses were built to accommodate goods from all over the world. Sugar from the West Indies gave its name to Sugar Island — the development alongside the 'new basin' (now the Basin car park), where a refinery had been built.

In 1769 a theatre was opened in High Street by James Parker. It was probably converted from an existing building and stood next to an inn called the Pope's Head, near the site now occupied by St Clare's Convent. The first performance there was George Farquhar's *The Inconstant*. Theatre proved popular in Newry and companies from Dublin and Belfast often played there. In 1778 Michael Atkins, a Newry-born actor, left Belfast to set up a company in his home town. However, troubles within the company meant that it did not survive for very long, although in 1779 it did stage *The School for Scandal* by Richard Brinsley Sheridan.

The first and only purpose-built theatre in Newry opened in 1783. The Theatre Royal stood at numbers 71—3 Hill Street — an indication of how important this 'new' street had become - near to a public house called, appropriately, the Shakespeare Inn. It was by all accounts a fine, elegant building, equal to anything Dublin had to offer. It opened in grand style with a ball, paid for by a patron of the actor—manager and owner, Thomas Betterton. Betterton had had previous connections with Newry; his daughter, Julia, who went on to become a well-known actress, was born there in 1779. He was an enterprising and dashing individual. He secured a mortgage to build the theatre and persuaded local patrons to finance its opening. He presented the Newry public with a lively fare of drama and engaged respected Dublin companies to bring their plays to his theatre.

However, like so many in his profession, Betterton had no head for business and by 1785 he was facing a financial crisis, for he could not keep up the payments on the theatre's mortgage despite the popularity of its plays. Faced with the prospect of bankruptcy and a debtors' prison, Betterton slipped away from Newry in the dead of night, taking his wife and daughter with him. By a strange twist of fate, years later the Bettertons returned to Newry as minor members of Richard Daly's company to perform in the theatre that had once been theirs. Time and Thomas Betterton's charm must have had their effect, for after a run of some months, the season ended with a special benefit night in aid of the theatrical couple. This was the last event to be staged in Newry in the eighteenth century, but the Theatre Royal continued to serve the town until 1832.

While Newry may never have equalled that 'Athens of the North', Belfast, it did have a rich cultural life. Not only did it support a theatre, but it could also boast of fine schools and a thriving printing industry that reflected the varied interests of the town's population. As well as the English classics — from Shakespeare to Robin Hood — books printed at Newry included numerous works by local authors, such as William Carr's *Rosstrevor, a rural and descriptive poem,* and John Corry's *Odes and Elegies.* Trade with foreign countries did much to widen the outlook of the Newry merchants. Writers from the Continent, such as Voltaire and Jean-Jacques Rousseau, had their works printed in Newry. A look through a catalogue of books printed in the town at this period shows a breadth of interest and a cosmopolitan outlook that would be exceptional even today.

This cultural wealth reflected the material wealth of Newry. By the late eighteenth century it was estimated that twelve thousand tons of cargo passed through the port and canal annually. In 1767 it was said that 1,082 packages were exported from Newry and also, in the linen trade alone, 1,151 boxes containing 128,133 pieces of linen cloth, valued at £300,000, were carried by ships from the port. A 1777 report ranked Newry as the fourth largest port in Ireland and the busiest in Ulster. Arthur Young passed through the town in 1776 on his famous tour, and wrote in his journal:

> Breakfasted at Newry, the Globe, another good inn. The town appears exceedingly flourishing, and is very well built; yet forty years ago, I was told, there was nothing but mud cabins in it. This great rise has been much owing to the canal to Lough Neagh. I crossed it twice, it is indeed a noble work. I was amazed to see ships of 150 tons and more lying in it, like barges in an English canal. Here is considerable trade.

The impressive archway of the white linenhall built for £14,000 in 1783. In 1927 the urban district council took over the property. The building behind the arch once housed the local fire brigade

By far the greatest trade was in linen. In Ulster, Newry was an important market for brown linen, along with Derry and Belfast. Traditionally, the finer white linen had gone to the market in Dublin. However, in August 1782 the Linen Board introduced new regulations to the linen drapers, which they regarded as being prejudicial to their trade in favour of the Dublin merchants. Such was their wealth and independence that they were able to withdraw from the Dublin market in protest. This seemed all the more important because in 1780 the London government had withdrawn the duty on white linen, so giving the Irish greater access to the English market. Hence Armagh, Belfast and Newry all built their own white linen halls. A letter from John Foster MP to Lord Massereene reports:

> The establishment of a linenhall at Newry for the sale of white linens has been judged essentially necessary from its central situation to manufacture, as it will occasion a saving of five per cent which the manufacturer has hitherto been loaded with, by sending linens for sale to the linenhall at Dublin.

The White Linen Hall in Newry was a huge building, situated beside the canal at the north end of the town. It cost £14,000 to build and represented a considerable investment by the drapers.

Newry also attracted a number of manufacturing industries on account of the canal, as it enabled easy transport of raw materials and easy export of finished products. Like any busy Irish town, it had its breweries and distilleries and it also attracted industries, such as a spadeworks, a tannery, a saltworks, a sugar refinery, an iron foundry and a foundry for casting brass. Stoneworking, both in local and Mourne granite, was important, the granite often providing the ballast for outgoing vessels.

One industry that remained prominent in the town well into the nineteenth century was the manufacture of glass — not just ordinary items like bottles or drinking glasses but fine glassware and cut glass. At one time cut glass from Newry was considered second only to Waterford in quality. The story of glass manufacture began in 1780, when, for the first time, Ireland was allowed to export glassware. It is probable that the first glassworks in Newry was established then. The records of the Irish customs reveal that between 1785 and 1790 glass goods were exported from Newry to Carolina in the United States. The first positive mention we have of a glassworks is in October 1792, when the following advertisement appeared in *Gordon's Newry Chronicle:*

> Newry Flint Glass Manufactory. Emanuel Quinn and Co. have pleasure in acquainting their friends and the public that they have now ready for sale at their glass-house a great variety of flint glass work, both cut and plain, which they are determined to sell at the most reduced prices, and will give every encouragement to those who buy to sell again. They will have a constant supply of tobacco pipes of their own manufacture.

Glass manufacture was an important trade in Newry. This 18th century decanter depicts St. Patrick's church. (decanter in possession of J. Anley; photograph by Dermott Dunbar)

The production of tobacco pipes often went side by side with the manufacture of glass. By 1795 ownership of this glasshouse had passed to Michael Dunbar and Company. Glass was among a number of products produced by the company, ranging from tobacco pipes and garden pots to fire bricks and floor tiles. It was quite a large concern - as well as owning the glasshouse in William Street, there was another factory and a showroom on Merchants' Quay. In August 1795 the company advertised in the *Belfast News-Letter,* stating that the flint glass that they produced was the equal to any in the kingdom.

In 1796 Samuel Hanna set up business in Newry as a glass manufacturer. He had no previous experience in this area but saw it as a potentially lucrative business. He advertised in the press for 'a person of experience and knowledge in a glass-house who would take a share in, and undertake the management of, the business'. Hanna found his 'person of experience' in John Chebsey, who had been a partner in the Ballybought Glass Works in Dublin. However, Hanna's company ceased to manufacture glass at the start of the nineteenth century and this would seem to have been the end of glass production at William Street.

At this point there seems to be some confusion as to whether or not glass continued to be manufactured uninterrupted in Newry. We do know that in 1800 the Belfast glass company, Edwards and Sons, established a branch in the town. They opened a warehouse, but there is no immediate indication of a factory being set up. However, in 1816 Benjamin Edwards,

Jr, was forced to sell off company assets to avoid bankruptcy. Among these assets was a glass foundry in Newry, which would certainly suggest that glass production had resumed in the town under the auspices of the Edwards company. Edward Street probably derives its name from the firm.

In 1824 John R. Watt established a glasshouse in Newry at number 6 Edward Street, perhaps reopening the Edwards foundry. In 1826 the *Newry Telegraph* comments:

> We are uncertain whether or not we have before now called the attention of the public to the beauty of the glass manufactured by Messrs. Watt & Co. at their glass-house in Edward Street, Corry Square. As a proof of the excellence of the manufacture, we have been shown some claret glasses ordered by His Excellence, the Marquis of Wellesley.

About a year after this notice appeared, John R. Watt entered into partnership with John Kirkwood of Belfast. Shortly afterwards, John R. Watt retired and Kirkwood made an announcement in the pages of the *Newry Telegraph:*

> John Kirkwood, late partner, takes into partnership Isaac McCune, and that the business will in future be carried on under the firm of Kirkwood and McCune, in Edward Street.

This partnership lasted until 1837, when Isaac McCune went to a glasshouse at Ballymacarrett in Belfast. Despite growing financial difficulties, Kirkwood continued to operate the glassworks in Edward Street until 1839. In that year it was announced to the public that the stock-in-trade of the Newry glasshouse was being sold off. This marked the end of the manufacture of glass in the town.

The establishment of such industries, its importance as a trading centre, and the increase in population had all put a great strain on Newry. The fact that the town coped and, indeed, thrived during this period, from the opening of the canal onwards, is a tribute to the adaptability and enterprise of its citizens. But the town faced one major problem: it had no form of local government, no corporation, such as in Belfast, to regulate affairs and look after the common weal. After the dismantling of the corporation established by James II in 1688 no attempt was made by William III or his successors to re-establish the old system. Every so often the citizens of the town tried to redress the situation. In 1787 a petition was presented to parliament by 'the merchants, traders and inhabitants of Newry' listing their grievances, chief of which was

> the want of proper regulations for cars and carts, for coal measurers and coal porters, in the market for bread, meat and other articles, for keeping the streets clear and free from rubbish and obstructions, and preventing swine from going at large, and also the excessive price of coal sold in small quantities to the poor.

We can well understand from this petition why Jonathan Swift complained of 'Dirty streets'. However, parliament took no action on this or any other occasion.

Trevor Hill, Newry, 1829. Women are doing their washing in the mill race which ran through the town. (lithograph by T. M. Barnes, Ulster Museum)

The vacuum left by the absence of municipal government was filled by the feudal institution vested in the lordship of Newry and Mourne. One thing that had survived the abolition of the old corporation and the destruction of the town in 1689 had been the special status of the lord of Newry as lay-abbot. The temporal powers of the abbot of Newry had been vested in Nicholas Bagenal in 1550 and were now exercised through the office of seneschal and the courts of the manor. Arthur Bagenal's successors continued to wield these powers and without any other form of local authority, they became increasingly important. The responsibilities for local government were assumed by the manor and the parish vestry — both under the control of the Nedham family: the former looked after public and legal affairs, the latter, moral and charitable issues. The parish vestry operated a poor house for the destitute of the town, and its widows and orphans. Unlike other parishes, the tithe - that is the tax paid to the Established Church — in Newry was paid directly to the Nedhams, and helped cover expenses incurred by the parish vestry.

The continued existence and the role of the manor as an instrument of local authority was much more unusual, but of greater importance. The seneschal appointed by the Nedhams was, in effect, the mayor or sovereign of Newry and through his courts public business was conducted in the town and he acted as the returning officer in elections to parliament. There was no formal assembly of citizens to deliberate on civil affairs, such as a corporation, but the seneschal could summon a town meeting, or be petitioned to summon one, so that a specific issue might be discussed and action taken. Through the courts of the manor, regulations regarding public order could be enacted and these courts also appointed constables and a Town Guard. In so far as it was possible, the courts of the manor assumed the role and responsibilities of the corporation. There was no election to the office of seneschal or to the courts. The Nedhams seemed to have used their power wisely and taken the sensibilities of the prominent people of Newry into consideration.

The seneschal was usually an eminent and respected member of the community, and it was considered an honour to be elevated to this office. Likewise the officers of the courts were respectable men who took their duties seriously. In the correspondence and petitions of the time there are many complaints about elections and the lack of a comprehensive system of local government, but the integrity of the office of seneschal seems never to have been questioned.

The exempt jurisdiction that existed in Newry contained some unusual features. The courts 'baron' and 'leet' were actual courts conducted like common law courts, in which civil and criminal cases could be heard with the seneschal sitting as magistrate. In his 1820 directory, Thomas Bradshaw tells us that the court 'leet' could try cases not exceeding £66 13s.4d. (£66.67) while the court 'baron' had a limit of £40 imposed on it. These courts appointed their own bailiffs, who had authority to serve writs, and acting through the courts, the seneschal could issue a 'town order' authorising the seizure of a defendant's property. The courts did not exist alongside ordinary courts, but replaced them. No bailiff, sheriff or minister of the Crown could enter the jurisdiction without the permission of the seneschal. It was not unknown for a magistrate's rod to be broken before the seneschal if the magistrate violated this rule. Other powers exercised by the seneschal included the right to hold an inquest into any death in Newry. Perhaps most curious of all was the right of any citizen of the manor to claim asylum at the seneschal court in order to avoid being summoned to appear before the courts at Armagh or Downpatrick. A residency of six weeks was long enough to qualify for this privilege, so it was a very useful device to anyone running foul of the law in counties Armagh or Down. Furthermore, any fines that the king's courts did impose on residents of Newry could be — and were — claimed by the seneschal and so paid to the lay-abbot.

As curious and anachronistic as this institution was, it was very important for the public welfare of Newry. Local government of some kind was essential and if the corporation were not to be restored, then this feudal system had to be relied on. In fact the office of seneschal and the manor courts continued to play their roles and to exercise these powers well into the nineteenth century.

By 1788 the remaining walls of the old Cistercian abbey had been demolished and much of the masonry used in the new buildings that were erected on the site. In their final years these ruins had provided shelter to vagrants in the town. The demolition of the abbey was in some ways symbolic of the transformation that Newry had undergone in the eighteenth century. The medieval town that had developed around the abbey was destroyed and in its place grew a bustling modern town. The eighteenth century saw Newry assume the dimensions and character it was to retain until the twentieth century. It became an increasingly important commercial centre, marked by the transference of the customs there, and in consequence began to expand in size and wealth. Symbolically, too, the lordship of Newry and Mourne passed from the old family of Bagenal to the new family of Nedham, and under the Nedhams the town changed from being the 'frontier town', a military base for the invasion of Ulster, to being a busy port, its importance lying in trade and shipping.

With the opening of the canal came the opening of new opportunities. Its significance cannot be emphasised too much, not only as the first major man-made waterway in the British Isles, but also as the means whereby Newry was catapulted from being a small port of secondary importance to being an international trading centre. The canal made Newry the natural export point for all kinds of goods - agricultural, industrial, commercial -from south-east Ulster. Likewise it was the natural point of entry into Ulster, and ships from all over the world anchored there — from America, the West Indies, the Baltic, the Netherlands, France, and even Poland and Russia.

The end of the eighteenth century saw Newry poised to become a major trading centre in Ireland. It had successfully survived the troubles of this century and as a port had surpassed its rivals in the north, achieving a prominent position in the commerce of the nation. It seemed as though Newry was set to go into the nineteenth century continuing on this course and so become the major city in the north of Ireland. However, commercial success is not the full story. The increasing commercial importance of Newry was complemented by its increasing political influence.

The ship sailing past Narrow Water castle is a Baltic trader carrying timber to Newry, its route having been secured by the opening of the ship canal. (19th century engraving by J. H. Burgess, Ulster Museum)

The town played a prominent part in the major political events of this era. It was one of the first to raise companies of Volunteers and the representatives from Newry were at the forefront in demanding political and economic reforms in Ireland. An MP from Newry, Isaac Corry, was not only a leading member of the 'patriot party' but also rose to become chancellor of the Irish exchequer, and he played an instrumental role in the passing of the Act of Union. In radical politics, also, the town was to the fore. It was home to the radical writer William Drennan and a stronghold of the United Irishmen, being one of the first places to come under martial law during the disarmament of 1797. As the town's prosperity continued into the nineteenth century, so too did its political importance. Newry played its part in securing Catholic emancipation and produced one of the greatest figures in the Irish nationalist tradition, John Mitchel.

5

PATRONAGE AND PATRIOTS

The state of Ireland at the start of the eighteenth century, where full rights as citizens were enjoyed only by those propertied men who were members of the Church of Ireland, left the mass of people — Catholics and dissenters — suffering to a greater or lesser degree from injustices under the law. The grievances felt by those people erupted into sporadic and violent protests. From 1761 onwards the south of Ireland witnessed the smouldering rebellion of the Whiteboys, peasants driven to take up arms against the iniquities of religion and property. The north also saw agrarian protests against the payment of tithes to the Established Church and against the unfairness of the system of leasing land. Although mainly rural in character, the protests sometimes threatened the tranquillity of the towns.

During one such outbreak of agrarian protest by the poorer tenants of Ulster, acting under the name of the Hearts of Steel, Newry itself was directly threatened. One of the town's inhabitants wrote to a friend about it in March 1772:

> Intelligence has just now been sent to the good people of Newry that they may expect a visit from the Hearts of Steel, Oakboys, etc.. They say that they do not mean us any harm provided we surrender all the arms of this place to them, and that the arms shall be returned as soon as they shall have effected their purpose of obtaining perpetual lease of land at their valuations.
>
> R. Scott [a local MP] is to be applied to by this post to lay this matter before government and to procure some troops, which if not immediately sent, I think they will effect their purpose, their numbers are formidable, and should they be opposed in their demand of the arms, it is most probable they would burn this town, so that the lesser evil is to be preferred.
>
> If government hesitate an hour in mobilising soldiers to us the inhabitants here will look upon themselves as sacrificed, and the ' Banditti' as count enanced —... for it is beyond a doubt that were these people reinforced with that supply of arms which this place affords they could ravage the country without opposition as far as the gates of Drogheda. In short things in Ulster (lately esteemed the free and happy part of Ireland) wear a dismal aspect.

Although at the time it may have seemed as if this was the greatest threat posed to Newry since the Duke of Berwick put it to the torch in 1689, in reality the Hearts of Steel were in no position to march on Newry. Nevertheless, the threat itself was a timely reminder that any peace and prosperity enjoyed by Ireland was built on a fragile foundation.

This romantic view shows how far Newry had spread from its Medieval limits across the Clanrye valley. The area in the foreground is Rooney's Meadow, now occupied by a housing estate. (lithograph by J. H. Burgess, Ulster Museum)

In Newry attention was drawn away from the rural disturbances when Robert Scott died in the final months of 1773. This left one of Newry's two parliamentary seats vacant, and a by-election was held on 3 January 1774. The by-election is of some significance because it marks the entry into national politics of a member of the Corry family. Edward, a merchant of the town and the seneschal, stood against Sir Richard Johnston, a gentleman from Gilford, County Armagh. Party divisions were of little or no importance during this era; personal or geographical loyalties were often crucial in deciding political allegiance and geography seems to have played a part in this election. Corry's successor as seneschal — he had to resign in order to stand in the election—George Anderson, excluded those citizens on the County Armagh side of the Clanrye river from voting by stating in the qualification oath that voters were obliged to take the words 'in the County of Down'. It seems likely that Anderson, a magistrate who had been Corry's deputy seneschal, wanted to ensure that only the trustworthy 'old' voters in the County Down part of Newry could vote and was afraid that those on the County Armagh side would be susceptible to the influence of Sir Richard Johnston. This manoeuvre introduced much acrimony into the election. The voting lasted for several days amidst great turmoil. One contemporary observed: 'Our election here goes on with the greatest spirit. Last night a poor fellow was killed and two or three are in custody for the murder.'

Corry was declared the winner but Johnston petitioned parliament to overturn the result on the grounds of illegal voting. Hot on the heels of this petition came one from the citizens of Ballybot, on the County Armagh side, complaining of their exclusion from the election. Parliament established a committee to look into the affair, which found that the election was invalid and a new writ was issued to hold a second one. This proceeded in a more orderly manner but the result remained the same and Edward Corry became an MP for Newry. This marks the last occasion

Isaac Corry, the most important politician to emerge in 18th century Newry. He was the last Chancellor of the Irish Exchequer and instrumental in passing the Act of Union 1801. (Public Record Office of Northern Ireland)

when the right of the inhabitants on the County Armagh side of the river to vote in elections was questioned.

Edward Corry remained in parliament until 1776, when in April of that year a general election was declared. It would seem that Corry's decision not to stand again was influenced by the death of his brother, Sir Trevor Corry. Sir Trevor was one of the first great merchants of Newry and had built his empire on trade. His wealth had contributed to Newry's growth and expansion. His major overseas enterprise was based in Danzig (Gdansk) in Poland, where he died and where he had made a considerable fortune, thus highlighting the international nature of Newry's trade. Edward's son Isaac stood in the April 1776 general election and so took the first step on a career that ultimately led to him being Chancellor of the Irish Exchequer and a prime mover in the Act of Union between Great Britain and Ireland.

Corry was entering parliament at a very exciting time for Ireland. July 1776 saw the Declaration of American Independence and Britain went to war against its colonies. There was no question but that Ireland would support the British effort with forces and finance. Even if it had been otherwise, the subordinate Irish parliament would have had no choice but to follow the lead of Westminster. Nevertheless, the American War of Independence was to have a profound effect on Ireland. For some time discontent had been growing about the conduct of Irish government; discontent that the executive was not responsible to the legislature and that the legislature was completely subordinate to the will of the British parliament sitting in Westminster. Opposition to this state of affairs centred on Henry Flood, and Isaac Corry soon attached himself to Flood's 'patriot party'.

There was much sympathy in Ireland for the Americans. Not only were there ties of kinship between them, many Irish having emigrated to the New World, but those who felt unhappy at the lack of independence of parliament and the restrictions on Irish trade saw similarities with the Americans' demand for 'no taxation without representation' and for a greater say in their own affairs. The principles upon which the new American republic was founded encouraged a move towards democracy and enlightenment among some of the Ascendancy. The Irish political thinkers not only wanted an unfettered parliament but more and more they wanted an end to the penal laws imposed on Catholics and dissenters.

In 1778 Henry Grattan, the rising star of the patriot party, made his famous declaration that 'the Irish Protestant could never be free till the Irish Catholic had ceased to be a slave'. This year saw the passing of an act for the relief of Catholics which removed many of the restrictions on property and inheritance. This act was of importance to Newry as the town possessed a large Catholic population. Corry's association with the patriot party helped to increase his support locally after the passing of the act.

Like other trading centres in Ireland, Newry was hit by the American War of Independence. Not only was an important market cut off but the activities of American privateers around the coasts of the British Isles resulted in the loss of ships and cargo. Matters were made worse when France became an ally to the Americans. John Paul Jones, the first great hero of the American navy, could not have operated with such effectiveness off the British coasts had he not had the safe haven of France to fall back on. When France entered the war on the American side, Ireland lay open to invasion, for Ireland's large standing army, paid for and supported by Irish taxes, was either in America or garrisoning Britain, while at home the Irish government could not even afford to raise a militia in order to defend the country. When Irish ships were taken by privateers within sight of land and raids were made on shore, it became obvious that the citizens would have to take their own measures.

The magnates and merchants of Ireland began to raise companies of Volunteers. These companies were armed and equipped from private funds and the men serving in their ranks received no pay, and without legal obligation subjected themselves to military discipline. To be seen in a Volunteer uniform was to have instant social success. Of the sudden rise of the Volunteer movement, historian W.E.H. Lecky says: 'A sudden enthusiasm, such as occurs two or three times in the history of a nation, seems to have passed through all classes.' Although the Government was alarmed at the appearance of a large body of armed men, it could do nothing to stop it. Even Catholics — despite the legal strictures — were eager to serve, and at its height the Volunteer movement claimed to have over eighty thousand members.

Newry was among one of the first towns to establish Volunteer companies. Being a port, it felt all the more threatened by invasion, and also the population of Newry had always taken a lively interest in public

Depiction of an Volunteer such as would have been seen in Newry

affairs and the state of the nation. To be a Volunteer was as much a political act -asserting national independence and support of the patriot party — as a military one. A number of units were associated with Newry: the 1st Newry Regiment, also known as the Newry Legion; the 2nd Battalion (or sometimes Company) of Loyal Newry Volunteers; and the 3rd Volunteer Company, also called the Newry Fencibles. There was a unit nicknamed the 'Newry Ladies' Fencibles', formed in 1781, 'in which no man under fifty was enrolled nor any who had not a wife and children'. The ranks of the Newry Volunteers were further swelled by the 1st Newry Artillery Company, formed in 1779. One of the units was nicknamed the Newry Rangers.

In the ranks, the companies were usually made up of younger sons and men of little property, and the wealthier men were elected officers and often met expenses from their own pockets. For example, the captain of the Newry Fencibles was David Bell, a merchant with interests in cotton and linen. His letter of 5 November 1779 to Lord Charlemont, the recognised commander-in-chief of the Volunteers, gives us an idea of the composition of a typical Volunteer company and of how they were equipped:

> [They were] composed of the principal gentlemen and merchants here to the amounts of fifty-four, who associated for the defence of this place, and who have provided themselves with arms and necessary equipment: my lord what makes me trouble your lordship with this, is this, a number of tradesmen equal to our original number have offered to join our company and clothe themselves, provided they can have arms from government. We offered to buy arms from them but they refused accepting of in consequence of which I am requested by the company to apply to your lordship for forty or fifty stand of arms.

The Earl of Charlemont was the commander of the Volunteers and along with Henry Grattan their leading political spokesman. (Armagh County Museum)

Like regular
soldiers, the
Volunteers were
awarded medals
for their
achievements.

Like the regular army, the Volunteers had official ranks and a uniform. While there were variations in accordance with taste and wealth, in general the Volunteers wore scarlet coats with different coloured facings and leggings to denote different companies or battalions. To prepare for actual combat they were drilled in military manoeuvres and the use of arms. The medals given out to Volunteers in training are one useful source of information. For example, one gold medal is inscribed 'Loyal Newry Volunteers, 2nd Company, The Gift of the Officers to Sergt. A. Michel as a reward for his efforts in Drilling and Instructing the Company.' Another is inscribed from the Newry Infantry Regiment to 'Ensign G. Foy for merit in the annual trial. C.F. Platoon firing, August 1786.'

Volunteers from different areas often worked together and reviews were usually grand affairs involving companies from more than one county. Writing to Lord Charlemont in 1781, Thomas Dawson, an MP and an officer in the Armagh Volunteers, said:

> Your Lordship's regiment will be by far the largest body of men that will attend the review at Belfast. They all mean to be at Newry, where I fancy there will be at least three times the number of that attended last year.

The Newry Volunteers had a reputation for being well turned out and well drilled. Even Dr William Drennan, a supporter of the Volunteers who had little good to say about Newry, admitted that the 1785 review of Newry Volunteers 'went off here with tolerable eclat. .. They were about 1,800 in number and I thought a good deal better than those at Belfast.'

Fortunately, there was no invasion from France and the Volunteers were never tested in battle — except when they assisted in suppressing the continuing agrarian unrest. However, they were to have an influence upon the politics of the nation and the so-called constitution of 1782. When what Grattan praised as 'the armed property of the Nation' was so assembled, it was only a matter of time before they turned their attention to political issues. The Volunteers were men of property and wealth, landlords and merchants. By organising to defend the nation, they had proved their loyalty and their ability to administrate for themselves. The increasing clamour within and without parliament and the strains of the American War of Independence made the British parliament eager to conciliate the Irish. In 1779 a bill to abolish the sacramental test for Presbyterians was passed by the Irish parliament and the following year was approved at Westminster. This bill removed the legal restrictions on Presbyterians holding public office. The granting of this concession to Presbyterians strengthened the case for lifting the laws excluding Catholics from civil liberties.

Since 1663, during the reign of Charles II restrictions had been placed on Irish trade with other nations wherever it was seen as a threat to English interests. This meant that Irish merchants were increasingly limited in what they could trade in. Like other trading centres, Newry was inhibited in the development of its trade, and so it is that we find the town's representatives to the fore in calling for an end to restrictions on Irish commerce. Between 1779 and 1780 a number of measures were passed that gave greater freedom to industry and trade in Ireland. New markets were opened to the Irish and manufacturers were able to sell a greater number of products abroad.

A 1784 ale glass of the 2nd Company, Loyal Newry Volunteers. By this date those who remained in the Volunteers were more radical politically. (Sotheby's, London)

Having achieved a degree of economic freedom, the patriot party sought to achieve political freedom also. Newry MP Isaac Corry was still a leading member of the patriot party and reflected the sentiments felt by the majority of people in his home town. Henry Grattan, now the recognised leader of the patriots, and Lord Charlemont, leader of the Volunteers, were the prime movers behind the Volunteer convention of February 1782. to discuss the state of Ireland. Delegates from 143 Volunteer corps attended the convention at Dungannon in County Tyrone, among them Captain David Bell of the Newry Fencibles. The grievances of Ireland were debated and resolutions passed that were to be the blueprints for Irish government and society as envisaged by these enlightened men of property. Besides the resolutions calling for an independent legislature and freedom from English influence, others were passed that probably meant more to Newry. One was a resolution that the ports of Ireland 'are by Right open to all foreign countries not at war with the King' and others calling for religious equality and liberty of conscience to be enshrined in the statute book were seen as a major step forward after almost a century of penal legislation.

The convention, of course, was not parliament and its resolutions were not law, but its voice was heard at Westminster, especially when the military defeats in America led to the resignation of British Prime Minister Lord North's government and its replacement by that of the Earl of Rockingham and Charles James Fox. This latter administration was more sympathetic to the Irish case and with the repeal in May 1782 of the Declaratory (or Sixth) Act of George I — an act that had been passed in 1720 which formally asserted the right of the British parliament to legislate for Ireland - it began to implement a series of measures that returned legislative power to the Irish parliament. This process was popularly known as the Constitution of 1782. Hailed at the time as the redemption of Ireland and the securing of real 'national' government for the kingdom, it was soon seen that reality did not match the patriots' expectations. Of the constitution of 1782, W.E.H. Lecky, a historian sympathetic to the patriot party, says:

> The extreme difficulty in making it work in harmony with the Parliament of England; the excessive concentration of political power in a very few hands; religious and historical antipathies, great ignorance and great poverty, the exclusion of more than three-fourths of the population from all political rights, scandalous abuses of patronage, and many forms both of corruption and of anarchy, still continued.

A series of measures was passed by the 'patriot parliament', as it has been called, which removed most of the legal and property restrictions on the Catholic citizens of Ireland and all those remaining on dissenters. This was done despite opposition from the government in England. This was of importance to Newry, since it meant that the majority of its citizens could now freely participate in the commercial and public life of the town. When in 1793 the Catholic relief act gave Catholics the same rights of franchise as enjoyed by Protestants and opened most official

Volunteer reviews such as this one in Lisburn, Co. Down, in 1782 could be magnificent spectacles. (painting by John Carey, Lisburn Museum)

posts to them, it meant that political influence was also open to the majority of citizens in Newry, and as it was a 'potwalloper' borough, this made the town one of the most democratic in Ireland.

William Pitt's British administration then changed its tactics in relation to the patriots in the Irish parliament. It was decided to weaken the strength of the patriot party by winning over as many as possible of its supporters to the Westminster government. To this end the viceroy, the Marquis of Buckingham, approached Isaac Corry in 1790. Corry was seen as an important member of the patriot faction and carried some influence in parliament. The fact that he had been elected on a popular franchise gave him a certain moral authority. In return for Corry's support, Buckingham offered him the post of Surveyor General of Ordnance, which was a sinecure that carried a salary but little responsibility. Corry accepted the offer, and so it might be said that a patriot succumbed to patronage. The acceptance of a government sinecure did Corry no harm in Newry. His personal standing and past deeds in the cause of the nation seemed to have ensured his popularity and he continued to be re-elected for the constituency. Indeed he held his parliamentary seat for a record thirty years. He had to stand for re-election in January 1798 on his promotion to Surveyor General of the Royal Lands and Manors, but no one opposed him.

Thus Isaac Corry transferred his allegiance from the national cause to that of British influence in Ireland. But it would be too simplistic to cast him in the role of a villain. In an age when political parties barely existed, even in name only, and political creeds had yet to crystallise into something hard and fast, it was not unusual for a politician to change from one faction to another or pass from opposition to government without a loss of integrity. Even the father of the patriot party, Henry Flood, went over to 'the other side' and accepted a government appointment.

Corry was a man of ability and talent, with a high standing among his contemporaries as the following description, quoted by John F. Small, illustrates:

> Mr Corry's person is manly, and his countenance expressive of spirit and good sense. There is not a more influencing speaker in the Irish House of Commons. His voice is strong and mellow, his diction correct, and his style fluent, copious, moderately ornamented, and always above mediocrity. . . It is principally upon subjects connected with finance, revenue, or commerce that he appears to the greatest advantage. To these he seems chiefly to have directed his attention, and in these he has acquired a very extensive and useful knowledge. Indeed, wherever clearness and strength can recommend a speaker to his auditory, Mr Corry is calculated to command applause, for his understanding is of the first class. ... His ornaments consist in extreme neatness of diction, smoothness and fluency of periods, and well judged arrangement of matter. These, added to the correct animation of his manner, the round fullness of his voice, and the effect of a good person, procure for his opinions a great degree of attention and respect.

Dr William Drennan, an acquaintance of Isaac Corry's for many years in Newry, was to have an influence upon events in Ireland. Drennan had come from Belfast to Newry in 1783 to establish a medical practice there, and he remained in the town for seven years before moving to Dublin. Drennan was an intelligent and learned man, with a deep interest in political philosophy. He was a supporter of the patriot cause, the Volunteers and more radical solutions to Ireland's ills. Like many people, Drennan was disappointed at the failure of the constitution of 1782 to thoroughly reform Irish government. The apparent success of that year and the signing of peace with the United States saw the end of the Volunteers as a mass movement. Those who remained in its ranks did so for mixed motives. Drennan commented in 1786:

> You will have a new company from [Newry] at the Belfast review formed from the saved remnants of the rest, and Corry, it is said, is to be their Captain. This is just a frolic of young lads to show their silver at the review and will die the day after.

Many of those who remained with the Volunteers were the more politically aware who wanted to continue with the agitation until real reform had been achieved. The eruption of the revolution in France in 1789 made a huge impact on the more liberal and radical elements in this reform movement. Drennan himself was inspired by the French revolutionaries and not only celebrated the fall of the Bastille but found satisfaction in the execution of Louis XVI. As he played a prominent part in the politics of Newry and was influential over the political activists in

William Drennan practised medicine in Newry for a number of years before moving to Dublin. He was an influential political thinker and came up with the idea for the United Irishmen. (painting by Robert Home)

the town, it is quite probable that the strong republican element in Newry owed much to his presence.

While the Volunteers came more and more under the influence of elements who sought to model the movement on the French National Guard, and had tried to obtain help from France and would actually have welcomed a French invasion, so too the reform movement came under the sway of revolutionary factions. Grattan and other moderates split with the radicals, the Catholic committee abandoned Edmund Burke's son in favour of Theobald Wolfe Tone as its secretary, and talk of revolution was in the air. At this point, while he was in Dublin, Drennan spoke of the organisation of a society that would overturn the existing order and establish a new one based on liberty, equality and fraternity. It was Drennan's idea that gave birth to the Society of United Irishmen in 1791. Although Drennan disassociated himself from the society before it became a secret organisation, the United Irishmen had many adherents in Newry.

In 1792 a gentleman by the name of John Hutton, who apparently was on holiday, visited Newry. Hutton was none other than Theobald Wolfe Tone, on a secret mission for the United Irishmen. He arrived in August with another leader of the United Irishmen, John Keogh. They were in the north in an attempt to reconcile the different nationalist factions and secret societies and unite them in common cause. In Newry, Wolfe Tone found that the Catholics were fighting among themselves and it took a considerable effort on his part to get them to sink their differences. He was also involved in an expedition to Rathfriland to meet with the Peep o' Day Boys, but nothing came of it. Wolfe Tone seems to have had more influence over the political activists in Newry than over the secret societies in the surrounding countryside. On leaving Newry he commented: 'We have materially contributed to restore peace in the county Down; we have created a spirit in Newry which never existed there before; we have reconciled their differences.'

Whether it was due to Wolfe Tone's influences or not, Newry was a republican stronghold. Plans were put into being to prepare for an armed rising and many eminent merchants of the town were said to be republican. One common activity was the cutting down of ash trees for use as pike staffs, as the following account by Samuel Murphy of Newry illustrates:

> The rage and complexion of our country becomes every day more alarming and serious; the vile mob have begun to cut down and carry off all the ash timber for shafts to their pikes; at Kinghill Cabra, and Lord Clanbrassil's, many hundreds assemble in the early part of the night, exult and huza on the fall of each tree.

This was not an easy time for the conservatives of Newry, who feared that events in France might be repeated on their own doorstep. George Anderson, a magistrate, wrote from Newry in February 1797:

> Our town abounds with dangerous and disaffected people and I assure your lordship [Lord Downshire] treason is not confined to the low orders; we should be proclaimed [as being under martial law]; a young Isaac Glenny of Glenville in a large company declared that all around his place there are frequent nightly meetings and that they have cut down the trees of all his neighbours, but have not touched him. I fancy he is indebted to his name for that favour.
>
> I astonished a parcel of our republican merchants in a pretty large circle speaking of the yeomanry corps against which their utmost rancour is shown on every occasion; they were censuring the yeomanry oath of allegiance when the thought struck me and I observed to them that they must soon all take it or they would cease to be wholesale merchants and entitled to the benefit of six per cent, for that it was intended to introduce such a clause in the next Revenue Bill; indeed they were completely panic struck. . . You may rest assured of it this would be a brain blow to the Belfast and Newry rebels and why should there not at these times be such qualifications and why should rebels enjoy the [advantages] of the friends and supporters of government?

The 'Newry rebels' were in a strong position. The yeomanry was openly insulted in the streets and attempts to arrest United Irishmen often led to their being rescued by the crowd. Nevertheless, some suspects were arrested and confessed to swearing United Irishman oaths and 'declaring they would join the French on their landing'.

The Government's policy was to break up the United Irishmen and to seize all stocks of weapons. Newry was singled out for particular treatment. Isaac Corry, once the darling of the town, was now seen by many as the villain and, justifiably or not, was held personally responsible for the arrests of many of the most important merchants. However, things did not all go the Government's way; in March 1797 one magistrate had to report:

> The disarming here yesterday rather failed; the Republicans were aware of it; about 18 guns with a great number of pistols and some sword

sticks composed the booty; the troops looked remarkably well; our town had quite a marshal appearance; some of the principal young Republicans went through the streets with green handkerchiefs and the most fiend like and frantic countenances; some disturbance was expected at night but all has been quiet.

Despite the light tone of this letter, it was a grim time for Newry, as for the rest of Ireland. Suspects were often arrested and sent to Belfast, where, away from family and friends, they found themselves condemned in a summary manner. One such case gave rise to a rather bizarre episode. On 22 May 1797 a detachment of the 22nd Light Dragoons arrested a number of Newry townsmen suspected of treasonable activities, among them John Gordon. In a further series of arrests four days later, ten men were taken. The prisoners were sent under armed escort to Belfast for trial. John Gordon's wife, on hearing of his arrest, set off in pursuit on horseback, with proof of his innocence. It is said that she did not stop for rest until she had reached Belfast. Fortunately, she arrived in time to save her husband, but the poor horse collapsed and died from exhaustion. The Gordons returned to their home at Templegowan, on the outskirts of Newry, with a curious memento of the affair as a keepsake - the tail of the unfortunate horse. This odd relic of those troubled times still survives and can be seen in the board room of Newry Town Hall. Although its tail is preserved, the name of the poor beast is not.

Theobald Wofe Tone, a leader of the United Irishmen, visited Newry in 1792 under the name of John Hutton. (portrait by T. W. Huffam)

The military operation against the United Irishmen begun in Ulster under General Lake was extended to the rest of Ireland by 1798. In that year Newry was occupied by the Ancient Britons, a Welsh regiment of horse under the command of Lord Carhampton. This was a time of arrest and atrocity, murder and execution. A gallows was set up on the hill below St Patrick's Church and a number of condemned men were executed there. Two in particular, Cochrane and Lowans, are still remembered in the town. After their executions their heads were displayed at the News Room in Margaret Street. The tradition in the town is that, before Cochrane's father was allowed to bury his son, he had to carry the head through the streets proclaiming him a traitor.

When the rebellion broke out in May 1798, Newry was not involved. The arrests, seizures of arms, and harsh treatment had left the republicans in the town disorganised and disheartened. They did not rise to support their comrades elsewhere in the north and so the town was saved from the worst excesses of the insurrection.

The defeat of the United Irishmen was followed by the implementation of plans to bring about a parliamentary union between Great Britain and Ireland. William Pitt's British government instigated a campaign of patronage and bribery on a scale unimagined before. It wanted to secure friends and win over waverers. Among the first to benefit was Isaac Corry - he was promoted to Chancellor of the Irish Exchequer in place of Sir John Parnell, who was opposed to the Union. Corry may have entered parliament as one of Grattan's patriots but now he was to exercise his not inconsiderable talents to undermine the patriots and bring about a union with Great Britain.

Patronage was exercised on a grand scale. Promotion to the peerage and appointments to government sinecures were handed out in an effort to win a majority for the Union. The episode that stands out most, however, in the campaign to force the Union through parliament is the duel that was fought between Isaac Corry and Henry Grattan. During one of the many fierce debates over parliamentary union, on 17 February 1800, Grattan had had as much as he could take from Corry and so challenged him to a duel. The two men met 'on the field of honour', with the result that Corry was wounded. He may have lost the duel but he won the battle, for in 1801 the Irish parliament was dissolved and the United Kingdom of Great Britain and Ireland was established. In the imperial parliament, in which the town had only one seat, Corry continued to serve as MP for Newry.

The majority of Newry voters supported the Union since it had been promised that union with Great Britain would be followed by the implementation of full Catholic emancipation, and so the Newry people were willing to continue to support Corry in the belief that the last vestiges of the penal laws would be removed. When the Union failed to fulfil its expectations, it, and Corry, lost support in Newry. When Corry moved to his new house at Derrymore in 1802, he had a road built that led straight from the Dublin road to his house, thus avoiding the town completely. This is still called the Chancellor's Road.

One of the last acts of the Irish parliament was to purchase the White Linen Hall from its owners at a cost of £5,000, less than half what it had cost to build. The white linen venture had failed and the hall had been used to house arrested United Irishmen in 1797-8. It was to become the army barracks for the town, a role it fulfilled until the twentieth century.

The war against Napoleon brought a measure of prosperity to Newry. Britain's need for supplies and the Continental blockade meant there was a greater demand for goods from Ireland. These years saw a growth in the businesses of Newry, leading to increased wealth and an influx of population, people wanting to set up businesses or looking for employment.

When he inherited the Newry estates the unpopular Robert Nedham, Viscount (later Earl of) Kilmorey altered the town seal by adding his name to it and replacing the abbot with an earl, as seen on this impression. (National Museum of Ireland)

For Ireland this was a period of relative calm, but for Newry it saw a change that was to have a profound effect upon its future development. In 1806 the last Nedham, William, died. He left no immediate family and there were no obvious heirs to his estate. However, he had willed all his estate and possessions to one Robert Nedham of Shavington, in Shropshire, who held the title Viscount Kilmorey. The apparent lack of any blood relationship between the two led one observer to call this bequest 'whimsical and absurd'. But William Nedham (or Needham as the surname was just as often spelt by this time) had good reason for his choice, as Robert Nedham was, in fact, a distant cousin of his. So the Kilmorey family replaced the Nedhams, and were to have an influence on Newry, not always welcome, for the next century.

Almost immediately the Kilmoreys began to exert their authority. A general election was called in 1806 and Isaac Corry, who had remained as MP for Newry after the Union, stood for re-election, and was opposed by the Honourable Francis Jack Needham, who was a lieutenant general in

One of the last acts of the Irish Parliament was to purchase the White Linen Hall on Canal Quay for use as an army barracks. (Lawrence engraving)

the army. Although an Englishman and a stranger to the town, General Needham received considerable support. Newry had not forgotten its sufferings in 1797—8 and was now opposed to the Union with Great Britain. The citizens wanted to see Isaac Corry ousted because of his involvement in the government responsible for the Union. This election seems to have passed with less violence and disorder than was customary in Newry, although feelings did run high. At the closing of the polls the result was 116 votes for General Needham and 74 votes for Isaac Corry. Another election was called in 1807 and once again Needham defeated Corry.

Newry continued to prosper. A new custom house was built on Merchants' Quay, in the heart of the business centre of town. In 1809 a Reading Society, to promote knowledge and literacy, was formed. In 1810 parliament sanctioned the building of a new Episcopalian church, as St Patrick's was no longer considered adequate for the congregation. In the same year the *Newry Commercial Telegraph* was published for the first time.

Although in 1815 Newry's population stood at 13,500, and a new periodical, the *Newry Magazine,* was established, all was not going smoothly. The first major concern to suffer from the depressed state of the economy in the wake of Napoleon's defeat at Waterloo that same year was the bank of Moore, Macan and Foxall which had come into existence during the war years through both commercial and political motives. The bank that Moore, Macan and Foxall were in opposition to was one owned by Isaac Corry and John Ogle. Of Corry, we already know; Ogle came from a prosperous commercial family who first came to prominence in the mid-eighteenth century. They lived in a mansion in Fathom, on the Omeath Road, and Fathom Park was for a time called

Ogle's Glen. Isaac Corry was still much resented in Newry and it was as much this resentment as commercial motives that brought the rival bank into existence. Sir John Moore owned the building in which the bank was set up and also a considerable estate at Drumbanagher, near Newry. He had been one of Newry's two representatives in the Irish parliament and was a committed opponent to the Act of Union. The Moores were an older family than the Corrys, having settled in Drumbanagher during the early seventeenth century plantation, when they were granted the confiscated estates of the O'Hanlons. Foxall was also a man of property and the third partner, Macan, was a merchant of the town but little is known of him.

The bank flourished during the Napoleonic Wars when the Irish economy was buoyant. However, the economy was hit by the depression that followed the end of the war. Despite attempts to save the bank, it was forced to close in 1816. This was not an uncommon occurrence in Ireland at the time. The biggest loser was Sir John Moore, as he had invested more money than his partners and was committed to underwriting the debts. He was forced to sell his estate at Drumbanagher but even it was not enough to pay all that was due. He retired, in comparative poverty, to Loughbrickland, where he lived until his death.

By the late 19th century warehouses were built on both sides of the canal. Boats came up as far as Merchants' Quay until 1956. The bridges being opened to allow this was often used as an excuse for being late for school. (Lawrence Collection)

The bank of Moore, Macan and Foxall was set up in opposition to that of Isaac Corry and John Ogle. It went bankrupt in the depression that followed the end of the Napoleonic Wars.

Despite such setbacks and the increasing rivalry of Belfast as a port, Newry's commercial position was never seriously undermined. Its trade was established on a firm footing and thanks to the canal it had access to a vast hinterland that continued to provide a steady flow of traffic. Thomas Bradshaw's commercial directory, published in 1820, reported:

> The total tonnage invoiced yearly at the port of Newry, amounts to 40,000 tons. . . The quantity of flaxseed imported, when the trade is open, is very considerable. On an average it may be taken at 9,000 hogsheads, yearly.
> Newry has a very considerable export of butter, provisions, and linen cloth. The export of [butter] may annually be rated at 80,000 casks, averaging £3.10s. [£3.50] per cask. Besides this, there are from 1000 to 1200 crocks sold at the crane for home consumption, averaging £1.5s. [£1.2.5] per crock.

The same directory gives a sketch of the town at this time; it had a News Room, a theatre, the army barracks and schools for children of the poor, one 'for the benefit of female children', as well as two classical schools. Among the societies were the Reading Society, a Humane Society, and a Bible Society. The Humane Society was founded to save people from drowning in the river or in the canal, apparently a common occurrence; the directory tells us that 'the society have purchased an excellent resuscitative apparatus, and have appointed a number of receiving houses in convenient situations. They have also published cards of instruction for restoring suspended animation.'

An insurance company of sorts existed in the town, by the name of the Newry Amicable Annuity Company, whose object was to provide an annuity for the members' widows. In 1819 its capital was valued at £25,000 and it had one hundred members. The 182.0 directory goes on to tell us that:

One of the major industries in Newry in the 19th century was the Duncan Alderdice distillery on Monaghan St. (Newry Museum)

there are at present two large distilleries in Newry. The old one, though not working at present, is one of the most complete concerns of the kind in Ireland. The distillery in Monaghan-street, is as perfect as possible, and produces excellent whiskey. In Ballybot, there are two extensive breweries, both of which are working at present.

Near Violet-hill there is an establishment for the manufacture of spades, shovels, and rod and hoop iron; and in Newry there is a foundry for casting brass and iron.

On 21 November 1819 St Mary's Church was opened for 'divine service'. This was the church that had been sanctioned in 1810 to replace St Patrick's, which had never fully recovered from the troubles of the seventeenth century and had only been partially rebuilt in 1720. In the building of St Mary's much of the decorative stonework was taken from St Patrick's, so the nineteenth-century church has stones dating back to the sixteenth century, including the memorial to Sir Nicholas Bagenal, which makes it look older than it actually is. Some of the congregation remained loyal to St Patrick's and a schism occurred in the Church of Ireland in Newry as one section went to the new church and another remained with the old. However, good relations were eventually restored in 1866, when St Patrick's — Swift's 'High Church, Low steeple' — was rebuilt in the form that it retains today.

In 1822 Viscount Kilmorey was elevated in the peerage, and thus became the Earl of Kilmorey. He was granted the second title of Viscount Newry and Mourne, to be used by his heir.

St. Mary's church was sanctioned by Act of Parliament in 1810 and opened in 1819 to replace St. Patrick's. Part of the congregation remained at St. Patrick's causing a schism in Newry that was not settled until 1866. (Ulster Folk and Transport Museum)

By far the most important commercial development in Newry at this period was in 1822, when the Newry Gaslight Company was established. London had first been lit by gas in 1812 and many cities in England followed suit. Dublin only introduced gas lighting in 1818. Both Belfast and Newry established gaslight companies in 1822. The social reasons for wanting the streets to be lit were obvious enough: attacks and robberies at night were common occurrences; prisoners often escaped custody while being moved at night; and, of course, the benefit of being able to see where one was putting one's foot was obvious.

The founders of the company were aware of the value of the service they would be offering to the public. The preamble to the articles establishing the company states that

> it would be of great benefit to the inhabitants of the said town of Newry in the Counties of Down and Armagh and the Suburbs if the streets and other public passages and places. . . public buildings, shops, and manufactories therein were better lighted.

To this end the Newry Gaslight Company was convinced that

> Inflammable Air produced from coal and other substances and conveyed by means of pipes may be safely and beneficially used for lighting and several streets and other public passages and places. . . and for lighting private houses, shops, counting houses, ware houses, public works, manufactories, Quays and public and other buildings.

111

The partners in the company obviously had grand designs and a great vision of what changes their 'Inflammable Air' could bring to the town. While these were important factors in their thinking — as well as the desire not to be outdone by Belfast, no doubt — the men who established the company were businessmen with a sound commercial sense. Unlike other methods of street lighting, there would be valuable side-products from the production of gas, as the articles of the company state:

> Coke obtained from such coal may be beneficially employed as fuel in private houses and manufactories, and oil, tar, pitch, asphaltum, ammoniacal liquor, and essential oil also obtained therefrom may be used and applied in various other ways with great advantage.

Many people in Newry castigated the gas company as an 'English' intrusion. This may have been because its establishment required an act of parliament, which gave rise to the myth that it was set up by Englishmen attempting to make a profit at Newry's expense. Whatever the case, this local chauvinism was misplaced, for the records show that the men who founded the company were locals. The Earl of Kilmorey owned the land on which the gasworks was built — down by the quay in present-day Kilmorey Street — and the company partners were all Newry businessmen, such as: William Greer, a coach proprietor from Hill Street; Robert Greer, an attorney from the town; Isaac William, a local merchant; Isaac Glenny, another local merchant; and Thomas Gibson Henry, merchant, and the Earl of Kilmorey's agent. The only person involved with the company who was not local was John Vazii, an engineer brought over from England to build and manage the gasworks.

Jonathan Swift's 'high church, low steeple' – St. Patrick's overlooking Newry was built in 1573, destroyed in Berwick's fire on 1680, partially restored in 1720 and eventually rebuilt in 1866 (Lawrence Collection)

ST. PATRICK'S CHURCH. NEWRY Co. DOWN 3094. W.L.

The Newry Gaslight Company officially came into being on 1 September 1822. Initially it had fifty-five shares of £50 each and a total working capital of £2,750. It had a board of twenty members which appointed the directors by rotation annually. The first directors were Trevor Corry, John Boyd and Samuel Reid. In the articles of agreement setting up the company it states that the company 'shall have full power to enter into any contracts with any person or persons, body politic or corporate, willing and desirous of contracting with the said Company or Proprietor for the lighting of the said town of Newry'. The reference to a 'body politic or corporate' is significant when we remember that Newry still had no corporation or council to regulate public affairs, and shows that the members of the company expected such a body to be established shortly. And this was indeed the case, for dissatisfaction at this vacuum in public administration had led the Earl of Kilmorey to take steps to institute a corporate body for the town. The members of the Newry Gaslight Company were fully aware of this move, as many of them were directly involved and were proposed as members of the Board of Commissioners that was to be set up to have responsibility for the lighting, guarding and cleaning of the streets. This body would have the power to levy a rate from the town's inhabitants to be put to public use. One such use would be to pay for more lights on the streets, which would have obvious benefits for the company.

In 1824, under the auspices of the Public Health Act, the Earl of Kilmorey's proposals for the establishment of twenty-one public commissioners came before parliament. The proposals were heavily weighted in the earl's interest. Of the twenty-one commissioners, only twelve were to be elected and the rest were to be comprised of the earl (and after him, his successors), the local MP, the vicar of the parish, the seneschal, the earl's land agent, the church wardens, the Marquis of Downshire and his agent, all of whom were either the earl's direct appointees or his political allies.

Murphy's Bridge and beyond it on the right is the Savings Bank and Assembly Rooms. Note the gas lamp on the bridge. (Lawrence Collection)

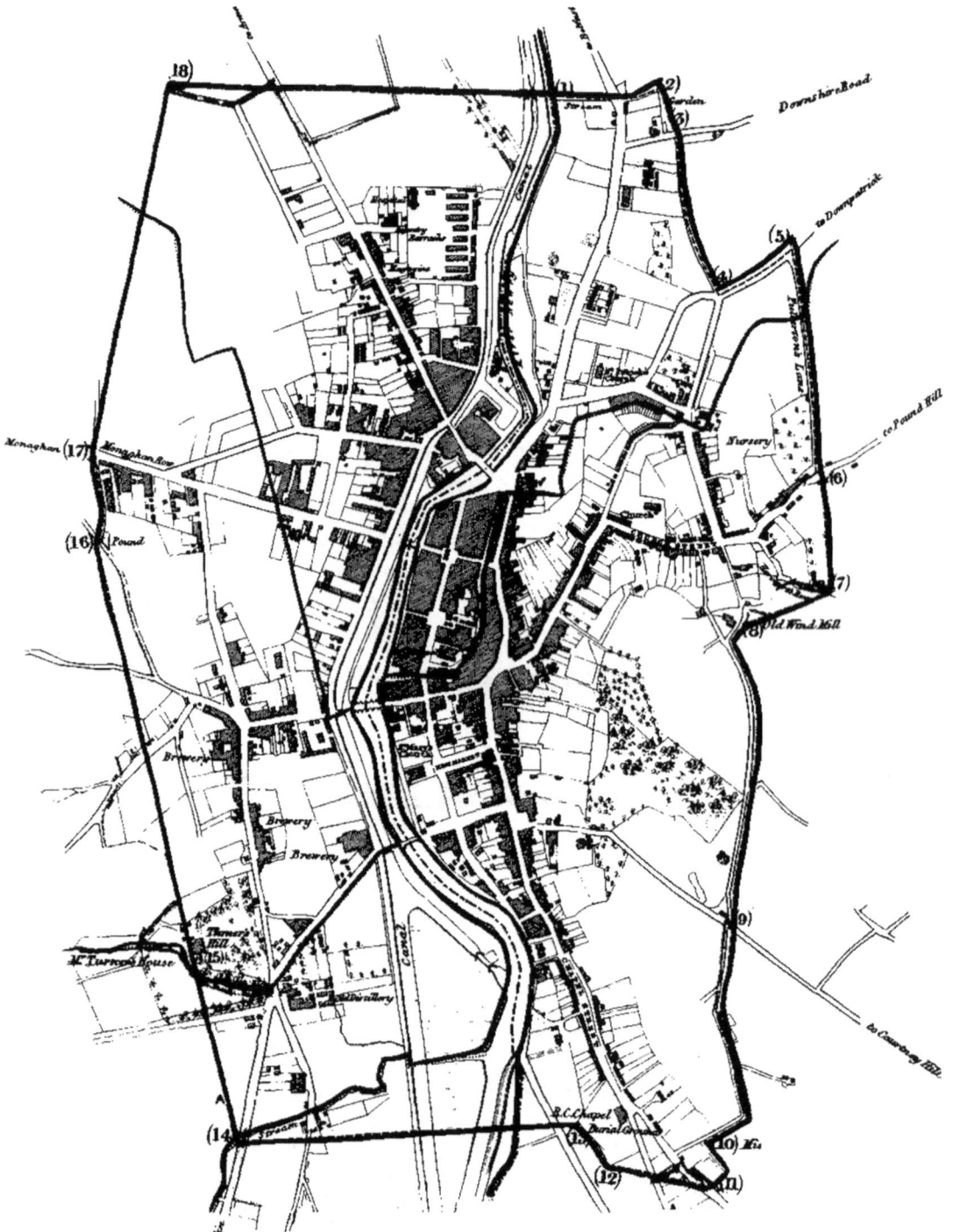

Not until the 1871 Improvement and Water Act was the municipal boundary of Newry officially defined. (Newry Museum)

Illustration of the Cathedral of SS Patrick and Colman showing the transepts and tower added in the early 20th century. (*Newry Telegraph*)

The other twelve commissioners each had to have an income of £1,000 per annum in order to be eligible to serve on the board, and even then the first twelve were named in the bill to serve for a term of five years only. These named commissioners were also by and large appointees of the earl. Newry, therefore, was to be administered by a Board of Commissioners on which the earl's faction had an automatic majority. The patent unfairness of these proposals and the widespread opposition to them among the people of Newry led to their being rejected by parliament. For a long time afterwards there was resentment at the Kilmoreys' attempts to influence affairs in Newry and years later a local politician and commentator, John F. Small, condemned them strongly for 'that interference in the political affairs of the borough, which they have ever since assumed with such a malign influence on the progress and prosperity of our town'.

While such acrimony flourished in the political affairs of Newry, there was a growing tolerance in religious matters. The Irish parliament had removed many legal restrictions on Catholics and most opportunities in commercial and public life were now open to them. The failure to grant full emancipation after the Act of Union did create resentment, but the position of Catholics had improved. In a town like Newry, as historian Francis Plowden informs us, where Catholics, 'from their numbers, being three-fourths of the inhabitants, and from their respectability and property, [were] the most important body of that persuasion in any town of Ulster', it was only natural that they should use their wealth and influence for the betterment of the Catholic Church. In 1825 ground was acquired in Hill Street and work began on what was to become the Cathedral of SS Patrick and Colman, which, when it opened in 1829, was the first such cathedral in Ireland following emancipation. Newry was to the fore in supporting the campaign for Catholic emancipation led by Daniel O'Connell, and with its implementation all except the highest offices in the kingdom were opened to Catholics on an equal footing with other citizens. In the following decades this was to have a significant effect on the nature of local government and parliamentary representation in Newry.

While the issue of Catholic emancipation was being fought out on the national stage, parliament passed an act which was of more immediate importance to the townspeople. The failure of the Earl of Kilmorey's attempt to establish a municipal government had not deterred others from trying and, in fact, prompted greater efforts on the part of the people of Newry to redress their grievance at being left without a corporation. Parliament finally responded in 1828, with an act establishing a board of twenty-one commissioners of police. Under this act, for the first time, the boundary of the town was definitively set out (the parliamentary borough took in part of the outlying districts). The commissioners were to be elected annually and had the authority to levy a rate to cover their expenses. In the first year the rate levied amounted to £1,150. The provisions of this act were specifically designed to deal with Newry alone, but its obvious benefits were extended to any Irish town that did not have a corporate public body. Newry, having been left without a proper system of local government for over a century, became the model for municipal administration throughout Ireland.

The establishment of the Board of Police Commissioners did not mean that the manor courts were immediately dissolved. The courts continued to exercise the powers previously held by them and it was not until the implementation of legal reforms in the middle of the nineteenth century that the courts of the lordship of Newry and Mourne were completely dissolved.

One of the first acts of the commissioners was to sign a contract with the Newry Gaslight Company for the lighting of the streets. Not all public lights were gas - some were fuelled by oil. One was used to supplement the other, and it may have been hoped that competition between the two would have kept prices down. Whatever the case, the cost of gas and oil lighting came to over £400 per year.

A formal patrol known as the Town Watch was established to enable the commissioners to fulfil their duty to 'light and watch' the streets. It comprised eleven men directly employed by the commissioners. In the early years they were paid 7s. (35p) per week, with the superintendent (sometimes called the inspector) of the watch receiving £50 per annum. They acted as policemen, patrolling the streets to ensure order and prevent crime. An important part of their duty was to monitor the street lights; every light was carefully logged in the watchmen's report book and at the end of his beat each watchman recorded the condition of the lights.

The minutes of the police commissioners' meetings frequently record disputes over the lighting of the streets, and the imposition of fines on contractors for not fulfilling their duties. Wherever possible they cut down on expenses, as witnessed in the following instruction issued on 19 February 1839,

A gas lamp post as would have been used in Newry.

116

that directions be given to the Gas Company not to light the Gas Lamps for five nights previous to the full moon and the night of the full moon but to light the night after the full moon.

Although ensuring that the street lights were working properly may have been the Town Watch's primary duty, its other responsibilities took up much more time. These involved removing drunks and other 'nuisances' from the streets, ensuring public order at the courts, sometimes attending at church and also escorting — for his own protection — the Collector of the Police Tax on his rounds. Its headquarters was the Watch House in Pollock's Court, where the superintendent also had his rooms. The first superintendent was John Henry. The watchmen had no uniform but were usually supplied with greatcoats. They each carried a halbert, and in case they needed to summon assistance, a rattle. This rattle sounded something like a corncrake, used then by farmers to scare away crows, and nowadays used by supporters at football matches. The watchmen patrolled at night. The standard beat was set in summer time, and in winter was extended to cover the hours of darkness, for which they received extra payment. For example, on 13 December 1841 the commissioners resolved 'that the Watchmen go on duty from 15th of December to 15th of February at 6 o'clock in the evening and that they be allowed 1 shilling [5p] in addition to their wages'. Two sub-inspectors were appointed to assist the inspector in supervising the watch and they also received an extra shilling in wages.

The cells in the Watch House were used for detaining drunks, nuisances and vagrants whom the watchmen had arrested. They were usually released after a warning but were sometimes brought before the magistrates at Newry or before a higher court in Downpatrick. An entry in the commissioners' records for 18 July 1836 refers to 'R.H. Jackson [the superintendent], expenses prosecuting vagrants at Downpatrick, £1 7s.4d. [£1.37]'; in those days anyone without money or steady employment could be committing a criminal offence under the vagrancy laws.

Newry being a busy commercial town and port meant that the nightlife there could be somewhat rowdy. This often meant trouble for the watchmen and, to judge from this entry in the commissioners' accounts, their jobs must have been hazardous:

Repairing Watchman's rattle .... 10d. [4p]
A new lock for the Watch House .... 2s.2d. [11p]
Repairing Watchmen's Halberts, rattles, etc....8s.6d. [42 ½p]

Maintaining public order — especially at election time — was the biggest single task faced by the commissioners. In the absence of a fully fledged police force a lenient approach seems to have been adopted, as witnessed in the following instructions issued on 18 November 1839:

In case of a riot, the Watchman is to caution the persons who may be acting improperly to desist, and retire to their houses, but if such disorderly person or persons will not consent to go quietly home, and persist in making Noise and Disturbances, the Watchman is to spring

A gas lamp post as would have been used in Newry.

his rattle, get assistance and convey the person or persons so disturbing to the Watch House, using, however, no unnecessary force or violence, and if he, or they, consent to go peaceably home with any Householder (known to the Superintendent) who will undertake in writing in the Watchbook with his signature affixed thereto to be responsible for the appearance of the Person or Persons in the morning, if required, the Superintendent in each case is allowed to permit such Person or Persons to go away with such Householders.

As the years progressed, the commissioners had to respond to more and more demands being made on them. It was no longer considered adequate to have a patrol at night only, as there was need for some daytime regulation of the streets. It was decided, therefore, on 12 January 1839, to appoint a 'Day Inspector of Nuisances' to patrol the streets by day. In November 1842 Mr McCormick, the day inspector, was ordered to pay particular attention to the problem of 'piggs perambulating the town, which are now complained of generally'. Another matter that the day inspector was asked to attend to was to see to it 'that the stand for jaunting cars be in William Street and no other places in town'.

While the Town Watch may have prevented crime and kept order on the streets of Newry, it did not always keep order within its own ranks. Because they were not trained as policemen and were often friends or neighbours of offenders meant that the watchmen were sometimes led astray. The most common charges brought against them by the superintendent were insubordination, drunkenness and leaving the beat.

A Town Watch inspector's written report to the Police Commissioners.

Some examples brought before the commissioners were:

4TH OF MAY 1835 Michael Boyle, Watchman, put under stoppage of 3s/6d [17 ½p] for being off his beat and found by the Overseer in the Glass House.

1ST OF FEBRUARY 1836 Resolved that Robert Freeburn, Watchman, be fined in the sum of twenty shillings [£1] in consequences of insubordination to the Superintendent of the Watch and that he pay four shillings [20p] per week until that sum be paid.

18TH OF MAY 1836 Resolved that Hugh Thompson be dismissed for being drunk and unfit for duty.

In June 1836 the superintendent himself was brought before a disciplinary hearing and it was 'resolved that R.H. Jackson be fined in the sum of 20/-[£1] for bad conduct to Mr James Irvine, and he be severely reprimanded and should such an offence occur again that he be dismissed'; Mr Irvine was one of the commissioners. In addition to the fine, Jackson was forbidden to carry a sword, the badge of his rank.

Whatever their failings, the watchmen continued to patrol the streets of Newry until local government reforms removed the police commissioners in the late nineteenth century. Even after the introduction of the Irish Constabulary in 1836 - renamed the Royal Irish Constabulary in 1867 - the Town Watch remained in being to fulfil their functions of 'lighting and watching'.

Not all the commissioners' time was taken up with the Town Watch. During this period they saw to it that the more important streets in Newry were paved. They employed people to sweep the streets and remove refuse, dirt and obstacles. After the introduction of the poor relief act in 1847, the contract for removing refuse was given to the Newry workhouse. Within a decade of their establishment the police commissioners had seen to it that Newry was adequately lit, that the more important streets were paved and that they were kept clean. Had Jonathan Swift returned to the town a century after his original visit, he would have had little cause to complain of dirty streets.

Two years after the setting up of the Board of Police Commissioners, another measure was taken that was to contribute to the public welfare of Newry, when the fever hospital and dispensary were extended. This had originally been housed in a deserted store beside the gasworks. In January 1830 eight beds were made available for the treatment of patients. It is a sad fact that fever was endemic at this time, encouraged, as this doctor's report says, by

open sewers, stagnant pools, yards, courts, lanes, and alleys, filled with putrefying heaps of every description. . . Fever at this time was a very prevalent disease, and that it was a very fatal one is but too evident from the appalling fact that four out of the five medical men who were first attached to the Institution [the fever hospital] lost their lives from typhus in the discharge of their official duties during the first four years of its existence, and the fifth most narrowly recovered from a violent attack of the same disease, when he at once resigned his charge, and soon afterwards left the town.

1858 view of Newry showing the workhouse, which was opened in 1841, became swamped by the influx of poor people forced off the land by the Great Famine. (lithograph, Southern Education and Library Board)

When the extension first opened in 1830 there were five to six hundred typhoid cases annually in Newry. Within a few years the cases were dramatically reduced to between sixty and seventy annually.

Typhus was bad enough in itself but in 1832 a cholera epidemic spread through the town. Its outbreak had been heard of the year before and in November 1831 two boards of health, one for County Armagh and the other for County Down, were appointed to take suitable steps in case of an epidemic. The first case was reported on 7 May 1832 and the disease remained in the town until July. During this period 271 people succumbed and 129, including the military doctor, died. There were so many victims that an old windmill on Pound Road was opened to treat the infected. Three years later this windmill was opened permanently as a hospital but was inadequate, so the medical officer began a campaign to raise money to build a proper hospital. Eight hundred pounds was raised by public subscription, which was matched by the Grand Jury of the County of Down, and a hospital was opened for the town on the Rathfriland Road in July 1839. It was a large modern building able to treat up to 9,800 outpatients for a number of ailments, including fever.

Other developments were taking place. In 1830 St Clare's Convent in High Street was opened. This was a teaching order of nuns and they contributed to education in the town, especially among the poor. Transport was improved when the Needham Bridge was built across the river in 1831. Five years later an adjoining bridge spanning the canal was opened — called Godfrey Bridge after the man responsible for its construction - so linking Monaghan Street directly to Margaret Street. In 1834 the Bank of Ireland on Trevor Hill was opened. This was not seen as a good thing, as, through government legislation, it had a monopoly on banking, thus limiting the source of capital available to the merchants and businessmen of Newry. It was ten years before this monopoly was removed, when the Government lifted banking restrictions.

In 1840 a Savings Bank was opened near Sugar Island and the street became known as Bank Parade. The same building housed the town's Assembly Rooms, where public business was conducted, social functions were held and visiting companies performed. Until the construction of the town hall, the Assembly Rooms was the most important public building in Newry. The courthouse was built in 1843, a tasteful Georgian-style building that still stands on Downshire Place and is one of the finest buildings in Newry.

Although the town was quite prosperous, it did, of course, have its poor, and throughout Ireland the nature of the economy and the system of land-leasing left many people living just above subsistence level, which shocked any visitor to the country and prompted some public figures to call for reform. Reform did come about in the shape of the poor law. Ireland was divided into unions for administrative purposes and each union had a workhouse from where 'outdoor relief' to the poor was organised, a measure which became the last resort of the desperate. The poor law was administered in each union by a board of guardians.

In 1840 Newry's guardians were elected and the following year the workhouse was opened at Carnegat on the west side of the town. The union contained twenty-two electoral districts returning thirty-one guardians, six from the town proper. The workhouse system was not intended to be a welfare system; it was there simply to provide the basic necessities of life and alleviate the huge amount of poverty in Ireland. Far from being a haven for the destitute, the system was designed to be so unattractive that only the most desperate would turn to it, and it was much criticised at the time, and has been since, for the nature of its service. However, before the poor law had time to develop and function as it might have, it was hit by a crisis that brought the system almost to the point of collapse: the Great Famine that resulted from the failure of the potato crop from 1844 to 1849.

The people of Newry were little affected by the Famine. After all, the town relied on commerce for its wealth, but it did have an influx of people fleeing the terrible conditions on the land. Some of these people ended up in the workhouse, some settled in town, but the vast majority passed through Newry en route to America. The effects of the Great Famine, and efforts by landlords, philanthropists and the Government to encourage emigration, forced many to leave Ireland for America and the colonies. Being a port of some significance, Newry became the centre of emigration for southern Ulster and northern Leinster. Ships carried thousands from Newry and Warrenpoint, sometimes directly to America or, more often, to Liverpool, the major centre for emigration in England. There were several emigration agents in Newry, merchants, solicitors and others who went into this business. These agents competed with one another, each anxious to prove that they offered the best service and that none of their vessels were the infamous 'coffin ships' in which passengers died by the hundreds because of the foul conditions on board.

The Great Famine touches on the story of Newry in another way, for it brought two of its citizens to the centre stage in Irish history —John Mitchel and John Martin. Of the two, John Mitchel has achieved greater prominence and he certainly had a more immediate influence on the Ireland of his day. It is said that his father, the Reverend John Mitchel, was a supporter, if not actually a member, of the United Irishmen and he passed his values on to his son. Mitchel was born near Dungiven in County Derry in 1815. He came to Newry when his father was transferred there in September 1823, and he always regarded himself as a Newryman. The Reverend John Mitchel had been the Moderator of the Presbyterian Synod of Ulster in 1822 and had so impressed the congregation at Newry that when their own minister, Dr Andrew George Malcolm, died, Mitchel was asked to replace him. He was a well-educated man whose writings and sermons had earned him a reputation as a man of intellect.

Vere Foster's Penny Emigrant's Guide *was influential in convincing many that emigration was the best answer to Ireland's economic problems in the 1840s. (poster, Public Record Office of Northern Ireland.)*

His son John went to Dr Henderson's school at number 6 Hill Street, where he met and became friends with John Martin. Ties of friendship between the two men were further strengthened years later when Martin married Mitchel's sister, Henrietta. Mitchel had something of a tempestuous youth, culminating in elopement and marriage to Jenny Verner, the daughter of a local merchant sea captain. In 1840 he was sworn in as an attorney-at-law and set up a practice in Banbridge, ten miles from Newry. In this year his father died, and Mitchel generously renounced all claims to his father's house at Drumalane, which went to his mother and subsequently his sister.

This was a time of great excitement in Ireland. Daniel O'Connell was on the march again, this time to achieve a repeal of the Act of Union. 'Monster' meetings were held throughout the country and it seemed as if the whole nation would rise in response to O'Connell's call. Mitchel's business trips to Dublin during these years had brought him into contact with a group of young men — like William Smith O'Brien, Thomas Davis, Thomas Francis Meagher and so on — who shared his radical views and ideals. They were given the nickname of 'Young Ireland' and soon Mitchel was accepted as one of the number. He was asked by Thomas Davis to write the life of Hugh O'Neill as a contribution to the 'Library of Ireland' series and he also wrote articles for the newspaper edited by Davis, the *Nation*.

FROM WARREPOINT, FOR

ST JOHN, N.B.

800 TON BURTHEN.

The Splendid Barque

LADY CAROLINE,

J. MALONEY, Commander,

To Sail on Friday, 4th June.

This is Ship will be found in Bread-stuffs, Water, and Fuel agreeably to Act of Parliament, and as a large number of Passengers are now engaged, immediate application will be necessary to secure berths

Apply at the OFFICE of

FRANCIS CARVILL,

9, SUGAR ISLAND

Newry, 17th May. 1847.

The Great Famine saw emigration on an unequalled scale through Newry and Warrenpoint. Here a Newry emigration agent seeks passengers to Canada.
(Newry Museum)

In 1845 Mitchel achieved national prominence when on the death of Davis, he became the editor of the *Nation,* and found that he had a flare for journalism. His passionately argued articles made the newspaper one of the most popular in Ireland. He had a way of speaking the truth that shocked his allies and alarmed his opponents. His family background, his debates with the other Young Irelanders, and his experiences as an attorney-at-law, often defending tenants against landlords, made him the 'angry man' of the nationalist movement, and he was not sorry at the split between Young Ireland and the more moderate Daniel O'Connell.

The tragedy of the Great Famine altered Mitchel's whole perspective. What moved many Irishmen to despair, moved him to anger. He was no longer content to talk of a repeal of the Act of Union and he now called for an active and, if necessary, violent campaign to drive the English and their landlord system out of Ireland. Fintan Lalor had already expressed these ideas but Mitchel took them to his own and in his book *The Last Conquest of Ireland* he gave a pitiful description of the starving peasants and delivered a crushing condemnation of the British government. Mitchel's advocacy of armed rebellion led to him leaving the Young Ireland faction and striking out on his own. He founded his own newspaper, the *United Irishman,* to propagate his ideas on revolutionary organisation and social reform. He had a large personal following in the country, and in Newry found support from all sections of the population. However, it was all to come to nothing, for the nation did not rise in response to his call, and in May 1848 Mitchel found himself before a court in Dublin. His writings in the *United Irishman,* his open letters to the lord lieutenant, Lord Clarendon, and a series of brilliant letters addressed to 'the Protestant Farmers, Labourers and Artisans of the North of Ireland' so alarmed the Government that it introduced and passed through parliament the Treason-Felony Act. It was under this act that Mitchel was tried and found guilty in May 1848, and was sentenced to fourteen years' penal transportation.

So John Mitchel was, in his own words, 'kidnapped and carried off from Dublin in chains'. His conviction provoked the rebellion he had called for, but the rising of 1848 was a sad, half-baked affair - Ireland's sorry contribution to the Year of Revolution throughout Europe. Newry, despite any regard it may have had for Mitchel, took no part in the rising and the ship that took him to Bermuda also carried him out of the story of the town.

Just as they had been friends in youth, so John Martin and Mitchel had become colleagues in politics. Although never as dynamic or extreme as Mitchel, Martin had played his part in the national movement and he was implicated in the Young Ireland rising. He was also convicted under the Treason—Felony Act and the two school friends later found themselves in exile in adjoining districts in Australia, to where Mitchel had been transported from Bermuda. Martin was able to return to Ireland and had a long political career with the Home Rule party. In contrast, Mitchel's life was one spent in a long, frustrating exile. His *Jail Journal* is now regarded as a classic of prison literature.

Nevertheless, Mitchel is important both to Ireland and to Newry. For Ireland, Mitchel represented the transition from the 'romantic revolutionary' vision of the United Irishmen period to the 'professional revolutionary' activity as later epitomised in the Irish Republican Brotherhood (IRB). For Newry, Mitchel personified the strength of the radical political tradition in the town — which continuously opposed the local dominance of the Kilmoreys — and of the real shift in influence in local affairs away from the conservative landed interest to the more liberal commercial interest. In the 1790s Newry had sent Isaac Corry to parliament, the man who went on to be a key figure in framing the Act of Union. In the 1840s the most prominent Newryman was a radical, agitating for an independent republic, who was not sent to parliament but into exile.

6

'MILLS, FOUNDRIES AND MANUFACTORIES'

In 1842 Newry was visited by one Michael Angelo Titmarsh, who was conducting a tour of Ireland. Of Newry, Titmarsh wrote:

> Newry is remarkable as being the only town I have seen which had no cabin suburb; strange to say, the houses begin all at once, handsomely coated and hatted with stone and slate; and if Dundalk was prosperous, Newry is better still. Such a sight of neatness and comfort is exceedingly welcome to an English traveller, who, moreover, finds himself, after driving through a plain bustling clean street, landed at a large plain comfortable inn, where business seems to be done, where there are smart waiters to receive him, and a comfortable warm coffee-room that bears no traces of dilapidation.. .
> .
> Steamers to Liverpool and Glasgow sail continually. There are mills, foundries and manufactories, of which the Guide-book will give particulars; and the town, of 13,000 inhabitants, is the busiest and most thriving that I have yet seen in Ireland: . . .
> Newry has many comfortable and handsome public buildings; the streets have a business-like look, the shops and people are not too poor, and the southern grandiloquence is not shown here in the shape of fine words for small wares. Even the beggars are not so numerous I fancy, or so coaxing and wheedling in their talk. Perhaps, too, among the gentry, the same moral change may be remarked, and they seem more downright and plain in their manner; but one must not pretend to speak of national characteristics from such a small experience as a couple of evenings' intercourse may give.

Michael Angelo Titmarsh was the pseudonym of the novelist William Makepeace Thackeray, author of *Vanity Fair* and *Barry Lyndon*. In *The Irish Sketch Book, 1842,* Thackeray seems to have found little that pleased him in Ireland and he cast a sardonic eye upon Irish society and pretensions. So praise from Thackeray was praise indeed.

Industry had continued to flourish in Newry and a variety of enterprises, from linen mills and brickworks to bakeries and distilleries, could be found in the town. Improvements to the canal made it more accessible as a port and steamers plied their trade into and out of Carlingford Lough. It has been estimated that in the mid-nineteenth century shipping in Newry was over 106,000 tons annually. It was this prosperity as much as the town's advantageous geographical position that led to an enterprising family of linen manufacturers, the Richardsons, establishing themselves not far from Newry in 1845.

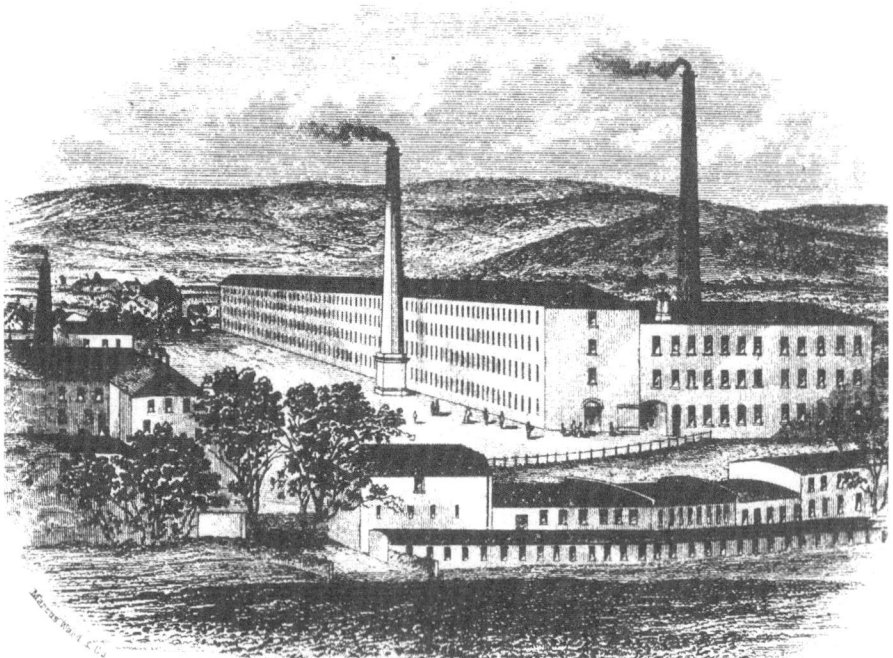

The Bessbrook Spinning Company's mill, like the village, was a model of its kind, noted for the use of innovative technology. (Armagh County Museum)

John Grubb Richardson, founder of Bessbrook

The arrival of the Richardson family was significant, not only because they founded a linenworks that was to be one of the most important in Ireland, but also because they set up what was perhaps the first planned 'model village' in the British Isles, Bessbrook.

John Grubb Richardson came from a Quaker family who already had a substantial linen business in Lisburn in County Antrim. Developments in the linen industry prompted the Richardsons to look for a new production centre, preferably one with a good supply of water, land for growing flax and conveniently situated to a point of export. All these criteria were met on a site two miles from Newry called Bessbrook, not far from Camlough. John Grubb Richardson was inspired by the work of another well-known Quaker, William Penn in Pennsylvania, and as well as establishing a linen mill he also wanted to create a community for the mill's employees based on sound moral principles, 'enabling us,' as Richardson expressed it, 'to control our people and to do them good in every sense'. The village built by him was planned around one main street with a square at either end, including a public green and shops. The village was deliberately left without the three P's common to most other villages and towns: the public house, the pawn shop and the police barracks.

The linen mill at Bessbrook prospered and grew and in a short time was one of the largest concerns in Ireland. The Bessbrook Spinning Company was to be a major local employer until recent times and the village itself thrived. In 1852 Caroline Fox, a prominent member of the Society of Friends, wrote of Bessbrook:

The Model School (left) and Masonic Hall (right), Newry (Lawrence Collection)

We went to a flourishing village which 5 years since had been a wilderness, but through the high-minded energy of our excellent host has grown into a centre of civilisation for the whole neighbourhood and a most happy prosperous place with its immense linen factory, beautiful schools, model houses for workmen, and lovely landscape, valley and water.

While its suburbs were flourishing, so was the town of Newry itself. Important developments were taking place, especially in relation to transport, that were to ensure its position as a commercial centre for decades to come. It had been realised from early in the nineteenth century that if the town was to continue as an international trading port, particularly in the light of Belfast expanding so rapidly, facilities at the docks had to be modernised to accommodate the larger ships now in use. If access to the heartland of Ulster was to be maintained, then the inland canal had to be overhauled, so that faults could be eliminated, enabling an easy flow of traffic to and from Newry to Lough Neagh and the other canals in Ulster. With the arrival of steam power the Newry merchants utilised transportation by train and became part of the nationwide network of railways that was beginning to dominate internal commerce.

The dissolution of the Irish parliament in 1801 had radically affected the authorities and enterprises under government control or relying on government patronage. Chief among these were the inland waterways of Ireland. The control of the Newry navigation had passed to the Directors of Inland Navigation, five commissioners appointed to look after those canals still in public hands. Their main objective, and the primary concern of the Westminster government, was to sort out the finances of the canals. In 1801 a report was submitted to the directors-general by Henry Walker, an engineer, in which it was estimated that it would take £32,500 to repair the Newry Canal and adapt it to modern navigation. However, a second engineer, John Brownrigg, argued that the faults that had developed in the canal since its opening could be corrected for much less and so he was appointed in place of Walker by the directors-general. Even so, Brownrigg was not optimistic about the prospects of revitalising the Newry navigation. On his appointment he reported to his employers:

> All the nine locks from Newry to Poyntzpass are little better than ruined makeshifts, pieced and patched from time to time these sixty years past, they were never right good, having been originally finished with brick and, as they failed, replaced with ill-cut or punched ill-jointed mountain stone and filled up with bad rubble-work behind, except in the lower parts, under water, where some of them are of rubble stone of as good as any in Ireland. The floors were of deal planks and the breasts and sill of oak. The gates and sluices are bad and of an ill construction, most of them now crazy and shaking, without copeing or upper heelstones to retain the iron land tiles of the gates. The iron work of a most wretched kind is generally naked above the ground instead of being bedded under the greatest stones that could be had.

For the next ten years he worked on the canal all the way from Lough Neagh to the end of the ship channel at Lower Fathom on Carlingford Lough. He enlarged the locks on the canal, rebuilding four of them completely, and widened and deepened the summit level. Three new bridges were built in place of older unsatisfactory ones. A new single lock was built at the end of the summit in place of the old double lock, and at the seaward terminus the lock was extensively repaired.

All this cost the directors-general £38,000, of which £23,000 could be recouped from the public purse. However, this rebuilding had meant that for long periods the lighters could not use the canal and by 1811 traffic had dropped to a level where the tolls only took in £2,500 annually. In an attempt to encourage traffic and so generate trade, certain goods were made toll-free, for example, limestone, lime, sand and manures. However, this measure failed to attract the anticipated trade and the canal continued to be run at a loss for some years to come.

One interesting feature of traffic on the canal during this period was the passenger service that ran from Newry to Knockbridge. It was the only passenger service to operate on a canal in Ulster and had been established by 'the respectable Quakers of Moyallan' as an alternative to the mailcoach and was managed for them by William Dawson. The fares were 3s.4d. (17p) for a first-class return ticket and 2s.1d. (10 ½p) for a second-class return. It was supplemented by a packet-boat service which could complete the journey in four hours at a cost of 2s.11d. (15p) for a single first-class ticket. This service operated successfully for thirty years until superseded by the railway.

In 1829 the directors-general relinquished control of the canal and it passed into private ownership in the form of the Newry Navigation Company.

This was largely a local concern, controlled by magnates from counties Down and Armagh under the chairmanship of the Marquis of Downshire, whose family had interests in Newry. The other chief director and stockholder in the company was the Earl of Kilmorey, whose family had already invested considerable amounts of money improving the channel and encouraging navigation. The company stepped in when the directors-general had despaired of making the canal viable. Despite Brownrigg's work, problems were still being caused by flooding in the low-lying region to the south of Lough Neagh, and at the seaward end silting had raised the floor to a dangerously shallow level. The water in the crater, or hole, outside the lock gates had decreased by four feet, due partly to the imprudent dumping of silt there that had been dredged from the canal. Once again the canal was seen to be too important to Newry's interests to allow it to become derelict, and in 1830 the Newry Navigation Company decided to institute a plan to revitalise it.

This time it was decided that little more could be done on the inland section and, as sea trade had become more vital, the eminent engineer Sir John Rennie was commissioned to improve access to Newry from Carlingford Lough. Over the next twelve years blasting was carried out at Narrow Water to remove rocks and islets blocking the channel, and the waterway from Warrenpoint to Squire's Point was deepened by three to four feet. This part of the plan cost £38,000. The second phase involved the complete rebuilding of the ship canal. Between 1842 and 1850 the old ship canal was replaced by a new one that was one and half miles longer. Most of this work was overseen by William Dargan, who was better known as being involved in railway construction. This part of the new ship canal was 160 feet wide and 15.5 feet deep. A new terminus was built at Upper Fathom, where the lock was 22.0 feet long and 50 feet wide. This part of the operation cost the company £40,000. In honour of the queen and her consort, the locks were called the Victoria Locks and the harbour named the Albert Basin. The first vessels passed through the locks to the basin in April 1850 and included three steamers of over five hundred tons' burden, the largest yet seen in Newry.

Fortunately, the traffic on the inland canal had been improving during these years. The old cargoes had been returning gradually, as it was more convenient to transport bulk goods by water than by land. In 1846, for example, the revenue from tolls was over £4,000, representing traffic of 120,000 tons. The cargoes being carried on the canal consisted of linen, butter, meat, coal, brick, tiles, and agricultural produce, coming from most of the counties in Ulster. A wide range of goods manufactured in the town or imported from abroad, such as grain, flour, flax, seed, tobacco, timber, iron goods, whiskey, hides and oil, was being transported into Ulster. One attempt to bypass the problems of the canal had been the development of docking facilities at Warrenpoint by the Newry merchants in conjunction with the local landowners, the Halls. In 1740 there had been only one house at Warrenpoint but within fifty years a village had developed around the quays, where ships too large to dock at Newry could unload. By the mid-nineteenth century three thousand people lived there. In 1850, travel writer J.B. Doyle described it thus:

> Warrenpoint is a noted watering-place, and from the purity of the water and its perfect safety, it is much frequented. . . Steamers sail twice a week for Liverpool. . . Probably in no part of the world is there a more secure or a more beautiful harbour, enclosed between the Carlingford and Rostrevor mountains.

Transporting goods on the Newry Canal provided a livelihood for generations of people. Journeys were so long that usually a bargeman took his family with him. Most barges were drawn by horses in the days before steam although this one appears to be employing a sail. (Newry Musueum)

At this time income from shipping was £5,000 per annum, representing more than nine thousand tons of cargo passing through the port. As well as being a port, Warrenpoint soon became a holiday resort. By the 1870s it had five large hotels and a number of boarding houses. It was the natural seaside resort for the rural population of County Armagh and much of County Down. Steamers brought thousands of holiday-makers from the industrial towns of Lancashire. Indeed, it is still within living memory that many English tourists came 'across the water' to holiday there. The national development of the railways was instrumental in the town's growth as a holiday resort as well as a port. Trains provided a cheap and convenient form of travel and when Warrenpoint became part of the national network, the town was accessible from all parts of Ireland. The first line to reach the town ran from Newry and opened in May 1849, under the management of William Dargan.

The railway boom had hit Ireland some years previously. Just as one hundred years before, it was believed that a network of inland navigation could save the Irish economy, so now all hopes were placed on the railways. The railway first came into the vicinity of Newry in 1844, when a line was opened between Dublin and Drogheda. Some time afterwards a line was built connecting Portadown to Belfast. There was an obvious gap in the centre, which left Newry, Armagh and points west outside the network. In 1845 and 1846 acts of parliament were secured to allow for the building of railways from Newry to Enniskillen in County

Fermanagh, and from Newry to Rostrevor. A third act licensed the building of a line connecting the Portadown and Drogheda termini. On 5 February 1849 the first train ran on the new line that connected Dublin and Belfast via Drogheda and Portadown. Curiously, the line passed to the west of Newry and did not link with the town. There are reasons to explain this: on a practical level, the straightest route did not go through Newry; and it was believed that the planned line from Newry to Enniskillen would automatically link with the Drogheda—Portadown line. At the time, of course, there were those who saw it as a Belfast-inspired move to exclude its rival, Newry, from the railway network.

It was many years before the proposed line between Newry and Enniskillen got under way. In March 1854 the line had reached Goraghwood, three and half miles from Newry, which was most important as this served as the junction with the Dublin-Belfast line. In 1855 management of the Newry, Warrenpoint, and Rostrevor Railway Company was taken from William Dargan when his lease expired and was vested in the company directors. In the same year the Dublin and Belfast Junction Railway Company built a station at Monaghan Street, to be known as the Bessbrook and Newry Main Line Station, which truly made Newry a part of the Belfast—Dublin network. Shortly after this, the locally based company, the Newry and Enniskillen Railway Company, linked its terminus at Edward Street to the Albert Basin, as John F. Small says, 'for the purpose of allowing direct transfer of coal and other commodities from the vessels lying in the canal to the railway waggons lying alongside, thus effecting a great saving of time and increasing the facilities for immediate conveyance into the interior'. By 1857 the Newry and Enniskillen Railway Company had decided that the project of building a railway to Enniskillen was too ambitious to be undertaken. A decision was made, therefore, to take the railway only as far as the next important town en route, Armagh, and so by act of parliament the company became the Newry and Armagh Railway Company. At the same time permission was given to form a junction in Newry with the Warrenpoint line. Further complications arose before the line to Armagh was built, and the following years were spent in improving railway communications in and around Newry itself. In 1861 the Newry-Warrenpoint railway was extended from Kilmorey Street across the river to the Dublin Bridge, thus bringing it within easy reach of the Albert Basin. On 2 September 1861 the link between the Armagh and Warrenpoint lines was completed at the officially named Newry Junction. Two years later an act of parliament allowed for the construction of a railway between Newry and Greenore in County Louth, the first privately built port in Ireland. This line was eventually opened on 1 August 1876, with the terminus at Bridge Street.

Some twenty years after the inception of the Newry and Enniskillen Railway Company, the line to Armagh was finally opened. From 25 August 1864 trains could travel from the station in Newry to Drummondmore Bridge, just outside Armagh city. Six months later the line was extended to the Ulster Railway Company terminus in the city itself. South-east Ulster and most of Leinster were now comprehensively united in a railway network, with Newry at its centre and Dublin and Belfast at the southern and northern extremities. The importance of this railway network cannot be overstressed. In the eighteenth century the building of canals had not brought commercial prosperity to Ireland as a whole, but the Newry Canal had brought wealth and importance to the town of Newry, making it a port of the first rank in the kingdom. In the nineteenth century the railways may not have industrialised Ireland, but they did save Newry from the decline that threatened it because of the deterioration of the inland canal. As John F. Small expressed it:

> It is from the arrival of the railway that we may date the present prosperity of Newry. No doubt it had always occupied a respectable position, and but for certain causes which operated prejudicially to its advancement, it would have held a still better one, but it cannot be denied that for some time heretofore it had not kept pace with other towns in Ulster less favoured by Nature, but more so by circumstances. The opening of the Armagh Railway appears to have given an impetus to its progress, which has been sustained ever since, and it may therefore properly be a ground of unmixed satisfaction to the townspeople, whether it be so or not to the shareholders. . . Be this, however, as it may, the fact remains that from this time forward our town has steadily advanced; it has increased both in population and in the number of houses; the condition of the people has greatly improved, and its commerce and manufactures have grown rapidly.

During this period of railway development, the town itself had indeed grown. The start of the new era of confidence was marked by the building of a new courthouse on the Downshire Road in 1843 by Thomas Duff, a Newry architect. Described by Myles Gilligan as 'the most important figure in the early development of the architectural profession in Ulster',

Duff went on to design many prestigious buildings, such as St Patrick's Catholic Cathedral in Armagh and the Old Museum Building in Belfast. He designed and built numerous churches, public buildings and fashionable homes in Newry and his influence was felt in the town long after his death in 1848.

In 1844 the Marquis of Downshire decided to build a 'garden suburb' on the part of his estate that bordered on Newry. The area was bounded by the Downshire Road, Sandys Street, Windsor Hill and Windsor Avenue. Within a few years the plan had been put into effect and until the late twentieth century it remained a pleasant suburb of Newry before being surrounded by more recent housing developments. At the same time, at the other end of Newry, Hyde Terrace was being erected. Described as Newry's 'best' terrace, this neo-Georgian row of buildings survives largely unmarred by more recent developments at St Colman's Park. In 1846 the oldest existing bridge in Newry, the Ballybot Bridge, was replaced by a new single-arch bridge. The new buildings that continued to be erected in the following decades reflected the wealth that the town was enjoying in this period. From 1850 onwards Thomas Duff's influence gave way to that of another Newryman, William J. Barre. A former pupil of Duff's, Barre too had a national standing as an architect. He worked for a time in Dublin and Gilligan describes him as 'the evangelist of ornament and of the decorated Gothic style'. Outside of Newry, he designed such works as the Crozier Memorial in Banbridge and in Belfast, the Albert Memorial, the Unitarian Church in York Street, and the Provincial Bank of Ireland in Castle Place. In 1860, when the authorities held an open competition to design a new hall for Belfast, Barre won the commission, beating forty-one other entrants, and the Ulster Hall remains his best-known work. In his home town Barre was responsible for many of the fine buildings erected in the 1850s and 1860s. In 1850 he initiated an entire change in

the style of architecture patronised by the Protestant dissenting community when he built the Unitarian Church in William Street. Until then, non-conformist churches had been quite plain and deliberately unobtrusive, and Barre's more elaborate design marked not only a new-found confidence among the non-conformist community, but also the continuing confidence of Newry as a pioneering town. Barre designed private residences as well, the most unusual being a commission from a Baron von Stieglitz to rebuild The Glen on Turner's Hill, near the Dublin Road.

This period of commercial prosperity, dramatic advancements in transport and improvements in the town's appearance, also saw important and radical developments in the municipal administration of Newry. In 1847 the first major assault was made on the powers of the manor court, which had been in existence in Newry since the sixteenth century and had been the only municipal authority before the establishment of the police commissioners in 1828. By 1847 many people viewed the manor court as an intolerable anachronism that could no longer be allowed to exercise the powers it did. In that year the seneschal's claim to have the exclusive right to hold death inquests within the manor was challenged by a coroner for County Armagh, a Mr Magee. The coroner had held several inquests into deaths that had occurred in the Armagh area of the Newry manor. The seneschal, John Boyd, objected and at the summer assizes of 1847 brought an action against Magee for infringing the rights of the manor court. The magistrate found in favour of Magee, whereupon a bill of exceptions was brought forward on behalf of the seneschal. This, however, was rejected by the Queen's Bench, and the seneschal lost the right to hold inquests which ever after were conducted by the coroners of counties Armagh and Down.

In the 19th century Newry had spread across the Clanrye valley and, as the chimneys here testify, was home to many mills, foundries and factories. (Lawrence engraving)

In 1848 the right of the manor court to issue 'town orders' was challenged. Following a claim of non-payment of debt against a Mr Costello, the senseschal issued a town order for the seizing of all Costello's property until the case had been heard. This procedure had long been the practice and although much hardship had been caused by town orders, no one had ever questioned their legality. However, Costello did object, and a case was brought before the Queen's Bench against the seneschal, John Boyd. He was no luckier this time than he had been the year before and the judge ruled that issuing town orders without a hearing was illegal. The authority of the manor court had been undermined by these two cases and it seemed only a matter of time before the court ceased to function. The end finally came in 1859, when, through the Probate Court Act, all irregular courts in Ireland were abolished. So it was that the last vestige of the exempt jurisdiction of Newry and Mourne, which had survived since the twelfth century, was taken away almost seven hundred years after the granting of the charter to the abbey by King Murtagh.

The year 1851 saw the death of Viscount Newry and Mourne, and his son succeeded to the title. He had been MP for the borough, and Edmund Gilling Hallewell, his successor, was elected unopposed, in deference to the deceased. By this time Newry had a population of 14,734, many of whom had the franchise. Although Newry's electorate had been dramatically reduced when it ceased to be a 'scot and lot' borough — where every householder had a vote — after the Act of Union, a reform of the franchise in 1850 had increased the numbers eligible to vote. In Ireland as a whole the electorate increased from 61,000 to 165,000 and in Newry many were placed on the electoral register, although voting was still by open ballot. A general election was called in 1852 and Hallewell found himself opposed by William Kirk, standing as a liberal. The result was that Kirk became MP for Newry.

The Unitarian Presbyterian congregation moved into their new church in 1850. Designed by William J. Barre, it represented a new departure for non-conformist architecture. (Lawrence engraving)

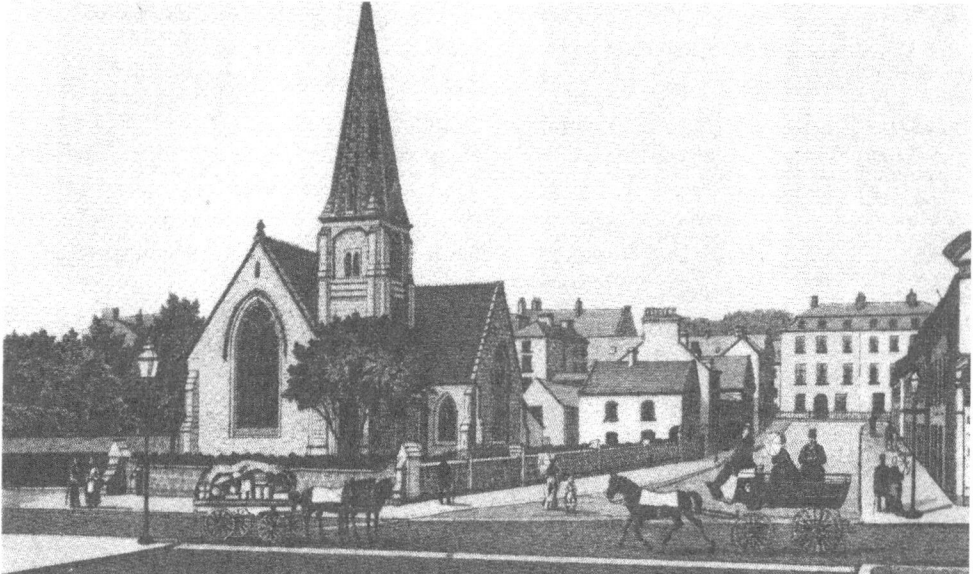

138

Completed in 1844, Hyde Terrace was considered the best terrace in Newry and epitomised the expansion in housing in the town in the 19th century. (Lawrence engraving)

In 1854 parliament was to introduce a piece of legislation that would greatly affect Newry. This was the Towns' Improvement (Ireland) Act, which allowed for any town which so wished to have a local authority, in the form of town commissioners, to take charge of all municipal matters. In accordance with the act, twenty-five Newry ratepayers petitioned the lord lieutenant and a public meeting was held in the courthouse on 3 September 1855 to decide whether or not the legislation should be adopted. Those in favour failed to win the day and the motion was rejected by a considerable majority. However, ten years later a second attempt was made. The intervening decade had shown the efficacies of the act and the population of Newry had also changed somewhat. At the public meeting held by justices Denis Maguire and Isaac Corry on 6 February 1865 in the courthouse, after much heated debate, the act was adopted. In response the lord lieutenant issued an order in council on 6 March 1865 bringing Newry under the provisions of the act, which meant that the Board of Police Commissioners was dissolved. The order divided Newry into three wards — north, south and west — to be administered by eighteen elected commissioners. Although the parliamentary borough had already been defined, this was the first time that the municipal boundaries had been definitively drawn and that the town of Newry had a legal, territorial meaning.

The terms of franchise for the commissioners' elections were the same as those for parliament. One-third of the commissioners had to retire or stand for re-election on 15 October each year. The first elected commissioners were: for the north ward - John Moore, John Linton Vallely, Felix O'Hagan, Robert M'Blain, Patrick O'Rorke and Robert Greer; for the south ward — Richard Downey, James Fegan, Arthur John Small, John P. M'Nally, Thomas Marron and Thomas Irvine; for the west ward—William Henry, Thomas Cardwell, Joseph Lupton, James Francis Erskine, James MacMahon and Robert Dempster. Most of the men represented prominent families in the commercial and industrial life of Newry, and their surnames will still be familiar to any inhabitant of the

town today. The first chairman of the commissioners was John Moore, but after three years he was succeeded by John James O'Hagan, who was probably the most important local politician of this period. Like the radical John Mitchel, O'Hagan had been educated at Dr Henderson's school in Hill Street, and on entering politics he described himself as a liberal nationalist. He dominated the commissioners for many years and became the first chairman of the gas committee. When he died in 1895, all boats in Newry flew their flags at half mast.

The main task facing the town commissioners was the implementation of schemes to improve sanitary conditions in Newry. Although some progress had been made by the police commissioners, the increase in population since they were instituted in 1828 and the continuing problem of the deterioration of pipes and outlets meant that bad health and poor sanitation continued to be the main challenge to the authorities. Over the next decade the town commissioners spent large sums of money on the construction of sewers and in ensuring that all parts of the town were serviced by them. The commissioners enforced health regulations for public places, shops and work places. Through these measures, disease was gradually being defeated. In 1864 there were 238 reported cases of fever in Newry; by 1865 the number had fallen to 192; in 1866 only 113 cases were found; and by 1868 there were just 48 cases.

National politics were once again the preoccupation in Newry when a general election was called in November 1868. This election arose because William Ewart Gladstone, the Liberals' leader, had put forward proposals in March of that year to sever the connection that existed between the state and the Church of Ireland. He had identified the anomalous position of the Church of Ireland, where only a small minority of the population belonged to it and yet it was the official state church, as being one of the chief causes of unrest in Ireland. When his proposals for the disestablishment of the church were accepted by the House of Commons, Prime Minister Benjamin Disraeli decided to appeal to the country. The 'church question' was the main issue of the election and was of particular relevance to Newry, where most of its citizens belonged to the Catholic Church and where there was a substantial and influential body of non-conformists. The electorate had been increased the previous year, when certain alterations had been made to the franchise. Feelings ran high throughout the United Kingdom and no less so in Newry. There had long been rivalry, if not open confrontation, between the liberal commercial interest in the town and the conservative landed interest. The 'church question' was one that brought the two sides into open opposition and left a stark choice for the electors, who numbered about seven hundred of the wealthier citizens. The Liberals, as they called themselves, put forward William Kirk as their candidate, a man who had already been elected twice for Newry. Opposing him was Viscount Newry and Mourne, Francis Charles Needham, grandson of the earl, who was described by one not very impartial observer as 'the champion of an odious ascendancy, and the asserter of the insolent prerogatives of landlordism'.

The voting took place on 20 November and was, for the last time, by open ballot. The two parties were almost evenly matched. The viscount received 377 votes, and William Kirk polled 385. In Newry, as throughout the country, those wishing to see the Church of Ireland dissolved had won the day. Gladstone's bill came before parliament the following year, and from 1 January 1871 the Church of Ireland became a voluntary body, with, as historian J.C. Beckett says, 'its ecclesiastical law no longer part of the law of the land, [it] would have merely contractual force, and its courts would cease to exercise coercive jurisdiction'. This, incidentally, removed the Earl of Kilmorey's last rights as the lord of Newry and Mourne, which he exercised through the parish's ecclesiastical courts. The material conditions of the Church of Ireland were not greatly affected by disestablishment, and in Newry the church continued to function much as it had done before.

By 1871 Newry was preoccupied with a matter that was of more import- ance to its citizens than the disestablishment of the Church of Ireland, and this was the 'water question'. For many years the problem of an adequate water supply to the townspeople had been a matter of concern. Newry had some two hundred wells but they were not always conveniently situated and as medical awareness grew, it was realised that they were not always hygienic. In 1861 the Newry Water Works Company had been established by some English businessmen, under Edmund Hallewell, to build two small reservoirs to supply water to the town. However, they were inadequate for the whole town's needs and there was a great deal of local resentment against an 'English' company controlling the water supply. In November 1867 the company publicly announced that it would approach parliament for an act enabling it to supply the town using Camlough as a reservoir. The town commissioners and the population at large opposed the scheme, mainly because it concentrated too much power in the hands of 'outsiders', and in January 1868 the bill was withdrawn. This still left the basic problem unsolved, and in January 1868 the town commissioners decided to take matters into their own hands by offering to buy out the Newry Water Works Company and supply the town themselves. The following year saw negotiations, public meetings and memorials, which failed to make any progress, as the company refused to sell. Towards the end of 1869 the company announced that it would again seek an act of parliament to supply the town with water from Camlough. Both sides were more determined this time. The town commissioners petitioned parliament in opposition to the scheme, and organised a subscription from among the townspeople to raise a fighting fund. The Bessbrook Spinning Company, which relied on water from Camlough, vigorously supported the fund and the petition was signed by 550 ratepayers.

When the company's bill was brought before parliament for its second reading on 9 March 1870, its opponents - in particular the Bessbrook Spinning Company - had exerted all their influence to have it rejected. The assault was led by the Newry MP, William Kirk. The bill was conclusively defeated and it was obvious that the Newry Water Works Company would have to relinquish its claims to supply the town. A board of arbitration settled on £3,948 as the price to be paid by the commissioners to the company in order to buy them out. The water committee of the commissioners then decided that a third large

reservoir should be built at O'Neill's Bog and in May 1870 the town commissioners accepted this proposal. The lord justices, however, on being petitioned, refused to allow the commissioners to raise the money for such a scheme, and instead only gave permission for the borrowing of £5,000 to buy out the company and begin construction.

It would seem that the commissioners' proposal to build a reservoir at O'Neill's Bog was unsound and motivated more by political considerations than by anything else. At the same time, in fear of things getting out of hand, the Bessbrook Spinning Company offered to establish a works that would supply Newiy with water from Camlough while assuring their own company of a plentiful supply for Bessbrook. This scheme was rejected. The commissioners then resolved to take expert advice in settling the matter once and for all. An engineer named Hawksley was commissioned to undertake a study of the three sites proposed for the new reservoir -O'Neill's Bog, the Glen Head and Camlough. Hawksley submitted his report on 3 October 1870, in which he argued that Camlough offered the best prospects. In the light of this, the commissioners approached the Bessbrook Spinning Company to re-open negotiations. On 10 October an agreement was reached whereby the Bessbrook Spinning Company agreed to supply Newry with 625,000 gallons of water Daily from Camlough at an annual rent of £525. This proposal was to be brought before parliament in the following session.

The death of William Kirk, Newry's long-serving MP, necessitated a by-election on 20 December 1870. Viscount Newry and Mourne came forward as a candidate, presenting himself to the different political interests in town as an independent who would attach himself to no party in parliament but who would look after Newry's best interests. He was accepted as such and so was returned unopposed. Whatever he may have said before being elected, Viscount Newry and Mourne was one of those who opposed the Improvement and Water Bill when it came before parliament. Despite the support that the bill enjoyed in Newry and the fact that it represented a compromise between the town commissioners and the Bessbrook Spinning Company, it did not have an uninterrupted passage. The committee of the House of Commons listened to evidence for and against the bill for thirteen days before approving it. On 24 July 1871 it came before the committee of the House of Lords, where two days were spent on the bill. On this occasion John James O'Hagan, the commissioners' chairman, made a memorable appearance before their lordships, arguing Newry's case for a full ten hours. The bill was approved, with certain amendments, by both houses of parliament and became law on 14 August 1871.

The act that was passed covered substantially more than the initial water-supply scheme, as the opportunity was taken to tackle other administrative problems facing the town commissioners. Previously, the Grand Juries of Down and Armagh also had responsibility for certain public works in Newry, while other matters, such as the markets, were irregularly controlled. The new act attempted to solve these problems by settling where authority for all public matters in Newry rested. Under the Improvement and Water Act the town commissioners were, for the first time, formally incorporated as a municipal body with perpetual succession. For the first time, also, they were given an official seal — that of the ancient abbey, the enthroned abbot between two yew trees. The authority of the Grand Juries in respect of maintaining and building public roads, bridges or any other public work was taken from them and vested in the town commissioners, who now had complete responsibility for all public matters, except the upkeep of the courthouse and the bridewells. Markets, too, were now within the commissioners' jurisdiction. Six market places were enclosed and tolls charged for the use of them. Only the market at Mary Street still survives.

As for the main motivation behind the act, the commissioners were empowered to strike a rate not exceeding 3s. (15p) in the pound on valuation for general purposes and a water rate not exceeding 1s. (5p) in the pound. The board members of the Bessbrook Spinning Company were incorporated in a parallel company as the Camlough Waterworks Trustees. They had responsibility for maintaining the works and for supplying the town with water. The commissioners might appoint an additional trustee on their own behalf. Although the trustees were also obliged to supply water to the mills on the river and to the canal, the town was to have the overriding priority in times of need. Instead of the £525 annual rent, the act laid down that the trustees were to receive an outright payment of £12,000 from the town for supplying water, and smaller sums of money from the mills and the Newry Navigation Company. A scheme was then enacted to close over the wells and to lay pipes to bring fresh clean water to all parts of town. Twenty-three fountains were opened, to be used by people who could not afford to have water piped indoors. The scheme took some years to implement and cost the commissioners £27,000.

The drama over the water question was briefly eclipsed by drama on a national scale, when John Mitchel, the former citizen of Newry, returned from his exile in the United States, to where he had escaped from Australia, to stand for parliament in County Tipperary. He had been invited to stand for the nationalists when the seat became vacant in 1875. Mitchel had not been in Ireland since 1848 and he was anxious to return and play his part in the national cause before it was too late. He stood as an abstentionist candidate, declaring that he would not 'creep up to the bar of the House of Commons and crave permission to take oaths and [his] seat'. He was elected without opposition, but Prime Minister Benjamin Disraeli moved a resolution in parliament nullifying the election on the grounds that Mitchel was an escaped felon. A second election was held and again Mitchel was returned. By this time he had come back to Newry, where he was staying at his former family home at Drumalane. He had supported the Confederate cause in the American Civil War of 1861 to 1865 and for a short time had served in an ambulance corps. Following the Confederate defeat, he had been imprisoned in Fortress Monroe; since then his health had been poor and electioneering in an Irish winter was too much for him.

Before parliament could nullify the second election, John Mitchel had died peacefully in bed on 20 march 1875.

The building of the Town Hall was the last achievement of the town commissioners. It was completed in 1893 and stands directly over the Clanrye River, the boundary between Counties Down and Armagh. (Linen Hall Library)

He was buried a few days later at the old meeting house in High Street, beside his parents. Mitchel's wife Jenny and his children had joined him when he was exiled in Australia; they followed him to the United States and were still there when he died, and so were unable to be at his funeral. The ceremony took place on a cold, rainy day, and John Martin, Mitchel's oldest friend, caught such a severe chill that he too died some days later.

The passing of the Improvement and Water Act represented a remarkable achievement for the town commissioners and was a major contribution to the welfare of the people of Newry. There was, however, another service that still remained in private hands and which many believed would be better controlled by the public authority, and that was the supply of gas. Ever since the establishment of the police commissioners, there had been strained relations between public and private interests. Although Newry was, on the whole, adequately lit and better off in this respect than many Irish towns, there were certain issues regarding the regularity of the gas supply and its cost that had led to arguments between the police commissioners and the Newry Gaslight Company. Even the replacement of the chartered company by a new limited liability company in 1857, called the Newry Gas Consumers' Company, failed to rectify the situation. Shortly after the establishment of the town commissioners in 1865, they had drawn up their own contract with the Newry Gas Consumers' Company. However, the developments relating to the water supply were a stimulus to taking action over the supply of gas. The commissioners established a gas committee with John James O'Hagan as chairman. In 1876 the committee proposed independent arbitration to settle a dispute over the costing of gas, in accordance with an act of parliament, but the gas company refused to agree. Following this, the committee proposed that if the gas company continued to overcharge and failed to adequately supply its customers, then, as the minutes of the gas committee state, the town solicitor, J. Carey, should 'be instructed to have the necessary notices published with a view to the introduction of a Bill in Parliament for the transfer of the Gas Works to the Town Commissioners'.

This proposal was brought before the commissioners on 6 November 1876. The chairman, James Fegan, did not vote - he was, in any case, a member of the board of the gas company. Another member of the board, Arthur J. Small, led the opposition against the proposals, supported by Robert Campbell and Robert Frazer; however, the majority voted in favour. It should be noted that many of these commissioners were also factory or mill owners, so it was as much their own commercial interests as a concern about public welfare that motivated their support. Robert Dempster openly declared that he was losing money because of bad lighting in his factory. The Newry MP, W.C. Whitworth, duly presented a bill to implement the commissioners' proposal. The Newry Gas Consumers' Company offered little opposition. Indeed the shareholders seemed quite disillusioned with the company. For some time they had even found it difficult to gather a quorum to conduct business at the shareholders' meetings. So unlike the water question, the Newry Commissioners' Gas Act had a relatively uneventful passage through parliament and became law on 4 July 1878. On 1 January 1879 the director of the company, Henry Woodhouse Wallace, formally handed over the keys of the gasworks to the chairman of the commissioners.

Despite being overtaken by Belfast as a port, Newry remained an important retail centre at the turn of the century.

Over the next ten years the gas committee improved and extended the gasworks. New retorts were built and extra offices were added. Under the town commissioners the price of consumer gas was reduced. In 1880 the price was 5s. (25p) per 1,000 cubic feet; by the end of the century it was 4s. (20p). By careful management of resources the commissioners were able to spend £8,000 in improving the gas service and also met all the loan repayments.

One of the last acts of the Newry town commissioners was to build a town hall. They raised a loan of over £9,000 to pay for its construction, and work on it was completed in 1893. The town hall was built directly over the Clanrye river — that is, the old county boundary. The reason for this is said to be that when the decision was made in 1891 to build a town hall, there was rivalry between the townspeople in County Down and those in County Armagh as to which county should have the honour. A compromise was reached by building the town hall over the river so that it was in both counties at once. Coincidentally, plans were in motion in Belfast to build a new city hall. Over £300,000 was spent on Belfast City Hall and the corporation did not have to borrow any money, as the revenue from gas alone almost covered the entire cost — in Newry the gas consumers were numbered in hundreds, but in Belfast there were over seventeen thousand. There can be no clearer illustration of the rapid growth of Belfast in the late nineteenth century and of the inertia of Newry in the same period.

M.W. Ward & Sons was a prominent retail outlet in Newry until recent times, when the premises in Hill Street was demolished

The ship canal enabled larger ships to come into the Albert Basin where cargo could be transferred to lighters for transport on the inland canal or to freight cars for the railways.
(Lawrence Collection)

Newry could look to the end of the nineteenth century with some satisfaction but not with the optimism with which it greeted the end of the eighteenth. A sharp decline had been avoided by the rebuilding of the canal and then by the development of the railway network. Unfortunately, neither was enough to retain Newry's leading position in the commercial life of the north of Ireland. Both forms of transport had involved vast outlays of money that were never fully recouped. In particular, the extension of the ship canal proved inadequate. Larger ships were being built year by year and soon even the ordinary vessels of international trade were too big for Newry. While the town had extended its ship canal, Belfast had abandoned the idea completely and instead excavated a deep-water channel from its port to the sea. Even the development of Warrenpoint was not on a scale sufficient to rival the facilities of Belfast. So while Belfast accommodated large vessels and was able to establish a shipbuilding industry that in turn generated further industrial development in the city, Newry was not in a position to do likewise. Opportunities for industrial expansion were limited and it was not heavy industry but linen manufacture that remained the most important.

Annual income from the inland navigation was only £1,832 in 1856 and after that it never exceeded £1,000. By the mid-nineteenth century shipping trade was already falling well behind Belfast. In 1841 Belfast handled 387,930 tons of shipping while Newry handled 106,080 tons. Attempts were made between 1884 and 1894 to deepen the upper reaches of Carlingford Lough and the Clanrye river for three miles beyond the Victoria Locks. The section from Warrenpoint to the Victoria Locks was made 120 feet wide. This cost the Newry Navigation Company £55,000 and enabled ships of up to five thousand tons to come into the port. However, it was too late to transform Newry into a viable rival to Belfast.

This is not to say that Newry had ceased to enjoy considerable wealth. The American Civil War and subsequent cotton shortages were a great boon to the linen industry in Ireland. Bessbrook increased its output during this time and additional housing for the employees was needed at the model village. Newry businessmen were not slow to take advantage of the conditions in trade to enter, or extend their interests in, linen production. In the 1860s Joseph Lupton opened his mill at Queen Street, Abraham Wilson his at Edward Street, and the huge mill at Drumalane was built by William Hill Irvine. These mills brought employment and additional investment to Newry. However, the fate of the Drumalane mill was a salutory lesson on the dangers of laying foundations on the strength of a temporary boom. Hill Irvine had no previous experience in the linen business but he spent £40,000 on the mill, which was designed by his cousin, William Hazlett Mitchel. After some initial success, the mill failed to live up to expectations and in the end it was the ruin of Hill Irvine. An interesting point is that Jenny Mitchel, John's widow and Mrs Hill Irvine's sister-in-law, provided the money that enabled the Hill Irvine family to emigrate to Australia, where William became prime minister of Victoria and founded the National Bank of Australia, which recently owned the Northern Bank in Ireland.

The 'mills, foundries and manufactories' spoken of by Thackeray had not all disappeared. Although Newry had been outstripped by Belfast in economic development, it was still by no means a poor town. G.H. Bassett, in his *County Down Guide and Directory* (1888), was able to give this favourable description:

> Newry occupies a position on the border line of Down and Armagh, and is an important trading centre for both counties. Its strong attractions, from the commercial point of view, were originally manifested when inland water ways were of more consequence than at present. Lough Neagh is connected with the sea by a navigation system which broadens in the Clanrye Valley, gives Newry a floating dock of respectable proportions, and permits the entrance of vessels of large tonnage from Carlingford Lough, five miles distant. In the matter of railway communication with the outer world, Newry is very well served. The Great Northern road, between Belfast and Dublin, passes at Goragh Wood, Co. Armagh, where it is met by a single track from town, three and a half miles in length. Belfast is 44 ½ miles by this route. There is a line between Newry and Armagh, which has proved of considerable advantage. A railway to Greenore provides daily communication with England *via* Holyhead. There is a five mile line to Warrenpoint, and an electric tramway to Bessbrook, opened for traffic in 1885. This net-work of railways has done wonders for the Newry markets, and has given a great stimulus to the general business. The manufacturing enterprises in good times would compare favourably with those of the best towns of Ireland. Three extensive flax spinning mills, two linen weaving factories, and an apron factory, give large employment to girls. There are five flour mills, three of them possessing immense power. Two iron foundries of long-established reputation, two mineral water factories, salt works, stone polishing mills, seven tanneries, cabinet furniture manufacture, and coach-building are among the leading industries. Minor branches are very numerous. Granite quarries, of high repute, exist in the vicinity, and are worked energetically, the products forming a valuable addition to the exports. A stranger entering Newry at the Edward Street railway station need not walk far to become favourably impressed. The principal portion of the town lies at the foot of a high hill on the

County Down side. Hill Street, the longest and broadest thoroughfare, is occupied by well-built warehouses ... The canal and river run through the town for the greater part, side by side, and are crossed by many bridges.

By the 1880s Newry had reached the extent of its growth. Physically, or geographically, the town had reached its limits, occupying all the level ground on either side of the Clanrye river, stopping where the steep hills of the valley began. Also physically limiting was the size of the sea channel and ship canal. Economically Newry had as much business as it could support. The local market was not large enough to act as a base for any great industrial expansion, and only the Bessbrook Spinning Company was able to capture a large export market. Once Belfast gained its momentum of growth, every success there attracted more to it, and so enterprises that in the eighteenth century might have gone to Newry went there instead, transforming it into one of the largest cities in the British Isles. Newry may have reached its limits but it did not stagnate. It was still a busy, bustling port and those industries that were there continued to produce goods profitably, even though on a small scale. However, just as in the past centuries the great national issues had affected the development of Newry, so too in the next century would the national upheaval result in irrevocable changes in Newry's position, and it would once again become the frontier town.

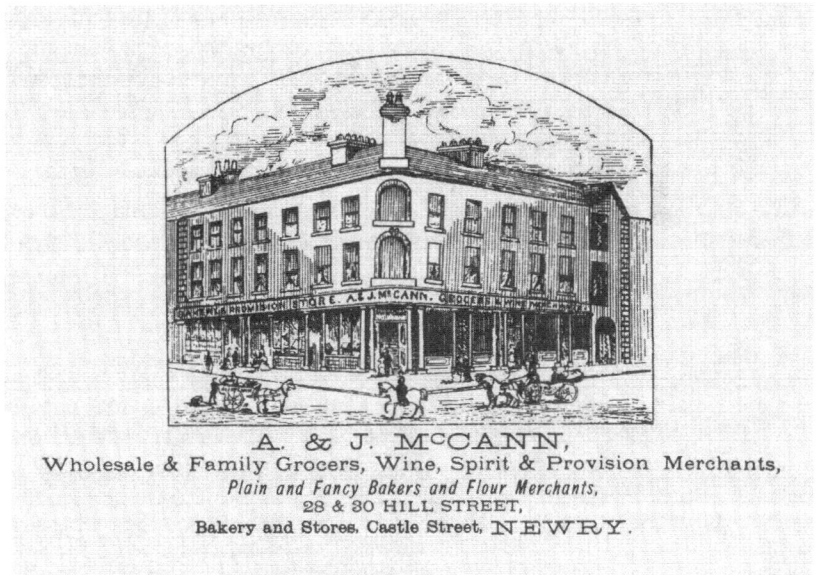

A. & J. M^cCANN,
Wholesale & Family Grocers, Wine, Spirit & Provision Merchants,
Plain and Fancy Bakers and Flour Merchants,
28 & 30 HILL STREET,
Bakery and Stores, Castle Street, NEWRY.

Newry continued to prosper at the close of the 19th century and was home to many wealthy businesses such as A. & J. McCann which survived into the 21st century.

7

A FRONTIER TOWN AGAIN

The founding of the Home Rule League in 1873 had been followed by a decade of agitation centring on the land and Home Rule questions. By 1880 there were sixty-one MPS in the Irish Parliamentary Party. However, it was not until changes in the terms of franchise and the basis of representation took place that the Irish Parliamentary Party, guided by Charles Stewart Parnell, began to make headway in the urban constituencies. The introduction of the household franchise in 1884 and the redrawing of constituency boundaries in 1885 were not designed specifically for Ireland but they had a profound effect on the Irish situation. Newry found that it had almost returned to its old 'scot and lot' status, as now every householder could vote in elections.

In November 1885 there was a general election in which eighty-five Home Rule candidates were returned to parliament. Among them was the MP for South Down, Newryman John F. Small. He had outspoken nationalist views and had published an interesting, if somewhat coloured, history of Newry in 1876, which has proved an essential starting point for any local historian ever since. He moved into the national arena as MP for Wexford, but in 1885, in order to make way for John Redmond, he stood in South Down. Small was a devoted follower of Parnell and was one of those who welcomed him to Newry in 1891, following the party split when Parnell's relationship with Catherine O'Shea became public. Support for Parnell did not damage Small's standing in Newry and he had a long career as a local councillor until his death in 1923.

Small's election to the South Down seat represented a distinct shift in the electoral balance, following the reform of the franchise in 1884. When a new Local Government Act established urban district councils elected on the household franchise in 1898, many towns passed from the control of the conservative and propertied interests to more liberal or populist elements. In Newry the urban district council was dominated by Home Rulers. One effect of the act was that all of the town - including Ballybot - was now considered to be part of County Down for administrative purposes. The first chairman of the council was James Aiken. He was an ardent nationalist and came to play a prominent part in the republican movement. (After partition in 1921, he quit Northern Ireland, and rose to become the Minister for External Affairs in the Dublin government.)

Charles Russell, Baron of Killowen, a Newryman of renown, died in August 1901. Russell was born in 1832 at number 50 Queen Street (now Dominic Street). He was called to the bar and had a distinguished and, for an Irish Catholic, unprecedented career. One of his outstanding successes was the defence of Charles Stewart Parnell, in 1888, in answering the accusations of *The Times* that Parnell had condoned the Phoenix Park murders of chief secretary Lord Frederick Cavendish and his undersecretary, Thomas Henry Burke. In 1886 he became the attorney general and received a knighthood. In 1894 he was appointed as a Lord of Appeal and shortly afterwards as Lord Chief Justice, the first Catholic to hold this office since the reign of Henry VII. He continued to have a distinguished career, twice arbitrating in international disputes. Russell had served as an MP for South Hackney in London. In politics he was in favour of Home Rule for Ireland but could not bring himself to join the Irish Parliamentary Party. In his home town reactions to Russell have always been mixed. While local pride is gratified that a Newryman rose so high, many of the townspeople had — and have — reservations over his politics and his acceptance of a peerage. Nevertheless, when he died in 1901 tributes were paid to him from all sections of the population.

The backdrop to the reforms in local government was the increasingly uneasy political situation in Ireland. The introduction of a bill by Gladstone in 1886 to grant Home Rule to Ireland precipitated a crisis that was not to be solved for some forty years. Resurgent Irish nationalism was met by committed Unionist resistance that brought Ireland to the brink on a number of occasions. At the same time the early twentieth century witnessed something of a revolution in industrial relations, as trade unions and socialism began to win support among urban workers and land labourers, the result being unrest, a series of strikes, and political agitation that ultimately became submerged in the struggle over the fate of Ireland.

Charles Russell represented Charles Stewart Parnell in *The Times* case and became Lord Chief Justice. (*Open Window*)

Newry played a pioneering role in the new trade union movement. The movement's chief protagonists were James Connolly, James Larkin and James Fearon. Larkin and Fearon had local connections. Larkin's father came from south Armagh and his mother from a farm near Warrenpoint; Fearon was born in Newry and did more than anyone to establish trade unionism there. He was born in Castle Street in 1874 but went to Britain in search of work, and he met James Larkin in Glasgow in 1905. Both men were committed socialists and soon became important within the National Union of Dock Labourers (NUDL). When Larkin was sent to Belfast to organise for the NUDL, the Newryman went with him. Fearon returned to his home town and began agitating there on behalf of the union. At this time the stevedore system operated in Newry and Warrenpoint. This meant that no one was guaranteed employment but everyone had to assemble each morning and hope that they were chosen by a stevedore to work in his gang. The system was rife with corruption: often only friends or favourites got jobs; every man employed was expected to reimburse the stevedore in some manner for the favour; and too often jobs were allocated on a religious basis. Fearon and the union promised an end to these abuses. In 1907 Belfast was caught up in the longest industrial dispute that Ireland had ever seen. Beginning in the docks, where the carters' strike was followed by lock-out, the dispute spread throughout the city and at one stage even the Royal Irish Constabulary (RIC) mutinied. Just as Newry had the reputation for being as 'rebellious' as Belfast during the period of the United Irishmen in the 1790s, so now the town was to be as 'socialist' as the city. On 27 September a branch of the NUDL was founded at a meeting held in Newry Town Hall, presided over by James Fearon and addressed by James Larkin, who received a welcome to match the reputation he had acquired among Irish workers.

James Larkin pioneered the trades union movement in Ireland. He had local family connections and with James Fearon played an important role in the 1907 NUDL dockers' strike in Newry and Warrenpoint.
(Belfast Central Library)

The strike in Belfast and the founding of a branch of the union were to have a decisive influence on Newry and the troubles that followed in the town were to bring to the surface grievances and injustices that had always been there but which had never been spoken of in the guidebooks or business directories and which had no channel of expression until the NUDL began to organise there. The trouble began in November, when three colliers that had been unable to unload in Belfast came to Newry as an alternative port. Since the members of the NUDL regarded unloading the boats as strike-breaking, they were 'blacked' and soon the port came out on strike in sympathy with the strikers at Belfast. The shipping firms then fell back on Warrenpoint in an attempt to carry on their business. However, a strike was called there following the dismissal of a crane driver who belonged to the union. On 30 November a mass meeting was held in Warrenpoint, which was addressed by Larkin. In the dispute that followed there was a great deal of ill-feeling on both the employers' and workers' sides, and long-held bitternesses began to be revealed. The employers offered a £1 bounty to any 'free' worker who would work during the strike and, in expectation of trouble, contingents of the RIC were drafted into Warrenpoint from all over County Down. Those men who accepted the bounty were housed in makeshift accommodation on the docks, guarded by the police.

In early December the men of the Newry gasworks, who had become members of the NUDL, threatened to strike if their demands for rates of pay on a par with England were not met. In fact, many employees of the gasworks could not afford gas in their own homes.

Newryman James Fearon played a key role in organising the NUDL in Belfast and his home town. He was the chief spokesman during the 1907 strike and a particular focus of hostility from the employers. (Irish Transport and General Workers' Union, Newry Branch)

They elected Fearon to be their negotiator. A strike at the gasworks was averted, but the situation on the dockside worsened. Two of the major shipping merchants, Fishers and Ferrises, issued a public warning that 'unless the men returned to work within 24 hours they would apply to the Shipping Federation for free labourers and request the military to send infantry to the town for the protection of their workers'. The Catholic Bishop of Dromore, Dr Henry O'Neill, was also bringing pressure to bear to force the strike to end. He warned his congregation that strikes were contrary to Catholic interests and that a continuance of the strike would put many businesses in Newry in jeopardy. He was also making efforts to bring both sides in the dispute to the negotiating table. He had little sympathy for the trade union activists and managed to cancel a public meeting scheduled for 11 December in Margaret Square.

On 12. December the settlement that the bishop had been working towards was announced, and the union case was argued by officials sent from central office. James Fearon had been excluded from the negotiations and he refused to endorse the agreement. Nevertheless, the union recommended a return to work and the agreement, which sets out the grievances felt by the workers, tells us much about conditions on the docks at Newry and Warrenpoint. While it conceded to the employers the right to employ union or non-union men and obliged the employees to work on any ship unconditionally, certain concessions were made. First, the merchants agreed to employ 'at their own expense a responsible man who shall engage and have charge of the men without any interference whatever'. This should have signalled the end of the stevedores. Second, the employers gave a guarantee that men would be employed 'regardless of their religious or political beliefs or whether they are trade unionists or non-trade unionists'. Discrimination against Catholic workers emerged as a major grievance during the strike and some employers, Fishers in particular, were said to be notorious for refusing to employ Catholics or political undesirables. It was hoped that this guarantee would end such discrimination. The final concession was the establishment of a Conciliation Board to arbitrate in future disputes. Since 1901, following the dissolution of the Newry Navigation Company, the canal and the port had been in the hands of a public body, the Newry Port and Harbour Trust, which was made up of representatives from the local merchants, the shipowners, and the ratepayers. The Conciliation Board consisted of two representatives from the Port and Harbour Trust, two from the employers and two from the workers.

On the face of it, it seemed to be an equitable settlement. However, the dockers refused to accept it. The agreement had been reached by union officials without worker consultation, and the men felt that giving up the union's position within the workforce, the obligation to unload ships involved in strikes, and effectively surrendering their own right to strike to the Conciliation Board was too high a price to pay for the concessions. James Fearon led the opposition but arguments over the deal were superseded when the strike flared up again on 15 December. Dockers at Newry had refused to unload a ship belonging to the Newry Provincial Coal Company. The collier in question had unloaded part of its cargo at Warrenpoint, in defiance of the strike, and now the men at Newry demanded payment for the full cargo before they would unload it. In response to this isolated dispute, all the shipping companies repudiated the agreement made with the union officials and a notice, signed by twenty employers, was posted throughout the town warning that 'no man connected with the union will receive employment'.

The docks in Warrenpoint were used as an alternative to Newry during the 1907 strike. When Warrenpoint dockers joined the strike, the RIC was drafted in to protect strike-breakers there.

This was in effect, if not in name, a 'lock-out'. The dispute was to continue for another two months, even after the lock-out in Belfast had ended. It was a time of great hardship for the strikers and their families. There are many reports of families going without food or fuel in the winter months, and the local school inspector reported that many children had little or no clothes to wear, so severe was the suffering. Matters were made worse when the poor law guardians refused outdoor relief to the wives and children of the striking workers on the grounds that their hardship was self-imposed. In this situation the odds were in the employers' favour and they only had to wait to bring the union to terms.

An attempt to achieve an acceptable solution was made at a meeting of the interested parties, held at the Dundalk Harbour Board. Both Larkin and Fearon were there for the NUDL. Neither side could satisfy the other and so the meeting ended with no agreement. However, by this time a drift back to work had begun. The hardship was proving too much and many of the returning men signed a document repudiating the union and promising not to be associated with it in the future. By February 1908 the strike was over with none of the men's demands having been met and with no official recognition of the union, following the repudiation of the 12 December agreement.

Fearon continued to be periodically involved in the industrial and political affairs of his home town. Although he never achieved the fame of James Larkin, he was recognised by some of his contemporaries as an equally influential figure. John Sexton, the chief official of the NUDL, said somewhat bitterly 'In Newry and Dundalk and every other port that could be influenced by Messrs. Larkin and Fearon, men were called out on strike and without the slightest consultation with us in Liverpool.' When James Fearon died in Glasgow on 24 October 1924, he was given one of the largest funerals the city had ever seen. The hall of the Irish Transport and General Workers' Union in Newry was named after him.

The beginning of the twentieth century also saw developments of a municipal nature — for example, in the Newry Volunteer Fire Brigade. The brigade had been founded by subscription in 1877 and in 1897 appointed its most famous captain, James Heather, who was to receive the Police Medal for his work in fire-fighting. The brigade was based in the town hall, where, in the event of a fire, a bell was rung to summon the firemen. At the same time two 'call boys' were employed to run from house to house fetching out the members of the brigade. In 1901 there was a disastrous fire that burned down the workhouse, despite the brigade's efforts. This left a huge gap in welfare for the poor and there was much hardship until it was rebuilt.

In 1910 it was decided to move the fire brigade alarm from the town hall to the gasworks, where a steam siren was installed. On one of the first occasions that it was used, 'such was the wailing, one old lady in Chapel Street died of a heart attack'. Following this tragedy, the siren was removed and the old system of 'call boys' was reintroduced. On 10 December 1910 the brigade had to fight one of the biggest fires yet seen in Ireland, at Duncan's flour mill, beside the cathedral. It was a tall building, 120 feet high, and strong winds soon spread the fire to the adjoining premises, including the printing works of the *Newry Reporter*. The whole block was destroyed and although the firemen could not extinguish the fire, it was contained from spreading further. The debris continued to smoulder for weeks afterwards.

The fire brigade's next innovation was more successful than the siren. In 1912 a full-time officer, Superintendent Hunting, was appointed. The brigade had purchased modern equipment and Superintendent Hunting's primary task was to train the firemen in handling it and increasing the professionalism of the brigade, which was completely reorganised around two officers and eleven men. The new professional standing of the fire service was then given official recognition when its name was changed to the Newry Municipal Fire Brigade.

The newly established urban district council was engaged on an important building programme in these years. In 1897 a new library was built for the town and a dispensary was opened the following year. The first council houses were erected in Erskine Street and Erskine Place at a cost of £4,800. The houses were originally intended to be rented by the army, who were still stationed in the nearby linen hall, but when the military declined them, they provided accommodation for some of the townspeople. A new post office was built on a derelict site in Hill Street, at a cost of £5,700, and was opened in 1900. It was a fine building with an elegant granite facade, which unfortunately fell victim to modernisation in later years.

Another major building project at this time was an extension to the Catholic cathedral. A tower and transepts had been added to the original church in 1888. In 1904 work began on extending the nave and decorating the interior with marble and mosaics. The project took five years to complete and Italian craftsmen came to Newry to work on the more intricate decoration of the interior.

In 1912 the council began a second programme of public housing when John Martin Street and John Mitchel Street were built. These houses were meant to provide affordable accommodation for poorer people, but there was no gas in most of them as it was too expensive, even though the same council owned the gasworks. The names of these new streets reflect the nationalist character of the urban district council and from this period onwards Newry was considered to be a safe nationalist seat in parliament.

Even though the majority of councillors were Home Rulers, they were more concerned with the affairs of Newry than with national matters, and for some time the town remained somewhat apart from the Home Rule crisis. But Irish affairs now dominated at Westminster; after years of a Conservative monopoly of government, the Liberal Party had come to power and one of its longest-standing pledges had been the introduction of a Home Rule Bill for Ireland. Previously, any bill that had been passed by the House of Commons could be sure of defeat in the Lords. However, the Parliament Act of 1911 meant that the House of Lords could delay the passing of an act but could not reject it. For the first time Home Rule for Ireland was a real possibility. When the bill came forward in 1912, it was acceptable to Irish nationalists, but republicanism, as espoused by Sinn Féin, was already becoming a force

157

The new post office opened in 1900. Unfortunately its impressive granite façade did not escape modernisation in the 1970s. (*Open Window*)

to be reckoned with. In Newry, Sinn Féin had a large following and its headquarters in Edward Street was the focus of republican activity in the town. Unionist opposition to Home Rule was increasing and by 1913 the probability of armed resistance by Unionists, especially in Ulster, was very close indeed. The determination of the Ulster Protestants to resist Home Rule was a surprise to the British government, and not fully understood by the nationalists. However, as historian J.C. Beckett has explained, for the Ulster Protestant the Home Rule issue was 'a revival of the seventeenth-century struggle between Roman Catholics and Protestants for ascendancy in Ireland, a struggle which his ancestors had twice fought to victorious conclusion and which he was prepared, should the worst come to the worst, to fight again'.

Unionist resistance to Home Rule had started in earnest when Edward Saunderson, MP for North Armagh, formed the Ulster Defence Union in 1893. With the formation of the Ulster Volunteer Force (UVF) and the signing of the Solemn League and Covenant in 1912, the dividing line between pro- and anti-Home Rule Ireland was set at the Ulster border, and Newry, a nationalist town, found itself on this line. The following year saw the formation of the Irish Citizen Army in Dublin, an organisation sponsored by the trade unions at the instigation of James Connolly and James Larkin. The Citizen Army had been formed in response to police actions during the lock-out of that year and had little influence beyond the capital city. However, shortly afterwards the Irish Volunteers were formed in order to protect, by arms if necessary, the Irish interest in the Home Rule crisis. The elements involved in the setting up of these Volunteers were a mixture of Home Rulers and revolutionary republicans influenced by the IRB, which saw it as a useful way of preparing an armed force for a rising.

Both the UVF and the Irish Volunteers found support in Newry and the surrounding districts. The Unionist, or Protestant, population of Newry felt threatened by the majority nationalist population, just as in

Ireland as a whole, the Unionist minority felt threatened by the majority. The nationalists of Newry felt that they had to defend themselves against the Unionists, especially after the declaration of a provisional government for Ulster in 1913. The question facing nationalists was: in the event of open war would this provisional government attempt to impose its authority over the nationalist town on its border?

The fact that Newry was on the dividing line and did have a sizeable Protestant population, some 25 per cent of the total, made it all the more important for the Unionists to show their strength there. Edward Carson, the Unionists' leader, addressed a mass anti-Home Rule meeting in Newry in 1913. The town was divided into six districts by the UVF and their organiser reported: '[I am] enrolling all good men I could get in each locality, about 150 in all. ... I am arranging for each locality being drilled weekly and once a month having one combined drill in Newry.' Arming these men seemed to present little problem, as a UVF officer, Robert Nesbitt, reported to his superior:

The Catholic cathedral, SS Patrick and Colman. In 1904 Italian craftsmen were brought in to work on the marble and mosaics during extension and decorative work. (Lawrence Collection)

As a border town
Newry was particularly
important for shows of
strength by the UVF in
1912. (Public Record
Office of Northern
Ireland)

The B.S.A.'S [British Small Arms rifles] are in great demand at
present, Monday and Thursday nights and Wednesday afternoons. If
you could let me have say a dozen more service rifles in addition to
the five we already have. . . only four men can be instructed at one
time in the rifle exercises at present and it is very slow work. The
squad organisation is nearly completed. … We are working away at
rifle exercises, skirmishing, signals etc.

On the nationalist side the Irish Volunteers had also been recruited in
the town. They too sought to arm themselves and drill in preparation for a
civil war. Newry had an active IRB cell and one of its members, Patrick
Rankin, has left an interesting account of his time as an underground
activist. The IRB'S chief aim was an armed rebellion to establish a
republic, but Rankin says of Newry: 'Very little progress was made from
1907—1913.' In 1913 Rankin went to North America to carry on
republican work there. He took with him, '[his] Stephen's Rifle, .22 bore,
which [he] purchased in Stephen Byrnes, Hill Street, Newry, 1900'. He
had to hand the rifle over to customs on his return to Britain. (Rankin took
part in the 1916 Easter Rising, cycling to Dublin after a rising had failed
to materialise in Newry.)

The close proximity of the UVF and the Irish Volunteers in Newry led
to some strange situations. In keeping with 'military' ethics, officers on
both sides tried to avoid confrontation with the 'enemy' until war should
officially be declared. Hence marches and drills tended to take place in
defined areas or at pre-set times in order to avoid clashes. Certain areas
were considered 'neutral' and it was understood that neither side would

enter them. However, as neither the UVF nor the Irish Volunteers were regular soldiers, it was sometimes difficult to restrain the men, and officers could face mutiny if the ranks' emotions got the better of them. One such 'unfortunate incident' occurred when a UVF company was marching in Bessbrook behind a local band. They were halted in the village by a policeman and warned that they could not go to the pump, as it was 'out of bounds' to both parties. The UVF halted but the band continued to march towards the pump, and Nesbitt later reported:

> Instructor Morrow called on the men to fall out and follow the band, inciting them to disobey orders (really mutiny) but I am proud to say when I called the Vols. to stand steady and obey my orders not a single Volunteer fell out, showing splendid discipline of which any line regiment might feel proud — it appears to have been a pre-arranged affair by the band and we would be well rid of them and also any others refusing to obey orders.

While the volunteers of both parties marched through Newry, the Home Rule Bill progressed through parliament. Opposition in the House of Lords could not stop it passing into law in August 1914. The crisis in Ireland had reached a critical point as Unionist leaders threatened open rebellion. In Newry both sides prepared for the civil war that now seemed inevitable. However, the fears of the Unionists and the hopes of the nationalists were made redundant by the action of nationalists on the other side of Europe. When Gavrilo Princip, a Serbian nationalist, fired the shots that killed Archduke Franz Ferdinand of Austria on 28 June 1914, he could have had no idea that his action was to have a decisive influence on the course of events in Ireland. When the outbreak of World War I, involving all the major European powers, followed this assassination, the British government decided, with the agreement of all parties in the House, that constitutional change of the magnitude entailed in the Home Rule Act could not be carried out while the country was at war. For Ireland, and for Newry, the moment of crisis had passed.

Many men from Newry and the surrounding districts enlisted in the British Army. The UVF members had no reservations about enlisting under the Crown and many became part of the 36th (Ulster) Division. On the nationalist side there were divided opinions. Many believed it was more important to fight for an Irish republic than for the 'Little Belgium' of the recruitment posters. The majority, however, followed the advice of John Redmond — the nationalists' leader — and joined the army. Newry was no different in this regard and when Patrick Rankin returned to the town after the outbreak of war, he found things 'very low in Newry as regards Volunteers or the I.R.B. There seemed to be no meetings of any organisations or preparations for the future.'

Many families, in all parts of the town, lost relatives fighting in France. War, however, was good for trade. Those who had not enlisted found plenty of work with good wages in the town and at the quayside. Disruption of international shipping meant that Britain turned to Ireland to make up shortfalls in supplies. The linen mills churned out cloth for uniforms, and workshops and factories produced all sorts of equipment demanded by the war effort.

The cattle trade, in particular, benefited from the needs of the British market and livestock exports going through Newry rose during the war. Ships belonging to firms such as the Dundalk and Newry Steam-Packet Company and the Dundalk, Newry and Greenore Railway Company (DN & GR) sailed daily from the Albert Basin with cattle to be sold in England. One of these voyages ended tragically off Greenore at the entrance to Carlingford Lough on 3 November 1916, when a boat belonging to the DN & GR, the *Connemara,* collided with a collier, the *Retriever,* belonging to Fishers of Newry. A severe gale was blowing at the time and visibility was bad. For some reason the *Retriever* was without lights and so the *Connemara* did not see it coming. Both ships sank on impact. Everyone on board the *Connemara* was killed: fifty-one passengers, thirty-one crew members and four railwaymen. Of the nine-man crew of the *Retriever,* only one survived. By some quirk of fate, many of the cattle on board the *Connemara* managed to escape the sinking ship and were later picked up on shore near Greenore.

The war, of course, also brought hardships. The people of the town suffered from shortages of fuel and a number of foodstuffs. The activities of German raiders posed as much of a threat to Newry shipping as anywhere else and trade was sometimes disrupted. It also meant that the price of goods rose as supply failed to meet demand. The local gas industry was hit by the rising price of coal and by the end of the war gas was costing 8s.4d. (42p) per 1,000 cubic feet, which was double the prewar price.

A general election was expected to follow the end of the war and so further reforms were made in the system of representation. Taking into account changing demographic factors, important alterations were made to electoral constituencies in 1917. As a result, Newry was no longer treated as a separate parliamentary borough but was submerged in the enlarged constituency of South Down. In the strict terms of the town's history, this was probably more important than the war, because Newry lost the status granted to it by James I in 1613. Since that time the town had returned representatives to the Irish parliament and subsequently to the imperial parliament at Westminster. The loss of its status as a parliamentary borough was not only a blow to local pride but it also represented official recognition that Newry had been left behind in terms of population and prosperity and now, by government decree, was declared a provincial town of the second rank.

The ending of the war would bring with it the reopening of the Home Rule question, as the Government was pledged to implement the Home Rule Act once peace had returned. In Ireland the situation had already changed beyond recognition. The Easter Rising of 1916 and the execution of fifteen of its leaders had so changed public opinion in Ireland that the demand was for nothing less than full independence. By September 1917 Sinn Féin had enough support to hold a public march in Newry despite an RIC ban. The British government had also changed its mind about Home Rule and in 1917 a convention had been called to try to find a form of government acceptable to all sides, but nothing came of it.

The death of the nationalist MP for South Armagh, Dr Charles O'Neill, necessitated a by-election on 2 February 1918 and this saw the first clash in Ulster between Sinn Féin and the nationalist parry. The Unionists decided not to put forward a candidate. Although not part of the constituency, Newry witnessed much of the campaigning that went on between Patrick Donnelly, the nationalist, and Patrick McCartan, the Sinn Féin candidate. The latter's campaign ended with a rally in Margaret Square on 31 January at which Eamon de Valera, Countess Markievicz and Arthur Griffith spoke. On the day Donnelly got 2,324 votes and McCartan, 1,305. It was a pattern being repeated throughout most of Ireland, in which Sinn Féin was becoming more active and was receiving more open support, and Newry was no exception. In April 1918 Frank Aiken, who was recognised as the local IRA commander, was arrested on a charge of illegal drilling and brought before the magistrate. Aiken was sentenced to one month's imprisonment and his trial was the occasion of a show of strength by local republicans who assembled outside the courthouse beneath the Irish tricolour and sang 'A Soldier's Song', the new anthem of an independent Ireland. Others drilled in military fashion before the courthouse. Although further arrests and trials followed this demonstration, republican support was not diminished. The story is told of how the magistrate threatened to send one defendant to prison for twelve months and the reply came,

'The Germans will be here by then.' The RIC commander in chief, Major General Sir Frederick Shaw, drafted extra police into Newry in anticipation of widespread trouble.

Margaret Square, one of Hill St's two squares, was at the heart of the retail centre of Newry. The golden teapot at the Kelly & Calvert grocery shop is still in place. (W.A. Green, Ulster Folk and Transport Museum

On 23 June, Sinn Féin held a large public meeting at a Gaelic football field at The Marshes, between Newry and Bessbrook, to protest at the proposal to introduce conscription into Ireland. After another protest meeting on 13 August, the president of Sinn Féin in Newry, Robert Kelly, was arrested and sent to Belfast for trial, where a court martial sentenced him to six months' imprisonment. August also saw something of a riot when republicans attempted to break up an army recruitment rally and police and soldiers had to be brought in for protection. More trials and convictions followed, which again were occasions of protest and propaganda by Sinn Féin.

The situation in Newry continued to deteriorate in the following months as resistance to the authorities grew. The end of the war in November 1918 brought with it an unproclaimed truce, as it became obvious that a general election was to follow in December. Throughout the country, Sinn Féin were determined to field as many candidates as possible in order to win seats from the Irish Parliamentary Party. However, in certain areas where there was no clear-cut anti-Unionist majority, there was a danger of splitting the vote and allowing a Unionist to be elected. Such was the case in South Armagh and South Down and after much hard bargaining and hesitation, Sinn Féin agreed to withdraw its candidates, allowing the nationalists, Jeremiah MacVeagh and Patrick Donnelly, a free run against the Unionists. The Sinn Féin candidate for South Down had been Eamon de Valera and in the weeks running up to the election he campaigned in Newry and the surrounding districts before the decision to withdraw was taken.

Left John Francis Quinn, Officer Commanding, 4th Northern Division, IRA, based in Newry. During the Civil War, on 22 April he was injured in a battle with Free State troops and died exactly a month later. (Séamus Mac Caibhead).

Right Newryman Thomas Carr in IRA Volunteer uniform. Even after hostilities ceased in 1923, he was still a wanted man and 12 February 1925 he was shot dead as the RUC attempted to arrest him. (Séamus Mac Caibhead)

The result of the general election was that Sinn Féin had seventy-three seats and the nationalists six, against the Unionists twenty-six. On 21 January 1919 the Sinn Féin members gathered in the Mansion House, Dublin, and formally declared themselves to be Dáil Éireann, the parliament of Ireland, inviting all elected representatives to attend. A government was chosen from the Dáil, which began to implement a strategy to make a reality of the Irish Republic that had been proclaimed in Easter 1916, and a provisional constitution was adopted. It was only a matter of time before there was open conflict.

In Newry the events in Dublin seem to have made little impact on the urban district council, whose chairman was Hugh John McConville, a nationalist. The council records suggest that the big issue was whether to introduce electricity into the town or not. The question of electricity had been on the agenda for some time, but the town commissioners, and then the council, had refused to make any decisions. By now electricity was becoming common in most towns and even Bessbrook had electric street lights. The council consulted a Dublin electrical engineer, Arthur E. Porte, who proposed a scheme for generating electricity by gas. A second scheme was put forward by an engineer from Dundalk, P.A. Spalding. Spalding proposed a straightforward plan for building a hydroelectric plant to supply the town. However, as the council's term of office was almost over, it was agreed to postpone a decision. The new council elections were held under proportional representation for the first time and no one could regard a seat as safe.

The success of Sinn Féin in the general election and the establishment of Dáil Éireann had gathered more supporters for the republican cause, and so it was in Newry. When the elections were held in January 1920, the make-up of the urban district council was now seven Sinn Féin councillors, five nationalists, four Unionists and two Labour.

The Irish Republic, not electricity, was now top of the agenda. The 'shooting war' had already started elsewhere in Ireland, and soon the Irish Republican Army (IRA), as the republican forces were now called, began operations in and around Newry. The war that followed was a 'dirty war', where ambush and assassination were the main tactics on both sides. In Newry the attacks began at Easter 1920. The first major assault by the IRA was the burning of the custom house on Merchants' Quay. Another operation the same night did not do so well, when Thomas Tait, the Newry battalion officer, was captured by a daughter of Robinett Gandy, the local income tax officer. Miss Gandy was trained in jujitsu and held Tait by the nose until the police arrived. However, future incidents were not to be so comical.

Among those arrested by the police in the following days was Patrick Lavery, a Sinn Féin councillor. On 6 April a meeting of the council was convened by Sinn Féin to express sympathy for the family of Thomas MacCurtain, the lord mayor of Cork who had been killed by the RIC. A week later, on 13 April, a national stoppage was called in support of hunger strikers in Mountjoy Prison in Dublin. On that day many Newry shops closed and workers came out on strike. The following months saw a series of incidents; ambushes by the IRA were answered by retaliatory measures by the police and army; gun battles became an accepted fact of life.

The first fatality in Newry did not occur until 21 November 1920, when Chief Constable Kearney of the RIC barracks in Canal Street was shot dead by the IRA, shortly after leaving church in Dominic Street. No witnesses came forward and the assassins were never identified. By this time a policy of reprisals had been introduced and in the following days republican suspects were arrested and property belonging to Sinn Féin and known republicans was destroyed. Few people could now have any illusions left about the nature of the conflict. The IRA launched its biggest attack in the area when an estimated two hundred men assaulted the RIC barracks in Camlough in the early morning of 13 December. A gun battle ensued that lasted for some hours and a second occurred at the Egyptian Arch, half a mile outside Newry, as the IRA ambushed police reinforcements who were coming from the town. The IRA was finally forced to withdraw.

In what was now the accepted practice throughout Ireland, three houses used by the IRA, which were opposite the barracks, were demolished, a local pub was burned down and the house of Frank Aiken was also set on fire. There were numerous police raids throughout the town. Four men with weapons were discovered on the Dublin Road and were subsequently brought to trial. They refused to recognise the legitimacy of the court and were each sentenced to fifteen years' imprisonment.

Two of the IRA men involved in the ambush in Camlough later died of their injuries and their funerals became occasions for a show of strength by the republicans. One man, Peter Shields, had died on the Christmas Day following the attack and was privately buried in Omeath in County Louth. However, the second man, John F. O'Hare, had been captured and did not die of his wounds until October 1921. Shields's remains were exhumed to be buried in Newry alongside O'Hare. On 8 October the centre of Newry was taken over by armed IRA members while the funeral service was held in the cathedral. Thousands turned out for the occasion. In the face of the large turnout the RIC thought it wiser to keep away from the scene.

The violence continued, following the set pattern of ambush and reprisal. In 1921, for the first time, republican, or 'Sinn Féiner', courts were in operation in the area. They had a sporadic existence but were quite often used as an alternative to the 'British' courts. Attacks on the police continued and casualties on both sides were now increasing. The intensity of the conflict was such that it seemed as if barely a week passed by without some incident in Newry or the surrounding counties.

In accordance with the Government of Ireland Act of 1920 a general election was to be held in May 1921. The act was an attempt by Lloyd George's government to settle the Irish question and for the first time it incorporated the concept of separate parliaments of 'Northern Ireland' and 'Southern Ireland'. In view of the number of incidents in Newry and because there was a fear of increased violence during the election, the following order was issued by the military commander in the town:

> I, Colonel-Commandant, G.T.C. Carter-Campbell, C.B., D.S.O., Commanding 15th Infantry Brigade, Competent Military Authority, in exercise of the powers conferred on me by regulation No. 13 of the Restoration of Order in Ireland Regulations, and of all other powers there unto enabling me, do hereby order and require: -
> That every person within the Newry Urban District, Co. Down, shall remain indoors between the hours of 9.00 p.m. and 5.00 a.m.; unless provided with a permit in writing from the competent military authority, or some person duly authorised by him. This order shall become force at 9 o'clock on the fourth day of May, 1921.

Although anyone breaking the curfew was liable to be shot, offenders were usually taken to court. Within a fortnight of the order being issued, over sixty civilians appeared before the magistrate, charged with being at large after nine o'clock.

The general election marked an important new stage in the Anglo-Irish War. It had been decided that the northern parliament should consist of the six north-eastern counties of Ireland, including County Down. In the other twenty-six counties Sinn Féin took advantage of the elections to reassert its right to represent the Irish people and thereby recognise the legitimacy of the Republic. In all but a few cases no one opposed them. Obviously the issue was not so clear cut in Northern Ireland and wherever Sinn Féin candidates stood, they met opposition. One constituency in which the Sinn Féin candidate was successful was South Down, where Eamon de Valera came top of the poll. He, as expected, would have nothing to do with the parliament due to sit in Belfast. Newry, therefore, found itself in the strange position of being represented in the Dáil by de Valera but falling within the jurisdiction of the Northern Ireland parliament. Despite anomalies such as this, the parliament of Northern Ireland was officially opened by George v on 22 June 1921, and he used the occasion to make a plea for peace.

In Newry the campaign of violence had continued. On 14 June the RIC barracks was extensively damaged by fire and a week later a troop train was derailed not far from the town. The establishment of the parliament of Northern Ireland had led to an even more determined effort by the IRA and the number of incidents increased. During July a member of the B Specials, the auxiliary police force, and six republicans were killed by ambush or assassination in and around Newry.

The king's plea for peace was not spoken in a vacuum, since for some months, secret negotiations had been taking place between representatives of the Republican and British governments. These initial negotiations led to the declaration of a truce on Friday 8 July 1921, to come into effect at noon on Monday 11 July. For Newry this meant a lifting of the curfew and months of uneasy peace while negotiations between the Irish and British delegates took place in London. The negotiations were of concern to everyone in Newry, whether Republican or Unionist. The establishment of the parliament in Northern Ireland on the basis of the six north-eastern counties placed Newry on the frontier between the North and the rest of Ireland. Whether or not this was to remain the frontier and what was to be the status of the rest of Ireland would be decided in London. In December 1921 the 'Articles of agreement for a treaty between Great Britain and Ireland' were signed and on 7 January 1922. they were accepted in the Dáil by sixty-four votes to fifty-seven. The bitterness of the debate and the closeness of the vote were to foreshadow the divisions in the country that would result in civil war within a few months.

In June 1921 a troop train carrying the 10th Huzzars was derailed by a number of IRA bombs at Adavoyle, near Newry. (Séamus Mac Caibhead)

```
                        MINISTRY OF HOME

                        AFFAIRS, SOUTHERN

                        IRELAND, BEDFAST.

    COPY.                              _19th April 1922.


    Sir,
        I am directed by the Minister of Home Affairs for Northern Ireland to inform you

    that the Ministry have, by Order under Seal, dissolved the Newry Urban District Council,

    and appointed Major James Hanna MoCorniok,D.S.O. to exercise and perform all the

    powers and duties of the said Council.

        Official copies of the Order will be sent you in due course, "but in the meantime

    you should formally communicate the decision of the Ministry to all the members of

    the late Council.

                        I am, Sir,
                                Your obedient Servant,

                                    I. W. HARRIS.



    The Clerk,
    Newry Urtan District Council,
    H B W E Y.
```

Newry UDC was dissolved in April 1922 for refusing to take an oath of allegiance to the new Stormont government.

The importance of the treaty for Newry was that it was constructed on an all-Ireland basis. However, Northern Ireland was given the option of withdrawing from the Irish Free State, as the new state was to be called, and the frontier between north and south was to be decided by a Boundary Commission, 'in accordance with the wishes of the inhabitants, so far as may be compatible with economic and geographic conditions'. Northern Ireland, as expected, did opt out of the Irish Free State and it was widely believed that the Boundary Commission would so determine the border that Northern Ireland would be left with only a small area of territory. The general feeling in Newry was that it and its hinterland would be part of the Free State. However, the continuing disturbances in Northern Ireland and the outbreak of civil war in June 1922 prevented the Boundary Commission from being convened until 1924.

Many IRA supporters in Northern Ireland, not surprisingly, rejected the treaty and partition and in Newry the IRA continued its campaign against the 'occupying forces'. A goods train was derailed in March 1922 and the following months saw further ambushes of police and military patrols. A curfew was declared by the Northern Ireland government on 31 May, which meant that civilians were to be confined to their homes between 11 p.m. and 5 a.m. The Royal Ulster Constabulary (RUC) and the B Specials were now at the brunt of operations against the IRA. Neither side showed much mercy for the other and the death toll continued to rise.

SPECIAL PERMIT FOR NEWRY.

The Bearer, *W John Edgar Connor.*

Address *Hill Street Newry*

has permission to be out of doors between the hours of 11 p.m. and 5 a.m. for the sole purpose of attending the Functions held by the **NEWRY SOCIAL AND SPORTS CLUB,** the Programme for which will be lodged with Police Authorities at Canal Street Barracks, Newry, each month.

DISTRICT INSPECTOR'S OFFICE
R. I. C.
16 NOV 1922.
NEWRY CO DOWN

W. R. H. HENNESSEY

A Henry

Head Constable.

On 31 May 1922 a curfew was imposed on Newry. An RUC permit was required for anyone wishing to be out during curfew hours. (Public Record Office of Northern Ireland)

On the political front the Northern Ireland government demanded an oath of allegiance from members of local councils. Members of the Newry Urban District Council refused to take the oath or to recognise the legitimacy of Northern Ireland. In April 1922 the council was suspended and a commissioner, J.H. McCormick, was appointed to administrate municipal affairs until such time as a new council was elected. The following authorities were also suspended for refusing the oath of allegiance: the Newry Board of Guardians; Warrenpoint Urban District Council; Newry number 1 and number 2 Rural District Councils; Crossmaglen Rural District Council; Kilkeel Rural District Council; and the Kilkeel Board of Guardians. New elections were not held until the following year. The elections were held under the old 'six shilling' franchise and not proportional representation, thus undoing the reforms introduced by the Westminster government in 1917. They were completely boycotted by republicans, and by nationalists generally, except for the Newry and Warrenpoint urban councils. Twelve nationalists were returned in Newry, giving them a majority and putting Hugh John McConville back in the chair. The suspension of the council had done little to change opinions in the town, but it had prevented the republican councillors sitting again and put in their place men who were willing to co-operate with the Northern Ireland government on a de facto basis in the expectation that they would be outside its jurisdiction once the Boundary Commission had published its report.

By the summer of 1923 IRA activity had all but ceased. The defeat of the Republicans by the Irish Free State left them without a base or any safe areas outside Northern Ireland. The new government in Dublin had no desire to see violence continue and sought instead to protect the interests of the nationalist population through diplomatic means. The cessation of the civil war left the way open for a return to 'normal' politics.

The issue that was uppermost in Newry returned — the supply of electricity to the town. The troubles of recent years had prevented any decision being made and consequently Newry was still without an electricity supply when other towns such as Dundalk in County Louth, just across the border, enjoyed its benefits.

On 25 October 1924
Eamon de Valera
crossed the Border to
speak at a political
meeting in Newry
despite an exclusion
order. He was arrested
and held in Canal St.
RUC barracks. (*Belfast
Telegraph*)

The matter was broughtbefore the council on 3 December 1923, and it was to lead to a dispute that brought to the fore the basic divisions between nationalists and Unionists on the council.

Renewed public interest in the electricity question prompted a visit in early 1924 by the council's electricity committee to Dundalk, where P.A. Spalding had installed a generating system. Both Spalding and Arthur E. Porte had submitted updated reports to the council but instead of choosing either proposal it was decided to advertise for a permanent electrical engineer. However, the Unionists on the council opposed this, saying that Porte was the acting engineer and so should be given the commission to introduce electricity to the town. In the event Porte refused to apply for the post and a field of ten candidates was narrowed down to two - Spalding from Dundalk and W. Pleasance, an engineer from Belfast. Unionist support was not enough to win Pleasance the post and Spalding was appointed. In protest at the proceedings the Unionists resigned from the electricity committee, their leader, W.R. Bell, declaring that 'he would not be a part of such a committee as no man of honour could serve on it', and the plan was shelved until 1927.

The fragile state of Northern Ireland in its early years meant that a controversy or crisis could easily arise to overshadow local issues. One such incident occurred in October 1924, when elections to the Northern Ireland parliament were called. Eamon de Valera was still the member for South Down and declared that he would return to the constituency to support the new republican candidate, Michael Murney. As with local council elections, proportional representation had been abolished and the 'first past the post' system introduced. De Valera was banned from the North under an exclusion order and he was warned by Dawson Bates, the Minister of Home Affairs in the Northern Ireland government, that

171

he would be arrested if he crossed the border, and extra police and armoured cars were drafted into Newry. It had been announced that de Valera would speak at a meeting in the town hall on Saturday 25 October. That morning the roads into the town were watched by security forces and all passengers alighting from northbound trains were questioned. De Valera had not arrived by the time the meeting started. Policemen occupied the stage of the town hall and more were stationed throughout the building. The arrival in the hall of some Unionists made the situation all the more tense and there was a general expectation of trouble. Nevertheless, the meeting went ahead, the organisers promising that de Valera would arrive at any moment.

In the event he was able to cross the border without being intercepted and even managed to breach the security inside the town hall. He was on his way to the stage when he was arrested and the police were forced to draw their guns in order to get him out of the hall and into an armoured car to take him to Canal Street barracks. The police held him in custody until Monday 27 October, when it was decided that it would be better not to prosecute him. Instead he was taken under escort to Adavoyle railway station and put on a train to Dublin, with a warning not to come north again. His departure eased the tension in Newry and removed the possibility of an outbreak of violence, but de Valera recrossed the border into Derry, where he was arrested again. On this occasion he was sentenced to and served a month in prison in Belfast.

Towards the end of 1924 the Boundary Commission that had been promised in the treaty was convened. The members of the commission were: Eoin MacNeill representing the Irish Free State; Richard Feetham representing Britain and also the commission's chairman; and J.R. Fisher representing Northern Ireland. The government of Prime Minister Sir James Craig, fearing a considerable loss of territory, had refused to co-operate and the British government took it upon itself to appoint a representative for Northern Ireland. The commission's task was to review the situation on the border as it stood, to listen to arguments from interested parties regarding its redrawing and to decide what the new border should be within the terms laid down by the treaty.

The sitting of the commission was of paramount importance to Newry and the urban district council made a submission for Newry to be included within the Free State. Warrenpoint council also pressed for inclusion as did a group representing the inhabitants of the Newry and Kilkeel poor law unions. However, opinion within this area as a whole was not unanimous. Those district councils that were being boycotted by the nationalists, such as Newry numbers 1 and 2 rural, and therefore Unionist-controlled, all asked to remain within Northern Ireland. Other interested parties making representation for inclusion in Northern Ireland were: the Newry Chamber of Commerce; a group representing property owners and certain inhabitants of Warrenpoint; John Kelly Limited, which owned the Warrenpoint harbour; and all of the Bessbrook business interests, that is the spinning company, the tramway and the Camlough waterworks.

On 27 October 1924, Eamon de Valera was taken under police escort to Adavoyle railway station and placed on a southbound train. (*Belfast Telegraph*)

The argument boiled down to two fundamentals — the wishes of the citizens and the economic conditions. In an attempt to weigh up the opposing viewpoints within the community, the commission adopted the formula of 'the members of the Protestant denominations being reckoned as wishing to be in Northern Ireland and Roman Catholics as wishing to be in the Irish Free State'. Using this as a guideline, it examined the 1911 census and concluded that the majority in south Armagh and south Down favoured inclusion in the Free State. This was reinforced by those bodies petitioning for inclusion, which all argued that the majority did not want to belong to Northern Ireland and that this had been proven by election results since the nineteenth century, as South Armagh, Newry and South Down were all nationalist strongholds. In Newry alone 75 per cent of the population was Catholic. The commission accepted these points.

The economic arguments were more complex and each submission had a different conclusion. Simply put, the pro-Free State lobby argued that Newry and its hinterland formed a definite self-contained economic unit, which included significant parts of County Louth and extended into County Monaghan. Therefore, especially since the inhabitants were nationalists, the whole area should be transferred *en bloc* to the Irish Free State, as it would be 'highly injurious, in fact almost disastrous ... if any portion of that area were cut off from contact with Newry, or if Newry was cut off from it'. The commission accepted the 'economic hinterland' argument but did not think that the Free State portions were of primary importance. The commissioners' view was that if Newry was included in the Free State then those areas economically locked into it would also be included, and conversely, if Newry remained in Northern Ireland, so too would they. On the other side, the pro-Northern Ireland interests argued in regional terms. They said that Carlingford Lough

173

formed a natural boundary and so should continue to act as a border. It was further argued that Belfast was the natural focus for all economic activity in the region and that most of the industries in Newry had little cross-border trade. All the mills, and many other industries, were owned or controlled by Belfast companies and that they, the Bessbrook Spinning Company in particular, objected to having a border separating them from the city. The most powerful economic argument came from the Belfast Water Commissioners. Since Belfast's most important water supply was in the Mourne Mountains, the commissioners could not allow this area to pass into another state. The problems of jurisdiction, of managing the supply, and implementing any further developments that would be created by having the supply in the Free State and the outlet in Belfast, they said would be too great. The commissioners accepted this argument as overwhelming, stating in their report that the circumstances regarding the water supply 'have led the Commission to adopt the view that such a separation must be avoided'.

In effect this meant that south Down had to remain in Northern Ireland. If this was to be so, Newry posed a key problem. If the town was to remain within Northern Ireland, nationalist south Armagh would also have to stay. However, if the town was transferred to the Free State, it would cut off those parts of County Down dependent on it, and it was this factor, plus the broader economic concerns, that weighed the balance in favour of Newry remaining in Northern Ireland. The commissioners had come to the conclusion that the town, as a centre of commerce and industry, was interlocked into the economy of the region and that it would not fare so well if it were included in the Free State. The commissioners, therefore, drew the conclusion that the economic integrity of Northern Ireland outweighed the desires of the inhabitants. Their report said:

> The majority shown on the basis of the census figures for the area as a whole in favour of inclusion in the Free State is a substantial majority, but the Commission has had to consider whether a decision giving effect to a change of jurisdiction in accordance with the wishes of the inhabitants as indicated by these figures would be compatible with economic and geographic conditions of a more general character than those hitherto referred to.

In the end the fears of the Unionists came to nothing and despite the hopes of the nationalists, Newry was to stay in Northern Ireland.

In the event the Boundary Commission made little difference to the existing border, but it gives us an invaluable analysis of the situation at the time and the opinions of those involved at all levels. When the commission report was written — recommending quite minor changes in the border—the political situation was such that it was not published. The three governments then thrashed out a different settlement that left the border of Northern Ireland intact, apart from some inconsequential alterations.

For Newry this meant an end to the uncertainty that had prevailed since 1911. The Unionist population was now certain of the security of its

British citizenship. The nationalists had to face up to the fact that Newry was in Northern Ireland and was to be so for the foreseeable future. Those who had already compromised, in the expectation of the town being transferred to the jurisdiction of the Free State, had to decide if they would continue to accept Northern Ireland as a de facto reality, or openly oppose it as Sinn Féin had done. Most chose to work within the state and to promote the interests of nationalists as best they could. The issue of the legitimacy of the Northern Ireland state and outbreaks of republican violence were sporadically to come to the fore, but for the next six decades the local political and economic issues were of more importance as Newry once again came to terms with its status as the frontier town.

8

CLOSURE AFTER CLOSURE

The report of the Boundary Commission affords an opportunity to examine Newry in the 1920s, since it provides a detailed economic analysis of the town and its hinterland. The commission's examination of Newry as a centre of commerce, industry and shipping, assessed the comparative importance of each and how they related to one another.

In terms of numbers employed, the most important industry was textiles, followed in descending order by shipping and coal, trade in timber, iron, slates and granite, and finally the flour and meal business. Other important employers in the area were the retail sector and transport - railways and carting. The town's commerce lay in two distinct areas: as a market and retail centre for the locality, and as a centre for shipping. As a market town, Newry enjoyed a wide catchment area that extended approximately halfway from Newry to the other important towns in the region, such as Dundalk, Banbridge, Portadown and Armagh. In County Down the catchment area was bounded by Hilltown and Killowen. The whole area represented a sizeable population, estimated at 34,500, excluding the town itself.

As a centre for shipping, Newry was well served by the Port and Harbour Trust, which had under its authority not only the port but also the whole of the inland canal as far as Lough Neagh, the ship canal, and control of the Clanrye river as far as the midway point between Warrenpoint and Omeath - beyond this the waters were controlled by the Carlingford Lough Commissioners. It was seen as a distinct advantage to have these interests under one authority and they were important factors in locking Newry into the economy of the region between the two loughs. Connected to shipping was the railway network, which acted as the primary distribution route for goods coming into Newry from the sea. There were two railways serving the town, the Great Northern Railway Company, and the London, Midland and Scottish Railway Company. In the view of the Boundary Commission, the necessity of going through the junction of Goraghwood in order to enter the Belfast—Dublin railway network was a disincentive to trade in either direction. On the other hand, the commission found that Newry was admirably suited to transport goods by rail to the major towns in counties Armagh, Tyrone and Monaghan, which constituted a significant part of its trade.

On examining the figures more closely, we can see that Newry's real importance was as a channel of entry for imports into south-east Ulster. Imports outnumbered exports by twelve to one. By far the main import was coal, which on average made up 80 per cent of the total. This is somewhat ironic when we remember that the Newry Canal was first built to export Tyrone coal. The other imports passing through Newry were maize, 12 per cent of the total, flour, 4 per cent, and general cargo — hardware goods, finished products, and so on — also 4 per cent of the total. These figures excluded the cargo handled by the Dundalk and Newry Steam-Packet Company, which in the main carried general cargo from Britain.

Once unloaded at Newry, 22 per cent of the coal was used locally, 15 per cent was sent across the border into the Free State, and the rest distributed in Northern Ireland. However, of the grain and flour imported, between 45 and 50 per cent (it varied from year to year) was sent across the border. The commission noted that while coal was a fairly regular trade, in grain and flour it was most uncertain, tending to fluctuate in response to climatic factors.

Newry's small export trade, excluding the produce of the local mills, consisted mainly of potatoes, which could be anything from 50 to 70 per cent of the total, depending on the size of the crop and the demand in any given year. The bulk of the remaining exports consisted of timber, and granite from the local quarries. An inhibiting factor on trade in Newry was the size of the ship canal. Unless it could accommodate the type of vessel that carried most of the international cargo, Newry could never hope to grow. The Port and Harbour Trust reported to the Boundary Commission that the Victoria Locks were 'so shallow that [they] could not be used by ships of modern dimensions when fully loaded'.

Margaret Square c. 1925. The prosperity that Newry enjoyed in the 1920s came to a sudden end with the Wall St. Crash of 1929. (W.A. Green, Ulster Folk and Transport Museum)

The nature of employment in the commercial sector was a mixture of full-time and casual labour, which made it difficult for the commission to assess the exact numbers employed at the Albert Basin or on the railways. However, there could be no doubt about the numbers employed in the linen mills. The three mills in Newry - Wilson's, Kerr's, and the Damolly Spinning Company — employed between them some seven hundred people, many of them women. The Bessbrook Spinning Company, throughout its different concerns, employed 2,500 people. The commission found that three hundred of the Bessbrook employees were residents of Newry, and that the spending power of the company's workforce was worth £75,000 per year to the retail trade in the town.

Just as linen was dominated by one firm, Bessbrook, so too one firm, Fishers, held a predominant position in the shipping trade. Joseph Fisher and Sons had been in Newry since 1852, when the father and two sons founded what was to be a considerable mercantile dynasty. The company acquired its first steamer in 1883, the *Kilkeel* (previously the *Celtic*). For many decades the fortunes of the Fisher company and of Newry as a port were inseparable. By 1925 Fishers had a fleet of over thirty ships, one of the biggest in the North. It had begun with just one vessel, the brigantine *Brothers,* in 1867. Developments in Newry - the building of the railways and the reconstruction of the canal - had ensured that the future economic activity of the town would be centred mainly on the port. Fishers benefited from this and became an important carrier of cargo into and out of the Albert Basin.

The turn of the century saw an expansion in Joseph Fisher & Sons' fleet beginning with the *Oak*, seen here on its sea trials on the Firth of the Clyde. (John Fisher)

The early years of the twentieth century were among the most prosperous for Fishers, reflecting the continuing importance of Newry as a port. In 1903 they built their biggest-ever vessel, the *Ulidia*, of 3,031 gross tons. This was Fishers' only venture into deep-sea trade, and it is a reflection of the company's, and more significantly Newry's, limitations that the *Ulidia* was too large ever to call in at her home port. Two years later the most important line of Fishers' ships was started with the building of the *Yews*. The name may have been inspired by the yew tree of Newry, and it set a pattern whereby all new Fishers' ships were named after trees or shrubs, which became something of an unofficial trademark. This period saw a rapid expansion in the company. Between 1906 and 1915 the *Oak*, the *Olive*, the *Elm*, the *Pine*, the *Alder*, the *Maple*, the *Walnut*, the *Mango*, the *Upas*, and the *Aspen* were all built in response to increased commerce. Fishers emerged from World War I in a relatively strong position, as a shortage in shipping was coupled with an increase in the amount of cargo carried.

The other shipping companies operating at this time were S. Lockington and Company, which also operated its own fleet, Moore and Dunwoody, O'Rourke and Company, and F.V. Hearty, who were all mainly coal merchants, while the chief grain importers were the companies of Robert Sands and John O'Hare. Sands's mill was on the canal at the north end of the town. Normally its cargo was unloaded at the basin and taken to the mill by barge through the town, and even after most other traffic on the canal had ceased, its barges continued to use this route, necessitating the opening of the bridges. The cattle export business was reasonably buoyant even after the war, and in the main this was handled by the Dundalk and Newry Steam-Packet Company, which was taken over by the British and Irish Steam Packet Company in the 1930s.

During the 1920s the actual work on the quayside differed little from the time of the 1907 strike. The men were still chosen to work on a gang rather than on regular shifts. The ships were usually unloaded without the help of machinery, the men going into the hold with large broad shovels to dig out the coal or grain, which was then lifted onto the quayside. The Irish Transport and General Workers' Union was now largely accepted but the stevedores were still employed by the companies to organise the workforce. Many of the stevedores' names are still remembered in the town, as the following recollection in the *Exploring Living Memory* project shows:

> Paddy McShane, stevedore to Fishers, looked after the discharge of all Fisher boats with a gang of approximately 36 dockers: Barney Maguire, who had a gang of around 20 dockers, looked after the discharge of coal for the other importers, and also discharged any cargoes of timber etc. which came into the port. In the case of timber, where every single piece had to be manhandled, Mr Maguire would employ extra men. He would pick all 'Card men' ['card men' were members of the union but not in the dockers' section] and then complete his gang with casual workers.
>
> Tommy Jennings, stevedore to the Steampacket Co., would employ anything from 18 men up to 60/70 men, according to the amount of cargo to be handled. He had 12 dockers and made up the others with 'Card men' and casuals.

During his tour of south Down on 8 February 1927, James Craig, Northern Ireland Prime Minister (front row, fourth right), was officially met in Newry by the urban district councillors and their chairman, Hugh John McConville (front row, fourth left). The Earl of Kilmorey, although having no official position, was also present (front row first left). (Newry Museum)

The docks provided an occasional supplement to the income of the local farmers, as they could often hire out their carts to help unload or distribute cargo. 'One of the most inspiring sights at that time, was to witness 30/40 horses and carts lined up in rotation along Buttercrane Quay, awaiting their turn to load direct from the ship.' Another group of workers associated with the docks were known as the 'cattle men'. Whenever livestock was sent across to Britain, usually to Birkenhead, anything from two to four cattle men would travel on board the ship to look after the animals. Once the cattle had safely reached their destination, the men returned to Newry by way of the Liverpool—Belfast ferry.

Away from the quayside, other things were happening. On the political front, Newry received a visit from the Prime Minister of Northern Ireland, Sir James Craig, and the Minister of Home Affairs, Dawson Bates, in February 1927. Ironically, the prime minister was officially welcomed by the council chairman, Hugh John McConville, on behalf of many councillors who had belonged to the council suspended in 1922. for refusing to recognise the legitimacy of Craig's government. Present also on this occasion was the Earl of Kilmorey. He and his family no longer held any significant local political influence but often added formality and colour to civic occasions.

In 1926 the council had begun another housing project. The continuing good fortune of the gas service enabled the gas committee to contribute £1,700 towards the building of forty-two houses near Chapel Street, in a new street named O'Neill Avenue in honour of the deceased Catholic Bishop of Dromore, Dr Henry O'Neill. The land for these houses had been purchased from St Clare's Convent at £100 an acre, so an ecclesiastical name for the avenue was not inappropriate. The following year the council undertook an even more ambitious scheme, following the abandonment of the linen hall barracks by the military. This was an opportunity to offer good houses at reasonable rents to the townspeople. In many of the older parts of town families lived in run-down terraced houses or shared tenements, which were old, dilapidated and virtually slums. The council's building programme had been largely in response to this situation. The linen hall was purchased and transformed into dwelling units at a cost of £20,000. It became home to nearly four hundred people, living in seventy-four houses, on which the rent was between 4s.5d. (22p) and 6s.10d. (34 ½p) per week. It was seen as a pioneering step in its day and the new housing complex was described as 'a paradise of sunshine surrounded by parklands'. The linen hall housing development attracted a lot of attention. The *Belfast Telegraph* described it in the following terms:

> Each house has three or four large bedrooms and a roomy kitchen, the only draw-back being that the houses stand back to back and there are no yards.
> The children have a playground of three acres and the whole area inside the walls is safe for the tiniest toddler, there being no vehicular traffic.
> In addition, provision has been made for the Fire Brigade, including a completely equipped station and residences for the captain and the six firemen on the permanent staff with their families.

Situated on the north bank of the Newry Canal, the Square overlooks some of the prettiest scenery in Ulster and could be made an ideal place of residence.

Despite the fears expressed by many, Newry seemed to be prospering in its new role as the frontier town of Northern Ireland. In one respect, however, Newry was still behind most other towns. It had been one of the first towns to introduce gas production for public and domestic use, but in 1927 it was still without electricity. On St Valentine's Day 1927, the council adopted the following resolution:

That we hereby direct in pursuance of Section 3 (6) of the Electric Lighting Act of 1882 that an application be made to the Electricity Commissioners, Ministry of Commerce, for a Licence or Special Order, authorising the Urban District Council of Newry to generate, distribute and supply and sell Electric Current for all public and private purposes as defined in the Electricity Supply Act of 1882 and 1919, within the Urban District Council of Newry, and for such purpose to authorise and carrying into effect the revised Electricity Supply Scheme prepared by Mr P.A. Spalding, AMICE, AMIEE, who is the Council's Consultant Electrical Engineer.

As had been the case in 1924, the Unionist councillors protested at Spalding's appointment and in this they had support from John Gallery, who was elected to the council as a Labour and Trade Union candidate. His objection was that Spalding should not hold the post in Newry 'as he already had a job in Dundalk'. However, the nationalist majority on the council could not be defeated.

Spalding had abandoned the idea of hydroelectricity in favour of a diesel generator and implemented a scheme accordingly. In July 1929 the generator, at the Buttercrane, began output and in the following year the old gas lamps began to be replaced, almost one hundred years after they were introduced to Newry's streets. Despite fears to the contrary, the gas industry did not suffer and in fact found many new customers. Within a few years the generation of electricity was removed from the council's hands, with the establishment of the Northern Ireland Electricity Board (NIEB). Similar to the Irish Free State's Electricity Supply Board, established in 1921, the NIEB set up a supply grid that superseded local arrangements.

For many people - in particular the children - the big event of the times was not the installation of electric lighting but the visit, on 6 August 1929, of a film crew from the Gaumont Company to record the 'Cranfield outing'. People were quite familiar with 'going to the pictures', but few had actually seen a film camera and certainly no one had taken part in a film. The children's outing to Cranfield, a scenic spot on the County Down coast, had become an annual event,

sponsored by all the businesses in the town. On the morning of the trip there were buses, taxis, private cars, all packed with upwards on 8 or 9 kids. The cars were decorated with streamers and the children were given balloons, and the Warrenpoint Road never saw a Road like it since, almost a mile long stream of traffic and hundreds of cheering children. On the Cranfield Beach everybody made for the water. Some had swim suits, some had none, but that did not stop them having a dip. After some games and tea it was time for home.

Before the Cranfield outing was shown in cinemas throughout the British Isles, the 'hundreds of cheering children' had a chance to see themselves on the big screen when the film was shown in the local cinemas in the week beginning 12 August 1929.

A spectacular event of a different kind occurred in the same year, when the bottom fell out of the Newry Canal. At the time — and ever after — many believed that the canal had a plug, like a bath, which had accidentally been pulled out, letting the water drain into the Clanrye river. The actual explanation is not so amusing, although the result was the same. A new pipe was being laid as part of a general scheme of improving sanitation and the water supply in town. Unfortunately, while the culvert was being built the canal wall was breached, allowing the water to escape. The accident seemed to have caused more mirth than alarm, and the canal was soon repaired.

This was an era of great change for Newry, symbolised, perhaps, by the opening in 1929 of an electrically controlled metal bridge at the bottom of Monaghan Street, to replace the old wooden one. Newry was experiencing its transition into the modern world. For the first time people spoke of 'Old Newry' in contrast to the modern town, as new houses replaced the old, as the streets were being lit by electricity, as motor vehicles replaced horses, and as the cinema replaced home-grown entertainment. The cinema was very important in changing people's perceptions of the world. Before World War I the first cinema had been opened in Canal Street by an Englishman who advertised it under the slogan 'Pinchin's Picture Palace Provides Pleasure'. By the 1920s the two most popular cinemas were the Imperial on the Mall and the Frontier in John Mitchel Place.

Bessbrook was connected to Newry via an electric tram opened in 1885. It carried both freight and passengers, taking twenty minutes to cover the two and half mile journey. Local engineer, William Barcroft, designed its flangeless wheels which enabled it to travel on the road as well as on rails. (Ulster Folk and Transport Museum)

Going to the pictures was a regular event for most people and everyone followed the adventures of the stars, from Pearl White to Charlie Chaplin. The usual admission price was 1d. (½ p) or a jam pot, but this went up to 3d. (1 ½ p) when the 'talkies' were introduced.

Motor vehicles affected people's lives as well, and brought the neighbouring towns and villages into closer contact with Newry. Regular bus services ran to the outlying areas; for example, Creggan's to Crossmaglen and Foots and Dunlop's to Banbridge. The coaches were sometimes little better than converted lorries or elongated taxis but they did bring Newry within easier reach. These small independent companies lasted until 1935, when the Government set up the Northern Ireland Road Transport Board, which took over responsibility for bus services.

Once the border question had been settled, it looked as though Newry had come to terms with its new status and would continue to develop as a market town and port. The town was enjoying a degree of prosperity in the postwar years. There was a definite sense of optimism and Newry traders were determined to make the best of what opportunities were offered them, and even introduced a 'shopping week' in July 1928. However, the prosperity and optimism were short-lived. The great stock-market crash of 1929 was to have a devastating effect on the world's economy and, in common with everywhere else, Newry was to suffer. The Wall Street Crash has entered into the mythology of the modern world and the following decade is universally known as the 'hungry Thirties'. For Newry this was a period of hardship and recession.

Hiring fairs continued well into the 20th century on the open ground in front of the Butter Market, the single storey arched building in this photograph. Here boys and girls would line up to be inspected by farmers looking for workers. (Newry Museum)

Those businesses that could not cope were forced to close down; those that did survive were often driven to introduce the harsh measures of wage cuts and lay-offs. Unemployment increased, and what little industry there was suffered. Emigration was once again a feature of life.

Fishers' shipping company was in a better position to cope than most. Nevertheless, even it was experiencing difficulties and in 1932 the ships' crews were faced with the choice of redundancies or wage cuts. As there was little hope of finding employment elsewhere, a reduction in wages was accepted. Such measures were not unusual, and even a concern of the size of the Bessbrook Spinning Company was forced to take cost-cutting steps. Luckily, large orders for linen, like those from the White Star Line, continued to come in. Despite considering themselves a model firm, wages at the Bessbrook company were always low and in the 1930s the average was £1 a week. For the first time the workers travelling to and from the linenworks were charged a fare of 2d. (1p) on the Bessbrook tram. Some preferred to make the journey on foot and so save money.

One effect of the economic depression was that certain institutions from the nineteenth century assumed a new importance. For example, pawn shops experienced a revival as desperate families turned to them for money. Another nineteenth-century institution that took on a new relevance was the workhouse. Not since the Great Famine of the 1840s had such demands been made on the Poor Law Guardians. The workhouse at Daisy Hill had been rebuilt after the fire of 1901, and the opportunity was taken to alter the layout so that the infirmary was now at

185

the front of the building while the rear was occupied by the 'inmates', that is, those people who were so poor that they had no choice but to fall on the mercy of the poor law union. The infirmary was now run by the Sisters of St John of God and had become a general hospital for the town, treating not only the poor but also those who could pay for treatment. The rest of the workhouse was still administered by the guardians and was not markedly different from what it had been in the last century. Inmates were still expected to do work of some kind and their lives were still highly regulated. Men and women, even husbands and wives, were kept in separate accommodation and only saw each other in the dining hall.

In the search for work — unemployment was never to be higher than in this period - many turned to another traditional institution, the hiring fair. Boys and girls could often find work of some kind at the fair, which was held each spring and summer. Newry had long been a centre for such events and any thoughts of them being on the wane were dispelled as the hungry Thirties saw a demand for cheap labour met by a desperation for work. Although the traditional length of employment was changing and the hiring of servants or farmhands was usually conducted on a weekly basis, the prospect of working on a farm, far from home, was never an attractive one. Farmers from areas that were not so economically depressed would come to Newry to find workers. The boys and girls thus hired would often have to sleep in makeshift accommodation after a long day's work in the fields:

> You slept really sound until you got the shout from the byre at 6.00 o'clock a.m. to get up. After doing the milking and the other yard work you went in for your so called breakfast — consisted mostly of porridge diluted with buttermilk, a little tea and very little bread — then off to the fields. The servant girls were no better off, only they slept indoors. Their work consisted mostly of yard work and in harvest, potatoes, etc; they also had to help out in the fields.

The fair continued for many years and there are a number of people in Newry and the surrounding districts who recorded their experiences in the *Exploring Living Memory* project.

The gloom of this period was alleviated to some degree when an ecclesiastical VIP visited Newry; on 1 July 1932, Cardinal Lauri, the Papal Legate to Ireland, came to town following the Thirty-first International Eucharistic Conference, which had been held in Dublin. The local Catholic clergy mustered their parishioners to welcome the cardinal, who found flag-bedecked cars awaiting him when he crossed the border. Newry was decorated with bunting and the local schoolchildren were marshalled to line the streets and wave flags. The children sang hymns as the cardinal drove to the cathedral, where he was met by Bishop Edward Mulhern and a civic delegation led by Hugh John McConville. After a service in the cathedral, the cardinal stood on the steps to bestow a papal blessing on the town. The splendour and scale of the procession by the cardinal and his entourage were such as had never before been seen in Newry and certainly had a greater impact than the official visit by Prime Minister James Craig five years before.

Although Newry continued to be a busy port, trade was badly hit during the 1930s. The inland canal was finding it difficult to operate profitably when faced with competition from the railways and roads. In 1933, 6,600 tons were carried on the canal compared to 120,000 tons a century before. As the economic recession worsened, the level of tonnage dropped and in 1936 a mere 600 tons were transported on the canal, and from now on, there was little or no use for the inland waterway. Towards the end of the 1930s the *Newry Reporter* commented that the town was 'noted for the multiplicity of its clocks and the scarcity of employment'. In 1938 the Newry board of poor law guardians reported that outdoor relief was costing an average of £200 per week. In one week alone in February of that year the board received 660 appeals for outdoor relief, that is, 660 families reduced to claiming relief payments as a result of their poverty, out of a population of 12,746. By this time, according to the *Newry Reporter,* Newry had lost 'two spinning, one weaving and two flour mills, two foundries and several other defunct industries'. By 1937 there were only two spinning mills, one rope and twine works, and one mineral water plant in Newry, and although five quarries operated in or near the town, they did not employ many men. The main business was generated by the retail trade, cattle-dealing and public houses, but these too had suffered. The optimism of the 1920s had vanished and few could see an end to the Depression.

In international affairs tension was mounting and many were predicting that before long the United Kingdom would be involved in a war with Germany. However, before this happened an event occurred that brought to the surface the communal divisions that existed in Northern Ireland. Patrick Fearon, a member of the IRA who had been prominent in the troubles of the early 1920s, died and his funeral took place in Newry on 4 February 1939. Fearon was well known in Newry and had been a member of the Garda Síochána (the Southern police force) after the establishment of the Irish Free State. A large crowd attended the funeral, including ministers of the Free State government. The *Newry Reporter* records that it was the occasion of 'deplorable scenes ... when police and people struggled and swayed around a coffin — the former to remove a tricolour flag, with which it was draped, with the latter to maintain it in its position'. As the display of the Irish tricolour was illegal, the RUC had decided that it had to be removed from the coffin. The family and mourners objected to this, and the result was scuffles and fights between policemen and mourners. When the police drew their revolvers, the officiating priest, Father J. Burke, persuaded the mourners to place the folded flag alongside the coffin until they reached the cemetery. This incident caused much bitterness at the time and was still spoken of for years to come.

Britain and France declared war on Germany on 3 September 1939. Although the announcement had been expected, when it came it took most people some time to adjust. One teenager at the time recalled:

After World War II the town section of the canal fell into disuse and showed signs of neglect as equipment was abandoned and its banks became overgrown, like here at Merchants' Quay.

We had all heard our fathers talk about the 'Great War', now 'we' were going to teach those 'huns' a lesson and it wasn't going to take four years either. ... Few of us realised then that many of us would never reach the end of that adventure. Suddenly during the next few months, all sorts of new things began to happen. We were issued with gas masks, identity cards, ration cards and many more things that we had never heard of before. There were announcements on the radio and in the newspapers, telling us how to use them. ... All food was on ration along with a lot more things.

World War II affected Newry physically as no war had done since the seventeenth century. The town was garrisoned and fortifications were built:

Suddenly all over the town sprang up massive reinforced gun emplacements called pillar boxes. Streets and bridges were semi-blocked by 'dragon teeth' [metal and concrete blockades]. The 'blackout' was introduced and we had ARP [Air Raid Precautions] wardens, who made sure you didn't show any lights. Car headlights were reduced to mere slits. Army barracks sprang up all around Newry, and we got used to hearing the sound of different accents around our town.

The Irish government, led by Eamon de Valera, decided that it would remain neutral during the war. The Irish state had been in existence for just seventeen years and it was widely believed that its new-found independence would be compromised if it were to follow Britain into a war in which it was not directly involved. As a result, the government of Northern Ireland decided that it was necessary to make the border with the South secure, and it was sealed off and movement across it restricted.

Rationing brought with it not only shortages but also enterprise. There was no rationing on the Irish side of the border and many commodities were cheaper there. Smuggling had been a fact of life since the border was drawn up, but now it became big business, as a regular black market in cross-border traffic developed. People travelled from as far as Belfast in order to cross into the South to obtain goods that were scarce. Those who would not risk actually crossing the border with contraband goods could usually find someone in Newry or Warrenpoint from whom to buy the products. The traffic was not all one-way, however, as certain commodities were scarce in the South; tea, in particular, was difficult to obtain and was often taken south to exchange for butter or other foods,

> certain 'smart boys' drying the tea from the pot, rowing across at Narrow Water and swopping it for butter on the Eire shore. Of course, if the customs man was waiting for you on the way back, the only thing to do was to 'drop it'. Many a load of butter floated out to sea in Carlingford Lough.

Smuggling became so common that the customs officials usually let it happen without interfering.

In some ways the coming of war was a welcome relief from the Depression of the 1930s and was something of a 'great game', with the influx of soldiers, the new rules and regulations, and the smuggling. Unlike most other civilians at the time, the people of Newry had the opportunity to see the 'enemy' face to face, or so they believed.

> Across the border, it was common to meet a chap with a foreign accent and a very close haircut, whom we soon learned [was] German. Of course Eire was neutral and many of the German Embassy staff spent a lot of time around Dundalk for very obvious reasons.

The home front became a reality in other ways. For example, 'Wings for Victory' campaigns started in Newry: 'We were amazed at the amount of money required to buy one "Spitfire", but money was raised and indeed a few of our townsmen flew the planes our town helped to pay for.' Conscription was never introduced into Northern Ireland, unlike elsewhere in the United Kingdom, but as in World War I, many volunteered for the armed forces and enlisted in the army, air force or navy.

The Albert Basin and the docks at Warrenpoint had barrage balloons and wardens patrolled the streets, but the reality of a raid never struck the people of Newry until April 1941, when Belfast was blitzed. Not only was this close enough to make people realise how vulnerable they were to attack but the Newry Fire Brigade was asked to go to Belfast to assist in tackling the fires. The attack on 15—16 April was so severe that the local brigades were inadequate and the town saw fire engines from Dundalk, Drogheda, Dún Laoghaire, and Dublin travelling north to help fight the fires. Belfast was struck again in May, and again these brigades sent engines to help control the fires that followed.

The decline in the gas industry was made worse when the council decided to light Newry's streets with electricity. This photo shows the last night of the gas lamps, 15 December 1952. (*Newry by Gaslight*)

One outcome of the German raids was that people, particularly children, were evacuated from Belfast and sent to safe areas elsewhere. Many of the evacuees were sent to Newry and Warrenpoint. They were housed wherever there was room for them and on the whole received a warm welcome from the locals. For children raised in the streets of Belfast, being sent to a small village or to a farm could be both wonderful and terrifying. Thousands of children spent some part of the war in or near Newry and when they grew up, they often returned with their own children on holiday. Probably the most notable of all the evacuees was a young boy called Rinty Monaghan who later became a world famous boxing champion.

Just as the demand for equipment and supplies in World War I led to an increased output from manufacturers in Newry, so too did World War II create a new market for Newry goods and present the opportunity of employment. Those who did not leave to join the armed forces often travelled to Britain to work in factories or on building sites to meet the demands of the war effort. In Northern Ireland there were also work opportunities in building installations and factories or in the manufacture of everything from ships to parachutes. The Bessbrook spinning mill produced 22,323,365 yards of cloth for uniforms and tents, and throughout the town, workshops produced all sorts of goods that were needed in the British market.

The necessities of war resulted in a shipbuilding yard being opened at Warrenpoint. The engineering firm of Smith and Pearson had a workshop in Merchants' Quay in Newry, producing the steel tanks that were used in the construction of Mulberry harbours. The firm was requested by the Admiralty to move to Warrenpoint and begin boat production. Construction began in 1943 and by the following year the first boats were hitting the water. These were the tank landing craft, LCT Mk 4, of which twenty were launched, and the larger Mk 8 landing craft, some of which were used in the D-Day landings in Normandy. The 'shipyard', as the locals called it, survived the war and continued to produce vessels for some years to come.

Of all the wartime experiences, probably the biggest impact was made by the arrival of the American soldiers. The United States entered the war after the Japanese attack on Pearl Harbour in December 1941. American soldiers were soon sent to Europe and many came to Northern Ireland for initial training. The Americans were stationed throughout the North and one of the arrangements made with the Westminster government was that the American army would be responsible for ground defence in the United Kingdom, leaving British troops free for the other theatres of war. After the austerity of wartime rationing, the Americans burst on the scene like something straight out of a Hollywood movie. As one woman remembers: 'Then came the Yanks and their PX [post exchange; government-subsidised shop for military personnel] stores. Food and luxuries were very short in Newry, but I can tell you the Yanks did not go short. They were a great attraction to all the kids and their families. If you had a Yank visiting your house, you never went short. We all learned to chew gum and smoke Camel cigarettes.' Many performers came to Northern Ireland to entertain the American troops stationed there: 'Professional stage people used to come regularly to entertain the forces. If you knew the right person you could nip into the Town Hall and see them. … People like George Formby, Glenn Miller, and Larry Adler were in Newry regularly.'

The American forces were stationed throughout Newry and Mourne. The 2nd Infantry Division took over Narrow Water Castle as their local headquarters and training centre. All around Newry, trenches were dug and fortifications put up to give the troops practice at defending and attacking. Tanks rumbled over the countryside as new crews were taught how to use them. At Ballymacdermot cairn today you will see that part of it has been 'stitched' together with steel rods, repairing the damage done when an American tank crashed into it. One of the most important airfields used by the United States Army Air Force was at Greencastle, near Kilkeel, on the County Down coast. It was built in 1942 and soon became home to air force units engaged in maintenance, training, and flying operations. General Dwight Eisenhower was among the distinguished American visitors who visited Greencastle. General George Patton also conducted a tour in March 1944, when he inspected troops at Greencastle and Warrenpoint. Not everyone reacted favourably to Patton; when he made a speech to the troops at Greencastle, which was broadcast beyond the base through loudspeakers, one lady 'was far from impressed by his well-known use of the vernacular'. On the other hand, it must be said that not all the Americans were impressed by what they found in Northern Ireland. The US troops may have brought colour and glamour to the region but many of the soldiers found it incredibly dull to be stationed there. One GI is reputed to have commented: 'Gee, Rostrevor's a swell little place, but why the hell don't they bury their dead?'

'England's difficulty is Ireland's opportunity' was an adage of the Fenians in the nineteenth century, and there was a faction of the IRA who believed it applied to the situation in 1939—45. They believed that Britain at war was the right time to apply pressure for a British withdrawal from Northern Ireland. In 1939 the IRA carried out over one hundred attacks along the border, against the RUC and customs' posts, many of the attacks occurring in the vicinity of Newry. The IRA made contacts with the Nazi regime, which was willing, of course, to help any group that might create trouble for Britain. The governments on both sides of the border responded by interning known IRA men, and some were even executed. On the whole, German attempts to supply arms to the IRA or to conduct their own sabotage operations in Northern Ireland were inept. The most spectacular IRA attack was the burning down of Lupton's mill in March 1942 on the grounds that it was supplying war materials. While never posing a major threat, this IRA activity was a constant worry for the RUC.

The war ended in 1945, but 'after all the celebrations we found it wasn't much different from other years. There was still rationing and shortages, but at least many of our mates came home again.' Rationing was to continue until 1953, as the newly elected Labour government in Great Britain thought it was the fairest way to cope with postwar shortages. These years were a time of great change and witnessed not only material reconstruction but also important social reforms. For example, the education policy of the Labour government, allowing grant-aided entry to grammar school and university based on merit, was to have a profound effect on Northern Ireland. Another measure that was to radically alter social conditions was the establishment of the National Health Service, which was extended to Northern Ireland in 1948. For the first time medical treatment was made available to all, irrespective of the ability to pay. In Northern Ireland it meant an end to the poor law system. In Newry it resulted in the board of guardians being dissolved and the functions of the workhouse being subsumed into the Welfare State. In its place a fully fledged general public hospital was established there, which became the Daisy Hill Hospital of today.

One major problem was the poor standard of housing and the prevalence of slums in many towns and cities. The Northern Ireland government established the Northern Ireland Housing Trust (NIHT) to implement a policy of house-building and it also offered grants to local authorities for house-building. In Newry the NIHT purchased Rooney's Meadow and built an estate there. Meanwhile, the urban district council continued its programme of building, beginning with James Connolly Park and Michael Mallin Park, and in 1954,136 new houses were built in Daisyhill Gardens, Barcroft Park and Monaghan Row.

Electric lighting again became a public issue when it was proposed that all the remaining gas lights be replaced with electric lamps. In 1949, after a deputation had visited Preston in England to meet with the manufacturers of the lamps, the council agreed to extend electric street lighting, at a cost of £3,700. This scheme was completed in 1952 and made Newry the first town in Ireland to be completely lit by electricity. One consequence of this was that the job of lamplighter, which had been in existence in Newry since 1822, disappeared. The remaining six lamplighers were made redundant and no longer would these familiar figures be seen walking the streets at dusk and dawn to light or extinguish the lamps. Despite the gasworks being extended in 1949, the gas service was running into trouble by the early 1950s. The loss of street lighting was a major blow and domestic consumption had dropped dramatically by 1954, when the council took the decision to instal gas in all new housing developments. Hence Daisyhill Gardens, Barcroft Park and Monaghan Row all brought captive customers that the service desperately needed.

Although this was an era of optimism, the difficulties of the gasworks were symptomatic of fundamental problems that lay beneath the surface. The postwar decade saw a number of Newry firms in crisis and some significant closures. In 1948 it was no longer considered economical to run the rail link to Omeath in County Louth and it was closed down; in fact, over the next twenty years Newry was to lose all its rail links. In January 1948 the Bessbrook Spinning Company was forced to close down the tramway, 'the track and the rolling stock, with the exception of no. 2 car, being disposed of for scrap'. The following year saw a closure that was symbolically much more important, when the inland Newry Canal was closed to traffic. It had ceased to be used for commercial transportation since 1936 and the last vessel to travel the canal was a pleasure yacht returning from Portadown in 1939. On 7 May 1949 an official warrant for its abandonment was issued. The canal route through the town remained open and was still used to carry goods from the basin to warehouses and mills on its banks, but this was also in decline. On 21 March 1956 this part of the canal was also officially abandoned, leaving only the section between the Albert Basin and the Victoria Locks open. For over a century Newry had relied on the canal for its prosperity as a port, but the canal's importance had been in decline since the development of the railways and there was no way of halting it. Traffic grew less with each passing decade until it was insignificant. It was not the fact that traffic once carried from the Newry port into Ulster by canal was now being carried by rail, since even the rail links from Newry were being dismembered, but that the port no longer took in sufficient trade for either.

This merchant's house illustrates the wealth that the canal brought to Newry. The area to the right was the new basin of 1760. The inland canal was abandoned in 1949 and this house demolished in 1989 to make way for a new road. (William Murdock)

World War II had given an unnatural buoyancy to commerce in the Newry port, but once the war was over, difficulties in maintaining that level of traffic were becoming obvious. Shipping firms based in Newry and Warrenpoint had to cope with increasing running costs and Belfast was attracting more trade. At the end of the war Fishers had a fleet of eleven steamers and one motor vessel. A general shortage of cargo ships in the immediate postwar period meant that there was still plenty of business, so Fishers invested in two new steamers, the *Ebony* and the *Balsa*. However, by the beginning of the 1950s the running costs of steamers were so great that Fishers, and the other local operators, could not compete with companies that had more modern fleets. From this period on, foreign shipping firms, most notably the Dutch, began to dominate the trade into and out of Newry. Fishers were forced to economise or face bankruptcy. Throughout the next decade their fleet of steamers was sold off, the last to go being the *Palm* in 1963, leaving the company with just the *Walnut* and the *Olive*. On the dockside itself other economies had to be introduced. In 1953 the company purchased two mechanical grabs to unload ships, which proved to be more efficient than using stevedores' gangs but also meant many job losses. More jobs had to go when the Port and Harbour Trust introduced a mobile diesel crane for the use of the other shipping merchants. These measures helped reduce overheads and alleviated the immediate problem but in the long term their efficacy was questionable. In 1962 the Port and Harbour Trust was given an ultimatum: either get the port operating on a profitable basis within two years or else face closure.

ROYAL ULSTER CONSTABULARY.

I hereby authorise _Arthur James DOLE_

of _9 O'Neill Avenue, Newry_

to be out of doors between the hours of _11 P.m._
and _12.30 A.m. each Night_ as and from this date.
for the purpose of _Returning home from to work
with the U.T.A._

(SIGNED) _[signature]_   Head Constable.
Sergeant.

(DATE STAMP)

SIGNATURE OF HOLDER _A. J. Dole_

Attempts to improve facilities at the port were severely hampered when the gates at the Victoria Locks were blown up on 13 May 1957, leading to the closure of the canal for many months. The explosion was part of a renewed IRA campaign against the border that had begun the previous year, although someone claiming to speak for its adjutant general denied that the IRA had sanctioned the attack. The IRA had reorganised itself after World War II; being a nationalist town on the border, Newry was to be central to its campaign. The IRA had been active for some years before the major offensive of 1956. When the Savoy cinema on Merchants' Quay announced that it was going to screen the coronation of Elizabeth II in 1952., it was bombed, and arms had been stolen from the Territorial Army hall in Newry in 1954. The renewed campaign began with the theft of explosives from a local quarry on 11 December 1956. The following months saw a number of incidents, such as an arson attack on the B Specials' drill hall, the bomb at the lock gates, and on 11 August 1957 an explosion that destroyed the NIEB offices. Even the capture of seven IRA men at Clontifleece, near Warrenpoint, in January 1957, had not deterred them and the attacks continued. In response the Minister for Home Affairs, W.W. Topping, issued a curfew order on the town, like the one imposed in the 1920s. No one was to be out of doors between 11 p.m. and 5.30 a.m. without a pass, and all incoming roads were sealed off from 12 August onwards.

However, this was not the 1920s and few people in Newry accepted that IRA activity was on a scale to warrant such measures. At 11 p.m. on the first night of the curfew a large crowd gathered in protest beneath the clock in Margaret Square. Attempts by the police to break up the crowd resulted in five arrests. The following night a crowd, estimated at two thousand people, found the square occupied by riot police and armoured cars. Fortunately, the protesters were satisfied with token gestures of

195

defiance and serious trouble was avoided. When the curfew was lifted on 9 September, a procession marched through the streets and fireworks were set off in celebration.

The IRA campaign continued. In November five IRA men, including three from Newry, were killed when the bomb they were carrying exploded prematurely at Edentubber, just south of the town. Over the next three years there were isolated bombing and arson attacks, which were of little more than nuisance value. The last attack occurred at Jonesborough, six miles from Newry, on 12 November 1962, when an RUC patrol was ambushed, resulting in the death of Constable William Hunter. Shortly afterwards the IRA called off its campaign.

While this campaign of violence was being conducted, Newry was continuing on the course established in the decade after the war. The fate of the canal was finally sealed when the swing bridge at Bridge Street was replaced by a pemanent structure in 1958. The following year the bridge at Sugar Island was also replaced by a permanent one and four years afterwards, the Ballybot Bridge. The gasworks, however, received something of a reprieve. In 1961 a new plastics factory, owned by Bessbrook Products, was due to open on the Camlough Road and it required up to 10,000 cubic feet of gas per hour. The urban district council was anxious to encourage new industry in Newry to help alleviate the unemployment problem and it assisted the gasworks in raising the £40,000 needed to facilitate the project. In the event it proved a wise move, for by the mid-1970s the factory consumed 25 per cent of the gas produced. The gas service received a further fillip when the council began work on the building of the Derrybeg housing estate, as all 350 houses were to be supplied with gas.

Building at Derrybeg was delayed because of a shortage of bricklayers, but in Newry as a whole there was a scarcity of jobs. In 1962 there were 1,779 unemployed people in town, about 10 per cent of the population. On the positive side there were hopes of a revival in the local quarrying industry. Newry granite was needed for a new post office being built in the town and also for a number of other public buildings that were to be constructed throughout Northern Ireland in the following years. In 1962 the council agreed to spend £9,100 in improving facilities at the variety market in Mary Street. Around this time the council was considering the building of a through-pass that would take traffic away from the town centre. The increasing volume of traffic travelling the Belfast-Dublin route was becoming a major problem and the through-pass was seen as a solution to traffic congestion. As a corollary of this plan, the town architect, John Smith, envisaged changing the Hill Street area into a pedestrian precinct. Generally speaking, the main thrust of town planning was on bringing industry and business to the town. The Northern Ireland government was actively promoting growth by encouraging foreign investment and by improving the infrastructure. Newry Urban District Council believed that it too had a part to play by encouraging growth in the town.

In 1964 the decision to close down the railway link with Goraghwood severed Newry's last important railway connection — that with the Dublin-Belfast line. The closure was part of an overall economising policy by the railway authorities in Northern Ireland and Newry was not the only place to suffer. The Northern Ireland government was actively encouraging road travel and most of the railways were shut down. Nevertheless, it was one more factor weighing the balance against the future growth of the town. In the mid-1960s Newry was experiencing a transformation, as the commercial activity moved away from the port towards industry and retail trade. A business directory at this time reveals that Newry was of greater importance as a market town than as an industrial centre. Although there were more than five factories, none of them, except the three linen mills, had very large workforces and few were to survive beyond the next decade.

By 1965 Newry was the fourth largest port in Northern Ireland. There were still at least seven shipping firms in Newry but most of them were agents rather than employers. Only Fishers remained as a large local concern in the port and its chief business was coal importation. Of the 131 cargo arrivals in the Albert Basin in the second quarter of 1965 most were deliveries of coal. Of all the ships operating in Newry at this period, only the *Walnut* was locally owned. The age-old problems of the size of the Victoria Locks and silting in the ship canal prevented larger modern ships using Newry. More of the large vessels were docking at Warrenpoint, which began to assume a new importance not just as a satellite port to Newry but also as a potential replacement. The situation was so bad that the oldest shipping firm, Fishers, could no longer afford to operate as an independent concern and in 1966 became a subsidiary of Cawood Holdings.

Demolition on a scale that Newry had not experienced since it was destroyed by the Duke of Berwick in 1689 was proposed in 1966, when the scheme, first discussed in 1962, to alleviate the town's traffic problems was put into effect. The idea was to build a dual carriageway that would meet the traffic at Trevor Hill on the north side of town and carry it around the town centre to join the road to Dublin on the south side. At the same time it was proposed that many old houses be demolished and replaced with modern flats. The scheme entailed levelling all the houses in an area defined by a line running from Abbey Yard to Trevor Hill and from Trevor Hill to tbe rear of the cathedral - in effect all of North Street and most of Water Street.

The new roadway may have bypassed the modern town centre along Hill Street, but it cut a swathe through the old town. The two streets due to be destroyed were the oldest in Newry; they were the first to be rebuilt after 1689 and corresponded to the streets depicted on the 1570 map of the town. Before the focus of the town shifted to the canal, these streets had been the busiest and up until the nineteenth century had boasted the residences of the wealthier citizens. The houses were among the finest examples of Georgian architecture in the north and had many interesting historical associations, not least of which is the legend that William of Orange slept in number 19 North Street. With their demolition, much of what constituted 'Old Newry' was lost for ever.

Demolished in the 1960s North Street was one of the oldest in Newry. It correspondents approximately to the street in the 'bayse town' on the 1570 map and was one of the first to be rebuilt after the fire of 1689. Legend has it that William of Orange slept in this house, number 19. (Newry Museum)

Newry had always prided itself on being a busy progressive town - a common expression in nineteenth-century Ulster described an active person as being 'as busy as half of Newry' — and the new road and housing schemes were in some sense part of that spirit. In common with the rest of Northern Ireland, Newry was experiencing change and a relative degree of prosperity. However, as events in Newry itself had shown, there had never been complete acceptance of the state of Northern Ireland among a sizeable portion of the population, and the Government, from local to central level, had created a sense of resentment and a feeling of injustice among the Catholic citizens. Newry, since ancient times, had been in the cockpit of war in Ireland, had always been radical and nationalist, from the early days of the United Irishmen, and in more recent years had been a key place in any campaign against the border. And Newry was to fulfil all these roles in the modern troubles that began with the civil rights demonstrations of 1968.

9

RIOTS, REFORMS AND RECESSION

Since its inception the stability and peace of Northern Ireland were fragile, even at the best of times. It harboured within its borders a sizeable population, of nationalists or Catholics, who questioned its legitimacy and resented its rule. Government at all levels was administered largely in the exclusive interest of that section of the population, the Unionists or Protestants, for whom the statelet had been established. However, attempts to reform or overthrow the regime had been isolated and sporadic and had floundered because they lacked support or internal cohesion. Since World War II society had changed, as Patrick Buckland points out in *A History of Northern Ireland,*

> as a result of the benefits of the welfare state, the growth of a new generation, the changing social structure and the empty rhetoric of the South. Some Catholics began to consider that they could play a more positive role in public life without prejudicing the ultimate aspiration to Irish unity. The new middle class — the graduates, managers and teachers — sought a much wider role in the economy and in society than the old small-town middle class and were less ready to acquiesce in the acceptance of a position of assumed or established inferiority and discrimination than had been the case in the past.

Due to the definition of constituency boundaries and the conditions attached to the franchise (where, for example, certain electors could cast more than one vote in local elections, based on the value of businesses and limited companies), the nationalists, despite being 40 per cent of the overall population, could only exercise a controlling influence over two public bodies of any significance, the urban district councils of Strabane in County Tyrone and Newry. In January 1967 a number of people, Catholic and Protestant, came together to found the Northern Ireland Civil Rights Association (NICRA) with the intention of eliminating the injustices within the region, initially campaigning under the slogan of 'one man, one vote'. Although its aim was to reform Northern Ireland, Unionists — within government and without — perceived NICRA as a threat to Northern Ireland's existence and they reacted accordingly. The Unionists' response was often violent in itself or resulted in violence. An early civil rights march through Newry was halted by the police, fighting broke out and some police land-rovers were pushed into the canal. Elsewhere the violence was to be much worse.

The temporary closure of Victoria Locks following the damage caused by MV *Saint William* on 30 January 1968 exacerbated the already precarious future prospects of the ship canal. (*Newry Reporter*)

In 1968 Newry Urban District Council was to experience its own crisis, which in some ways was indicative of the wider conditions prevailing in Northern Ireland. The year began with a government announcement that Warrenpoint was designated as the official port for the new city of Craigavon. This new city in County Armagh, formed out of the boroughs of Portadown and Lurgan, was to be a major development, envisaged as holding a population of one hundred thousand and being a major input into the economy. Consequently, the official port was to be of a considerable size and the Government promised investment for expansion and improvement of facilities. This clearly signalled the curtailment or run-down of Newry but it was expected that the new port would provide employment and business. As Vincent W. Hogg of the Newry Port and Harbour Trust expressed it, the port of Newry would not decline but would be 'developing towards Warrenpoint'. However, in February 1968 the Albert Basin was closed to traffic; the Victoria Locks had been damaged on 30 January when a collier, the MV *Saint William,* inexplicably crashed into the lock gates. It was not until March that boats could once again use the ship canal. The closure came at a bad time, when the future of the port itself was being questioned.

The commercial issues were overshadowed by a political argument that was to erupt in the council and cause long-standing bitterness. The redevelopment scheme, first planned in 1966, was coming into effect, resulting in the demolition of houses in the area between Trevor Hill and William Street and their replacement by flats and a new dual carriageway.

NICRA and PD had many supporters in Newry and demonstrations like this one, 18 June 1969, became common occurrences in the town. (*Belfast Telegraph*)

The question then arose as to how the new flats should be allocated to tenants. The traditional method was that the three parties in the council -the Ulster Unionist Party, the NI Labour Party and the Newry Labour Party (formed after Thomas Markey's expulsion from the Labour Party) would each provide a list. However, Councillor Pat McMahon, the chairman of the housing committee, argued that in this instance former residents of the area should be given priority. Thomas Markey, the council chairman, disagreed, and refused to allow McMahon's proposal to be discussed. McMahon took the matter to court and on 30 January 1968 the High Court in Belfast issued an Order of Mandamus requiring Markey to allow McMahon's proposal to be brought before the council.

At the subsequent meeting held on 2 February, the press were excluded from the council chamber. Making it plain that he was acting under duress, Markey was uncooperative towards McMahon and the housing committee. The debate continued until well after midnight when a compromise was reached whereby the parties would each submit a list but previous residents would be given priority. Exactly how the compromise was reached, no one outside knew. At one point Jim O'Neill, a Labour member, resigned in protest at the proceedings and a month later another Labour member, Michael McKeown, was co-opted on to the council to replace him. Matters in the council were not improved when in April, the start of the new financial year, it was forced to set a rate of 48s. (£2.40) in the pound, the highest in Northern Ireland. Gerald Cronin, the clerk, warned the councillors to keep within their budget in future, and Councillor Colman Rowntree accused the council of 'having run amuck on spending'. One bright note was the adoption of a scheme to allocate housing on a priority-of-need basis.

Housing again moved to the top of the agenda following complaints from Newry number 2 Rural Council that the urban council was building houses in rural areas. Under pressure, the urban district council agreed to cease its building programme. This was opposed by some, including Colman Rowntree, who said that he saw 'political corruption entering the council' and that 'it was time someone stepped in and took over the authority'. Rowntree was expressing an unease felt by many. Patronage and allocation of housing along party lines ran contrary to the growing demands for government reform, and there was increasing discontent about the running of Newry Urban District Council.

Other events drew attention away from the controversy. Thomas Markey resigned his position as chairman on health grounds and was replaced by his former critic, Pat McMahon. The new chairman's first official duty was to attend the opening ceremony of the Civic Week on 24 May at which Prime Minister Captain Terence O'Neill presided. The prime minister said he was pleased to be in Newry and - despite previous squabbles among the public representatives — he saw fit to praise 'the constructive and co-operative spirit so obviously shown by all sections of the community'. The following month saw the beginning of the demolition of North Street and Water Street.

Controversy again hit the council in September, when the question of housing allocation came up. Sensitive to criticism, it supported Councillor Aubrey Wylie's proposal to send the press from the room. As before, there were heated arguments over allocation and Michael Murphy stormed out of the boardroom in protest. Afterwards Thomas McGrath, the local Labour leader, said that the priority scheme was set aside and houses were being allocated on party lines. The *Newry Reporter* commented bitterly: 'Once again the men at the head of affairs in this Frontier Town have stooped to petty squabbling in the name of public representation.'

There was subsequent in-fighting between the Northern Ireland Labour Party councillors, as six Labour councillors had voted for Councillor Wylie's motion in defiance of the rest of the party. These same six — Terry Hogan, Pat McMahon, Stephen Ruddy, Michael McKeown, John McKevitt and Matt McAteer — further outraged the party by voting alongside Unionists to co-opt Unionist Robert Niblock in replacement

In 1968 Pat McMahon, chairman of the UDC's housing committee, led the campaign to have housing allocated on the basis of need rather than the controversial practice of allocation along party lines. (*Newry Reporter*)

for Joseph McCullough, the Unionist member for the north ward, who had died. The other Labour councillors had wanted to co-opt a fellow party member, despite the fact that this was a Unionist seat and would not upset the balance of power in the chamber. Nevertheless, Thomas McGrath and his Labour committee accused the six men of betrayal and expelled them from the party. At the same time the six announced that they were forming their own party, so the council was now divided into four blocs: six Unionists, two Newry Labour Party (Thomas Markey and Gerard Sloan), four NI Labour Party, and the six Labour dissidents. As one local paper put it, the council was now split 'down the middle and up the sides'. Every issue, no matter how petty, was now bitterly debated and normal business came almost to a standstill. Anger at this state of affairs prompted the Newry Chamber of Commerce to hold a meeting at which they declared Newry to be 'the worst council in Northern Ireland' and called for its suspension. To the people of Newry the agitation against corruption at Stormont seemed unimportant compared to their own troubles. At the council meeting on 14 October the chairman, Pat McMahon, made a generous plea 'to sink our personal and political differences and work for the common good of our town'. In the face of mounting public criticism of their conduct, there was little else they could do if they were to have any respect among the ratepayers. The councillors may have been willing to sink differences, but the questions of misconduct and unfair allocation of houses were now in the public domain and there were protests over these issues in the following year.

In some respects the criticism and crisis of Newry Urban District Council echoed the criticism and crisis of government throughout Northern Ireland. By October 1968 NICRA had begun its campaign of protest and marches. Violence had already flared up, most notably the rioting in Deny on 5 October, and there were already indications that Newry's own political problems would become part of the wider troubles. In October the local Unionists were addressed by Senator Nelson Elder from Derry. At this meeting Senator Elder accused the press of stirring up trouble in the North, saying, 'the press went out of their way deliberately to make certain that this back lash would be seen everywhere. [I do] not give two hoots about the National or the Newry Press.' The senator ended his speech ominously, asking, 'How many Protestants hold top jobs in Newry?'

On 9 November a branch of People's Democracy (PD), a radical, left-wing, civil rights group, was established in Newry under the chairmanship of Thomas Keane, a local schoolteacher. Almost immediately it began agitating not just against the widespread abuse of power in Northern Ireland but also against its abuse in the Newry council. They specifically called for the allocation of housing and employment on merit not party favour, a criticism of particular poignancy when directed against a 'Catholic'-controlled council. On 21 November PD demonstrated at the council meeting, calling for the allocation of houses 'on need, not greed'. The meeting itself witnessed more arguments and Councillor Murphy, feeling powerless to halt the unfair allocation of tenancies, stormed out. When Brian Faulkner, the Minister of Commerce, visited Newry the following week, PD staged a demonstration calling for action to create jobs. At this time the average rate of unemployment in Northern Ireland was 7 per cent — double the UK average — and in Newry it was twice that again.

The year ended on a far from optimistic note. At a local level there was an undignified quarrel between the council and the Chamber of Commerce over their respective contributions in paying for the Christmas street decorations. Throughout Northern Ireland the violence following the civil rights agitation and the reaction among many Unionists to Captain O'Neill's proposed reforms were causing a crisis of confidence in his government. On 9 December he made an appeal on television to end the violence and called for support for his policies. The following day Newry council held an extraordinary meeting at which they passed a resolution supporting the Government and the increasingly beleaguered O'Neill.

The situation continued to deteriorate in the new year. A civil rights march from Belfast to Derry was ambushed at Burntollet Bridge and the worst rioting yet seen followed. Newry was made the occasion of a test of Unionist strength, when on 7 January 1969 the local PD announced that they would hold a march on Saturday 11 January. The PD's press officer, Paddy O'Hanlon, said that the aim of the march was to call for 'one man, one vote', an end to discrimination, and the allocation of housing and jobs in Newry on the basis of need and merit. The following day in Belfast, Major Ronald Bunting issued a statement on behalf of the 'Loyal Citizens of Ulster', saying his organisation planned 'to hold our biggest yet protest demonstration' in Newry to counter the PD march. A further statement was supplied to the media, claiming to come from the 'Ulster Volunteer Force, South Down', stating: 'We will not permit any band of rebel anarchists to parade through the Protestant section of Newry.' In response to both these statements, Kevin Boyle of the PD stated that they would neither cancel the march nor accept its being re-routed. Rumours spread that people were converging on Newry to support or attack the march and the RUC drafted in reinforcements. At a special meeting of the Stormont cabinet on 10 January it was decided that the march should not be allowed to follow its announced route and would be barred from Sugar Island, Kildare Street, and Upper Hill Street. At 2 a.m. on 11 January, Major Bunting announced that he was ordering his supporters to withdraw from Newry 'in the best interests of Protestants'.

Knowing that some of the streets were sealed off, the PD issued printed instructions that, at the RUC cordon, the marchers were to sit down with their backs to the police and let the stewards handle the situation. The re-routing had attracted many people to the march, and well-known civil rights figures from all over Northern Ireland, such as John Hume, attended. Even a Unionist councillor, Aubrey Wylie, was there, although his party later criticised him for this. When the march reached the police barriers, the leaders attempted to negotiate their way through but the RUC adamantly refused to deviate from its orders. The talks continued for some time and patience was wearing thin on both sides. At some point, no one seems certain when, violence did break out. Despite attempts by John Hume and others to calm the crowd, scuffles became open fights between protestors and the police and by the end of the afternoon ten policemen and twenty-eight civilians were injured, some being taken to hospital. Six RUC vehicles were damaged, some burned and others tipped into the canal. The damage was estimated at £10,000.

In Newry the universal reaction was one of shock. Although most people had expected violence, no one was psychologically prepared for the reality of it. The *Newry Reporter* spoke hysterically of a 'blazing inferno of hooliganism', while John Hume and NICRA distanced themselves from it. Many people preferred to think of it as an aberration that would not occur again. The urban district council laid the blame for the riot on the decision to re-route and in this were supported by the Chamber of Commerce, who handed in a petition signed by 180 ratepayers asking the council to forget about the whole thing as they felt 'that a lengthy debate on the issues involved could be nothing but detrimental to our town'. Those most profoundly shocked were the Newry PD. Their naive expectations of what might result from political agitation had been shattered and they held an 'inquest' into the riot, resulting in the election of a 'much more adult' committee. In Belfast the PD office announced it was establishing a fund to reimburse the RUC and local traders for damage.

On 13 March two banks, the Bank of Ireland and the Northern Bank, were raided by armed men and in all £12,000 was stolen. This was the first use of firearms in Newry in the current Troubles. Initially no one claimed responsibility and there was much speculation over the perpetrators. 'Was it a political action by Republican elements, a plain criminal exercise, or a combination of both?' the *Newry Reporter* asked. Curiously, in the end, responsibility was claimed by the 'Welsh Free Nationalists'. The first explosions near Newry occurred on 20 April, when the Protestant Ulster Volunteer Force (UVF) blew up the Silent Valley reservoir in the Mournes.

For Northern Ireland as a whole the situation was growing more serious. Terence O'Neill found that the reforms he promised were not enough to satisfy the demands of those in the civil rights movements, and at the same time they frightened many Unionists into believing that they were being betrayed. In an effort to strengthen his base of support, O'Neill called a general election in February 1969. On the nationalist side the old spokesmen were being challenged by the new leaders emerging from the ranks of the civil rights campaigners. In South Down the sitting nationalist, Michael Keogh, had a hard fight to retain his seat against Fergus Woods of PD and in a surprise result in South Armagh, Independent Paddy O'Hanlon came top of the poll.

The involvement of the civil rights movement in the election campaign marked the beginning of a period of intense activity by them. The following months saw protests by PD and NICRA on the streets and in the council chamber. In March and again in April, 'six bearded young men' carrying placards interrupted council meetings. In common with many towns, Newry witnessed sit-down protests and street rallies almost weekly. Significantly, on 6 April the Oliver Craven Republican Club was able to muster about two thousand people to its rally commemorating the 1916 Easter Rising. After a PD march on Sunday 20 April, a small crowd threw stones and bottles at the police station.

Local protest centred on the poverty in Newry and the corruption within the council. Unemployment in the town remained at 14 per cent and the councils of both Newry and Warrenpoint complained to Stormont that the promised new industries and port facilities had yet to materialise. Following a report by James Meehan, the public health inspector, even the council had to admit that the housing stock in Newry was in an appalling state. In one house in Bridge Street that was typical of many, three families lived with 'one sink, cold water on tap, hot water from gas geyser, one gas cooker, four rings (situated in communal kitchen). For common use — one water closet in yard, one water closet bath first floor.' For this Dickensian squalor the rent was over £2 per week. Meehan advised the council to take immediate action in setting standards for rented accommodation and in limiting the number living in any one house. In response the council expressed the fear that by limiting tenants or closing down unfit houses they would only be creating large numbers of homeless that the council could not accommodate.

The housing question took a dramatic turn on 20 May when, as the *Newry Reporter* records, 'following a James Bond type of exercise involving three cars, possession of one of the houses [in The Glen] was taken by a young couple, 22 years old Francis Hanna and his 19 year old wife, Lynn'. The Glen was a prestigious private housing development in which five houses were owned by the Ministry of Commerce. The following week a second house was occupied. In response to the squatters' actions the ministry issued a statement saying that the houses were being reserved for key workers who would be coming to Newry with the advent of new industry. A spokesperson for NICRA, who had organised the squat, said that 'a situation where a family is forced to walk the streets of our town, or live in squalor and degradation constitutes the real violence in our community'. There was talk of the other residents of The Glen getting up a petition to remove the squatters. When the squatters were brought before the courts, a large crowd of supporters accompanied them and the case was adjourned indefinitely.

The other main local news during the summer of 1969 was the announcement at the end of June by the Newry Port and Harbour Trust that yearly profits to 31 March 1969 stood at £6,320. This was a great improvement on the loss of the previous year. A fortnight later it was announced that Wright Industries, which manufactured carpets, would soon be coming to Newry with 165 jobs. Terence O'Neill had resigned as prime minister in April and on 31 July, Roy Bradford, the Minister for Commerce in James Chichester-Clark's new administration, announced that the Warrenpoint port scheme would soon commence and that £1.5 million would be spent on it. This was considerably less than the Warrenpoint district council had expected but was nevertheless welcome. However, one blight on this optimistic outlook was the report to Newry Urban District Council on 3 July that there was a deficit of £16,000 in the housing budget. Some councillors spoke of suspending the council's building programme altogether.

The backdrop to these local events was that the summer of 1969 was one of the most violent in the history of Northern Ireland and August was one of the worst months. In Derry the annual Apprentice Boys' parade provoked violence that rapidly escalated into open battle between the residents of the Bogside, and the RUC and B Specials. Barricades were erected and the streets of the city resembled Paris of 1870 rather than a city in Northern Ireland in 1969. With the inability of the police to cope in Derry, the facade of ordinary government in Northern Ireland finally collapsed and Westminster was obliged to send in troops to take charge of law and order. Sixty years previously, republicans had risen in Dublin against British government and the people of Newry knew little about it, but now they, and the rest of the world, could see the events in Derry on their television screens, and their reaction was immediate.

In Newry street protests developed into full-scale rioting as the police attempted to halt marches. Barricades were erected, often using hijacked vehicles, and shops were attacked. The local PD failed to contain the situation and a new ad hoc group calling itself the Citizens' Action Committee tried to orchestrate the anti-government protest. The rioting lasted for three days, the worst of it being in the working-class area between Monaghan Street and Bridge Street. The *Newry Reporter* recorded that 'the battle continued for some time, the crowd drawing the police further along Patrick Street where a parked cattle lorry blazed furiously. Back and forth, back and forth, the fortune of the two parties continued.' By the weekend both sides were exhausted. Violence had erupted throughout Northern Ireland, shaking the state to its very foundations. A special meeting of the urban district council called for the suspension of the Stormont parliament and direct rule from Westminster. On 18 August the annual Civic Week was cancelled 'because of the present emergency'. In the following days refugees escaping the violence in Belfast — where whole streets had been devastated — passed through Newry on their way to relief camps set up on the southern side of the border. A committee was established to collect bedding, medical supplies and food to send to Belfast and some families from the city were temporarily housed in Newry.

Although Northern Ireland was on the verge of open civil war, this, in fact, did not materialise. The deployment of troops and the promises of reform brought with them a lull. In Newry the housing question again dominated public debate, when the council decided to make up its budget deficit by increasing rents. Many tenants decided to withhold rents in protest and so the council then decided, in September, to transfer money from the rates revenue. This in turn brought objections from members of the Chamber of Commerce, who were the main ratepayers. At the same time pressure from Stormont forced the council to adopt a points scheme for housing allocation, although some councillors protested that this system was unfair.

The council now found itself facing the combined tenants' associations on one side, staging a rent strike, and the Chamber of Commerce on the other, threatening to withhold rates. In the midst of all this one councillor quite illegally ordered a halt to the demolition in North Street, claiming that some property owners were not happy with their compensation. This resulted in the clerk, Gerald Cronin, delivering a lecture to the councillors on their responsibilities and legal obligations.

Under the promised reforms, a new RUC Chief Constable, Sir Arthur Young, was appointed and on 7 November 1969 he paid a carefully organised and highly guarded visit to Newry. Following the disbandment of the controversial B Specials, a publicity campaign was launched to encourage Catholics to join the new army unit, the Ulster Defence Regiment (UDR), which was meant to fill the gap left by the disbanded B Specials. On 26 March 1970 the first parade of the Newry Company was held at the Territorial Army centre on the Downshire Road. The parade was not a complete success as the company had yet to reach its full strength, and although it was soon on active service along the border, Catholic recruitment remained a problem.

The council found itself surrounded by controversy again; a report by John N. Benn, the Commissioner of Complaints, published on 20 July 1970, found Newry council guilty of maladministration. The case arose from the appointment of a non-qualified candidate as supervisor for the newly opened town swimming pool in place of a suitably qualified applicant for the post. Despite being given the opportunity to reply, the council had refused to do so and was rather indignant at its conduct being questioned. The commissioner made it clear that he did not think the council had acted out of religious or political motives but rather out of 'local patriotism', as one commentator put it, in that the new superintendent, unlike the rival candidate, was a Newryman. However, almost immediately after a suitably qualified candidate was appointed as pool supervisor, another argument erupted over the employment of pool attendants. Councillor McKevitt said that, as far as he could see, there was a policy of appointing local people. Again properly qualified candidates had been rejected and inexperienced people appointed instead. The issue was hotly debated in the council chamber and in the press until finally, in October, the councillors agreed to adopt the points system issued by the Association of Local Authorities with regard to employees. Many locals felt that alleged corruption and discrimination within their Catholic-controlled council at this time was the sort of publicity Newry could do without.

During the summer of 1970 there were important developments. In June the Government announced that a major hydroelectric scheme would be built at Camlough, bringing a welcome boost to the local construction industry. Shortly afterwards it was made known that Bairnswear would be opening a factory that would employ four hundred people. The UK general election on 18 June aroused little interest; the local MPS retained their seats, but a change of government brought the Conservatives to power under Edward Heath. The following month the Macrory Report on Northern Ireland recommended that local government be reorganised around twenty-six district councils which would have limited powers - responsibility for health and social services, and education and libraries, being vested in area boards. The report received the support of the urban district council when it was discussed in October and the scheme was implemented in 1973.

The route of the first civil rights march in Newry on 11 January 1969 was restricted by the RUC. Violence erupted when the PD members attempted to march their chosen route. (*Belfast Telegraph*)

Newry was an important focus of the civil rights movement. Leading activists spoke at rallies there such as Bernadette Devlin addressing a rally in St. Colman's Park, 5 July 1969. (*Belfast Telegraph*)

It had been a summer of significant political developments. In April a new party hoping to promote non-sectarian politics was formed, the Alliance Party, and shortly afterwards a branch was founded in Newry. In August a number of civil rights activists and nationalists came together to found the Social Democratic and Labour Party (SDLP) which, in Newry as elsewhere, soon ousted or subsumed existing parties on the nationalist side. The previous month had seen the first protest march against the UDR, in opposition to its alleged sectarian treatment of Catholics, when '200 youths, young people and some females' marched to its Downshire Road depot. In August the local Protestant Imperial Grand Black Chapter marched, despite a government ban, and twelve men were subsequently arrested.

The year 1970 also saw the re-emergence of the IRA as a 'military' force. It had gone on the offensive shortly after the deployment of the British

Army into Northern Ireland in August 1969. Newry had avoided the worst excesses of the feud resulting from the IRA split between the 'Officials' and the 'Provisional' in early 1970. Its bombing campaign in Newry began on 4 August of that year when the offices of Ulsterbus and the British Legion Club were blown up. The Official IRA denied any involvement. On 11 August two RUC constables were killed in an explosion at Crossmaglen in south Armagh; on 19 September the customs post on the Omeath Road was destroyed; and on 3 November all of Rostrevor was blacked out when a bomb exploded at an electricity sub-station. From this time onwards the IRA campaign was to be a predominant factor in the Troubles.

In January 1971 the Scarman tribunal, set up to investigate the early Troubles, came to Armagh for three days and listened to conflicting evidence on the riots in Newry. The IRA campaign intensified dramatically and in the first six months of the year there were almost twenty bombs and arson attacks in Newry, and army patrols along the border were frequently fired on. The offices of the two Newry rural councils were destroyed when a bomb was planted there on 27 February. On the same night an arson attack badly damaged Fishers' premises. On more than one occasion clashes occurred between stone-throwing youths and the security forces. Parades by republican supporters were now as frequent as once the PD marches had been. On 29 May the Shadow Home Secretary, James Callaghan, visited Newry. Most people seemed indifferent to the visit, but a small crowd of republicans jeered at the Callaghan entourage.

The council had the embarrassment of being reprimanded by the Ministry of Development for illegally allocating a house to Pat McMenamin, the pool superintendent. There had been a proposal to operate a points scheme, giving priority to incoming workers, but the council had rejected it. However, McMenamin, who had never been happy in the post, solved the problem by resigning. The council was shown in a better light on 21 April, when the first traffic travelled along the new through-pass and then a week later it ordered the closure of three houses on Mill Street as being unfit for human habitation, two years after the health inspector's report. In May the Government's development plan for Newry was unveiled, promising industrial and social improvements.

However, the political situation was soon to overshadow other affairs. On 1 May there was some trouble when buses carrying Linfield Football Club supporters passed through Newry on their return from a game in Dublin. The following day a more serious incident occurred at the football ground on the Warrenpoint Road. The army was involved in a search operation and it was believed that soldiers were going to enter the ground and conduct a search there. As the soldiers approached the ground, they were met with resistance from a small group of people that rapidly became a large crowd which surrounded the army land-rovers and 'escorted' them back into town. The soldiers took no action but as the strange procession reached the town it was confronted by other soldiers in riot gear. It was this confrontation that provoked the subsequent rioting. The following night trouble also broke out but on a smaller scale. Ever since the troops' arrival, their relations with the townspeople had been uneasy and the local nationalist MP, Michael Keogh, now called for their withdrawal. Matters were not helped by the implementation of a policy of blanket house-search operations, beginning in the early hours of 5 June, during which two brothers were arrested for possession of explosives.

The town suffered a severe blow on 18 June when it was announced that the Ulster Textiles mill was going to close down. So much local attention was focused on the Troubles that few people had been aware of the crisis that was affecting the company, which announced that it had debts of £620,000 and unless the Government baled it out, closure was the only option. The factory had been in operation in Newry since 1962 and employed three hundred people. Their redundancies would raise the unemployment figure in Newry to three thousand. Local councillors and prominent businessmen urged the Government to 'save the Ulster Textiles Mill in the same way as Belfast shipyard was saved'. Robin Bailie, the Minister of Commerce, said that he was 'conscious of the blow which the closure meant to Newry with its high level of unemployment and its previous industrial setbacks'. But despite reassurances, the Government refused to commit itself to a rescue package. A march held by Newry and District Trades Council, in an attempt to save the mill, received widespread support.

Northern Ireland officially celebrated its fiftieth anniversary in 1971. Belfast and many towns had special events to mark the occasion. Newry did not hold any celebrations, but the Orange Order in Newry and Bessbrook held a golden jubilee dinner in the model village's town hall.

Divisions among nationalists split the urban district council when an extraordinary meeting was called by Pat McMahon following the shooting of two men in Derry by the army on 8 July. The chairman and

On 27 February 1971 an IRA arson attack caused extensive damage to Fishers' timber yard on Merchants' Quay. (*Newry Reporter*)

others called for a boycott of local and central government if a public inquiry was not held. This was opposed by the former chairman, Thomas Markey, who instead proposed a motion asking for action to be taken against those who 'were acting like wild Indians on the streets' of Newry, a reference to the recent disturbances. On the streets an army search operation on 23 July resulted in more riots. When a landmine exploded beside a fire tender on the Drumalane Road a few days later, firemen were lucky to escape injury. Following further army operations, a torchlight procession of two thousand people marched through the town in protest.

Newry was to witness its most serious rioting after the introduction of internment on 9 August 1971. Prime Minister Brian Faulkner had taken this step in response to increasing violence and mounting criticism within his own ranks. With no prior announcement a massive search-and-arrest operation began just after midnight. It was said that over one hundred people were 'lifted' in Newry. Soon after the first arrests, people came on to the streets banging bin lids and blowing whistles. By first light the security forces had met with serious resistance, escalating into the worst rioting yet seen. The *Newry Reporter* recorded:

> Arson and rioting broke out … early on Monday morning and continued on Tuesday and Wednesday. There were numerous fires, bombs, looting and shooting. … On Monday and Tuesday it was shops and offices which were under attack and [on Wednesday] explosions occurred at two customs posts. … Scores of vehicles have been hijacked and used as barricades.

Many areas of Newry were cut off by the barricades and throughout the town all traffic was halted at army checkpoints and even ambulances were stopped and searched. Following telephone threats, two factories closed down.

The introduction of internment on 9 August 1971 resulted in the worst rioting Newry had yet experienced. Throughout the town vehicles were hijacked and burned, like this lorry and bus in Hill St. (Séamus Mac Caibhead)

If the object of internment was to break the organisation and morale of the IRA, in Newry it would seem not to have had this effect. On Wednesday 11 August a statement signed by 'John Mitchel' was issued to the media by the south Down IRA:

> We wish to state that we the above are responsible for the operations carried out in Newry. We also intend to carry on with these activities until all persons are released and until such times as the British Army are withdrawn. We will also ask the Council and the Fire Authority not to send their men out to interfere with barricades or put out fires as there are mines planted.

On 16 August a mass meeting was held at Newry town hall at which the speakers called for a plan of civil disobedience that would 'smash the state'. The PD outlined a campaign consisting of the boycott of public authorities and a rates strike. Some councillors were on the platform at the meeting and Pat McMahon announced that he was '100 per cent behind the campaign' and subsequently resigned as council chairman. These events echoed those throughout Northern Ireland, but in Newry support for the campaign was particularly widespread.

Although the council still had a quorum for business, there was difficulty in finding members for the various committees. In any case the Unionists decided it was futile to continue and they too decided to stay away. The rent-and-rates strike subsumed the existing anti-council rent strike and at its height it was claimed that 95 per cent of tenants supported it. In October the town clerk reported that the strike was costing £30,000 per week and forty council employees had to be laid off. The swimming pool committee reconvened to take any action needed to save the pool from closing down.

While civil disobedience continued, there was no lull in the IRA campaign. Before the end of the year there had been over twenty serious explosions in Newry and about twenty-five robberies and ambushes, some resulting in loss of life. On 29 August a soldier was killed in a gun battle near Crossmaglen. A few days later an arson attack gutted the offices of the *Newry Reporter*. (It continued printing with the help of the other local papers.) In one horrific incident two men, Eamon Henry and Brian Hamill, were trapped in a Hill Street drapery store following an arson attack. Firemen were unable to reach them and they were burned to death. Violence was also perpetrated against private houses. On 28 August a petrol bomb was thrown into the home of the Preece family in Emmet Street; Herbert Preece was a member of the Northern Ireland Territorial Army Volunteer Reserve and his father was a full-time sergeant in the UDR. No deaths resulted from this attack, but in the weeks following a number of Protestant families left the Derrybeg housing estate, saying that they had been threatened and intimidated. Throughout Newry and the surrounding area the sectarian lines were being drawn and both Catholics and Protestants were moving to where their co-religionists dominated.

Serious rioting broke out again towards the end of October. On the night of 24 October an army foot patrol shot dead three young men, who, they later claimed, were attempting to rob a bank in Hill Street. The army's version of events was questioned and so once again Newry witnessed battles between the security forces and local people. Stones and petrol bombs were thrown at the army, which replied with rubber bullets and cs gas. Cars were hijacked and barricades erected across main streets. When the three men, John Ruddy, Thomas McLoughlin and Robert Anderson, were buried, Newry was quiet again. At a protest meeting Rory McShane, speaking for the Civil Rights Association, called for non-cooperation with the troops in Newry. He also called for an end to the army's control of street lighting, which meant that after 9.30 p.m. Newry was left in darkness. The rioting on this occasion was the prelude to further bombings and attacks by the IRA.

An announcement that Wright Industries planned a £300,000 expansion was offset by the news in November that Reckitt and Colman, who made cleaning materials, would be closing down. They had been in Newry since 1944 and their closure meant 110 job losses. On the border the IRA bombed the customs post at Killeen and on 27 November its members shot dead two customs officers, Ian Hanklin and Jimmy O'Neill, when they attacked the post again. There was a virtual blitz on Newry in the week before Christmas. On one day alone three bombs went off in the town centre one after the other.

The new year opened with a threat from the Government that if the Newry Urban District Council did not resume normal business, it would be disbanded. The council had not sat for four months and had accumulated a debt of £500,000. On 17 January 1972 the official order to disband the council was issued. Almost fifty years after the council had been suspended for refusing to recognise the legitimacy of the government of Northern Ireland, it was dissolved for seeking the removal of that government. The Ministry of Development now had responsibility for public affairs in Newry.

The pattern of bombing set before Christmas did not decrease and almost every week saw bomb attacks on factories or offices. The worst day, in an 'attempt to raze Newry', was 26 January 1972, when bombs destroyed Vincent Toner and Sons on Hill Street, Sands's mill on the quay, the new inland revenue offices on Bank Parade and Etams boutique on Hill Street. The bombs not only destroyed their targets but created such massive fires that the Newry fire service had to seek assistance from Kilkeel in County Down and Keady in County Armagh before they were made safe.

On Sunday 30 January, fourteen people taking part in a civil rights demonstration in Derry were shot dead by the army in what became known as 'Bloody Sunday'. It was decided to make Newry the venue for a demonstration against the army's action. People came from all over Ireland and the news media came from all over the world to witness the largest rally Newry had ever seen. A crowd estimated at between twenty and fifty thousand attended a silent rally on 6 February. Three days later, the six-month anniversary of internment, there were more riots and in the following days four members of the security forces were killed and there were numerous bomb attacks, including an arson attack on the town hall that caused £30,000-worth of damage.

In February it was announced that three hundred more people would be employed at the Camlough hydroelectric scheme; at that time the unemployment level in Newry stood at 3,160. On the wider front, Edward Heath's government suspended the parliament at Stormont, introduced direct rule from Westminster, and William Whitelaw was appointed as the first Secretary of State for Northern Ireland. The move was welcomed in Newry, but did elicit protest from Unionists throughout Northern Ireland. The suspension of Stormont seemed to have little effect on the level of violence. IRA attacks continued unabated, despite the capture of a unit attempting to blow up the Victoria Locks and the discovery of a training camp near Rostrevor. On 19 April the body of UDR Corporal Jim Elliott, who had been kidnapped, was found on the border. On 26 June a policeman was killed while trying to prevent the IRA planting a bomb in Water Street. On the same day an IRA ceasefire came into effect as the result of secret negotiations between its leaders and the Government, but it did not last long, ending on 9 July when the post office in Jonesborough was blown up. A fortnight later the army launched 'Operation Motorman', a massive military movement into 'no-go' areas throughout Northern Ireland and the arrest of known IRA members. Even this tactic failed to decelerate the level of violence and in Newry the bombing continued. On 22 August an IRA attack on the Customs Vehicle Examination Centre went badly wrong when a bomb exploded prematurely, killing not only the two bombers but also six other people, and many more were injured. On the same day another bomber was killed in a nearby petrol station on the Dublin Road, when the device he was planting exploded.

August saw the final issue of the *Frontier Sentinel*. This weekly paper had been published since 1904. After a change of ownership, the paper was finding it increasingly difficult to make a profit and it decided to cease operations. At the end of August work at the hydroelectric scheme was halted yet again. Three months previously arguments over land acquisition had brought the scheme to a standstill and now attempts to resume work were once again stopped by local farmers. In fact, the scheme was ultimately abandoned because of these problems.

By now bombs were an almost daily occurrence. Many were shocked by the death of a local hotel owner, Edmund Woolsey, on 21 September, when he attempted to recover his stolen car that had been found on the border by the RUC. The car had, in fact, been booby-trapped in the expectation that the police would drive it away. A week later a soldier was killed by the IRA at Crossmaglen. On 1 October several hundred people attended a peace rally in the town, in Soho car park, to express their revulsion at the continuing violence. Good news at this time was the occupation of the Local Enterprise Development Unit's factory by Norbrook Laboratories, a pharmaceutical firm, on 27 October. In January 1973 the *Irishgate* became the first vessel to enter the new port facilities at Warrenpoint. This month also saw the Irish Republic and the United Kingdom join the European Economic Community.

On 6 February 1972 Newry was the venue for the protest rally following Bloody Sunday (30 January 1972). An estimated 50,000 people were led by prominent political figures including John Hume, Austin Currie, Gerry Fitt and Paddy Devlin. (*Belfast Telegraph*)

Relations between the army and the local population took a serious turn for the worse on 28 February, when a thirteen-year-old boy, Kevin Heatley, was shot dead by a soldier. The whole community was shocked at his death and outraged when the authorities could give no satisfactory explanation as to why the soldier, Corporal Francis Foxford, opened fire. The incident gave rise to outbreaks of violence and in the following weeks there were many gun attacks on soldiers on patrol. Subsequently, Corporal Foxford was charged with the manslaughter of Kevin Heatley. He appeared before the Crown Court in March 1974 and was found guilty and sentenced to three years' imprisonment. He appealed the verdict and in October 1974 the High Court found him not guilty of manslaughter.

The year 1973 saw the implementation of important political initiatives in consequence of direct rule. In March there was to be a referendum on the border issue. Two months later there were to be elections to the twenty-six district councils put forward in the Macrory Report, to be followed by elections to an Assembly at Stormont, in which it was proposed that Unionists and nationalists would share power. Civil rights groups and many nationalists organised a boycott of the border referendum, arguing that a simple yes or no to the border did not adequately address the problem and that there could be no guarantee that voting would not be rigged in certain areas. On 8 March extra troops were drafted into Newry and the ballot boxes were kept under armed guard at all times. In the event the boycott received widespread support in Newry and the surrounding areas. Of two thousand registered voters in South Armagh, only six voted. In the town itself one thousand ballot papers were burned at a boycott rally and Rory McShane, the civil rights spokesman, claimed a further two thousand had been destroyed. When the result of the referendum was announced, there was, not unexpectedly, a majority in favour of retaining the border.

Bombs and incendiary devices continued to be planted but there was also a renewed assault on the army along the border. In the week immediately after the referendum a soldier was killed by a landmine near Crossmaglen, and a few days later a second soldier was killed there. On 26 March a farm labourer, Samuel Martin, was killed by gunfire from an army post at Newtownhamilton in County Armagh. The military authorities claimed to be returning fire but some months later Private Gavin Spencer was charged with manslaughter and found not guilty. However, it was the soldiers themselves who remained the most common victims of the violence. On 8 April, not far from Newtownhamilton, two soldiers were killed when a landmine exploded and a month later three soldiers died in an explosion near Crossmaglen. In a follow-up operation, involving troops on both sides of the border, the Gardai arrested five men in possession of explosives.

The district council election campaign came to an end on 30 May, when the voters went to the polls to decide who should sit on the new Newry and Mourne District Council. After petitions from various bodies in the town, the local government boundary commissioner, F.A.I. Harrison, had agreed to add the town's name to that of Mourne for the new district. We do not know if he realised that in doing so he was evoking the old abbey, whose exempt jurisdiction covered much the same area and which ultimately gave the secondary title of Viscount Newry and Mourne to the Earl of Kilmorey. This new council incorporated the urban districts of Newry and Warrenpoint, the two Newry rural districts, the south Down rural district, and the rural district of Kilkeel, with 47,930 electors using proportional representation for the first time in over forty years when casting their vote.

The council now consisted of thirteen SDLP members, four Alliance Party, eight Unionists, two Republican Clubs members, and three Independents. The councillors elected an Independent, John McAteer, as chairman, with John McEvoy, SDLP, as vice-chairman. The new clerk was PJ. O'Hagan, formerly clerk to Newry number 2 Rural District Council. Over the next few weeks the councils that had not been suspended formally handed over to the Newry and Mourne District Council. However, the new council had considerably less power than the old one. The new area boards had responsibility for education and libraries, and health and social services. All public housing was now administered by the Northern Ireland Housing Executive, and other powers, like control of building and the regulation of traffic, were vested in the Department of the Environment. The council's new powers amounted to little more than 'collecting bins and running the swimming pool', as one observer put it.

A second round of electioneering got under way almost immediately as thirty-four candidates in South Down and Armagh fought for fourteen seats in the new Assembly. In a bitter campaign contested over the constitutional question, extremists on both sides played influential roles. On the republican side there were calls for a boycott, while loyalists demanded a return to the old Stormont. This election was also on the basis of proportional representation and the new Assembly would only be given power if both communities were represented in its executive. Such was the difficulty in getting a majority to support almost any combination of parties that it was not until November 1973 that Brian Faulkner, the chief executive, could announce an agreement.

In Newry, at this time, there was an example of ordinary people overcoming adversity. On 22 June, Stark Brothers' factory was destroyed in an arson attack; the IRA denied responsibility. Starks, a popular firm employing 150 people, was in danger of closing down but the workforce was determined not to let that happen. In response to their petition, the Government offered Starks a factory in the Greenbank Industrial Estate and by August the company was back to normal production. Shortly afterwards it was announced that a Canadian firm, Yardmaster Steel Fabrication, would be opening a plant in Newry, employing one hundred people. This was part of the Whitelaw administration's attempts to boost the Northern Ireland economy.

These initiatives also entailed devising new strategies for every area, and a plan was published for Newry, looking twenty years into the future and promising new developments in everything from industry and transport to housing and leisure.

GEBR. BROERE B.V. - DORDRECHT (HOLLAND)

The ship canal was finally closed to commercial traffic on 26 March 1974. The last ship through the Victoria Locks was the *Anna Broere* from the Netherlands. (Joseph Fisher & sons)

It must have seemed to many that these optimistic plans for the future were not a solution to Newry's problems and were produced without really addressing those problems. In the same week that the Newry Area Plan was published, Isaac Scott, a former UDR, was killed (a month later a local Catholic, Charles McDonnell was killed in retaliation) and a week later a UDR soldier, Frank Watt, was also killed. The 9 August rally against internment — in spite of the absence of the SDLP - had a huge turnout but was followed by violence. There were to be six more deaths in and around Newry in the subsequent months and the IRA was so strong, according to local reports, that it was mounting its own vehicle checkpoints in south Armagh.

The council had its first argument in August — over whether to hold its monthly meetings in the afternoon or evening. More seriously, the two Republican Clubs councillors declared that they were boycotting the council until the ending of internment. This was a divisive issue among nationalists. At the outset of the civil disobedience campaign almost every nationalist political leader had supported it. Also, the rent-and-rates strike was still being supported by many people, but now some politicians argued that the campaign should be suspended since the nationalist minority were offered this opportunity by the new Westminster initiative. This was to cause great bitterness among the nationalist community in Newry as elsewhere, and the question was never satisfactorily resolved, and the strike eventually petered out.

The Assembly executive took office officially on 1 January 1974. A local member for Armagh, Paddy O'Hanlon, was the SDLP'S chief whip and an influential voice in the executive. In Newry the new year opened with talk of the port closing. Coal imports had dropped by 10,000 tons and the Port and Harbour Trust realised that the closure of the docking facilities was unavoidable. The run-down began and equipment was formally abandoned and workers paid off. By March the process was complete and on 26 March the last ship, the *Anna Broere,* entered the Victoria Locks. The *Newry Reporter* said:

> Television and press cameras were there to cover the historic occasion. Undoubtedly the voyage was a sad one for the many people who have been proud of Newry's link with the sea. ... Apart from the news media and the lockmen operating the gates there were few members of the public there to witness the end of an era.

While local attention was focused on the closure of the ship canal, Northern Ireland was tottering on the edge of disaster. The IRA campaign continued and nine more people were to die in the Newry area before May. Power-sharing at Stormont had divided nationalists and brought Unionist hardliners to the fore, for whom any compromise was unacceptable. When Edward Heath's political difficulties forced him to call a UK general election in February, in Northern Ireland it was fought on the issue of the executive and the result seriously undermined the position of Brian Faulkner and his partners in cabinet.

The aftermath of the attack on the Miami Showband, 31 July 1975, when three band members were killed and others injured by UVF gunmen. Two of the terrorists were also killed when their bomb exploded prematurely. This incident marked the beginning of attacks in the Newry area by loyalist terrorist groups. (*Newry Reporter*)

`The following months were among the most violent in Newry, and when the Ulster Workers' Council (UWC) called its strike against the executive in May, most people were taken unawares. Although there was little support for the UWC in Newry and south Armagh, there was enough support in the neighbouring towns and surrounding countryside to make it bite. People not only kept away from work but barricades were set up, blocking incoming roads. The electricity was cut, resulting in the closure of shops and factories, homes were left without light and even the Daisy Hill Hospital was threatened. The district council found it impossible to carry on — for instance, the swimming pool had to be shut down. However, the gasworks remained operational. Then the following notice appeared in the press: 'As and from today Thursday 23rd of May, all Petrol-filling stations in Newry and District will close each day at 7 p.m. (including Saturday). Sundays all-day closing.'

Newry felt like a town under siege. The Government remained inactive -the executive had no legal powers to intervene, in any case, since the Northern Ireland Office still had responsibility for law and order - and the UWC seemed to be running the region. It was as if the threat made in 1913 to set up a provisional government of Ulster in defiance of the British parliament had at long last become a reality. On the weekend of 25—6 May some local trade unionists called on their colleagues to form a workers' action committee. Their intention was to organise relief efforts for the needy and where possible to maintain normal services. They called on the Government to reopen the canal and bring emergency supplies in through Newry, which they said they could transport to Belfast. In Dublin the cabinet watched events with increasing unease. It feared a loyalist takeover in Northern Ireland, but also feared that precipitate action on its part might do irrevocable damage. Irish troops were moved to the border and, as Robert Fisk relates in *The Point of No Return,* 'Justin Keating, the Minister for Industry, also drew up a spectacularly ambitious secret plan for hiring a fleet of ships, loading them with food and sailing up Carlingford Lough to the predominantly Catholic town of Newry'. In the event the British government moved first. On 27 May certain petrol stations were commandeered by the army in order to distribute petrol. Within a few days, the strike had been called off, not in defeat but in victory, since the UWC had achieved its aim of destroying the Assembly and by June the executive had been prorogued.

The street lights in Newry had continued to be controlled by the army and this not only caused resentment but also a number of car accidents were blamed on the lack of lighting. On 25 July the SDLP's Frank Feely led a deputation asking for street lighting to be returned to civilian control and a few days later the district council made an official request to this effect. Matters came to a head when following two days of rioting after the third anniversary of internment on 9 August, the IRA blew up the offices of the Northern Ireland Electricity Service (NIES) and issued a statement threatening to kill any NIES employee engaged in maintenance work, until the army relinquished its control of street lighting.

Within a few days 50 per cent of Newry's electricity was cut off as essential maintenance work was not done. Within a fortnight there was almost a complete blackout. The situation continued into September — the town had never suffered for so long, even during the UWC strike. Finally, on 5 September, the council chairman, John McEvoy, led a delegation to Stormont Castle, which, after two days of negotiations with Merlyn Rees, the Northern Ireland Secretary of State, secured the restoration of lighting to civilian control. However, in the following nights some soldiers from the UDR and the regular army shot out street lights in parts of the town. Few people believed them when they claimed to have been caught in ambushes.

October found the controversial British politician, Enoch Powell, knocking on doors in Newry. Another UK general election had been called for 10 October and Powell was selected to stand as the Unionist candidate in South Down. The main rival for the seat was Sean Hollywood, standing for the SDLP. In the event Powell was returned for the constituency, and Harold McCusker retained his Armagh seat. The election had little impact on the violence and five more people were to be killed in the area by Christmas.

One bright point at this time was the opening of the Newry Gateway Club on 17 October. It was the 317th to open in the UK, and was the first organisation in Newry to be concerned solely with the care of mentally handicapped people. Funds for the club were raised from public subscription and it proved to be a cause that transcended political and religious barriers. Gateway continues to provide an invaluable service in Newry, relying mainly on the townspeople's generosity.

On 18 October a sixteen-year-old boy, Michael Hughes, was shot dead by an army patrol. There were conflicting accounts of how the boy had died and once again relations between the townspeople and the security forces were strained. The Newry and Mourne District Council called for a public inquiry but none was forthcoming. Subsequently, an inquest returned an open verdict. The following months saw further bombings and the death of a UDR member at the hands of the IRA. In December there was a no-warning bomb attack on a public house in Church Street in which one man was killed and many injured. A few days later a member of the RUC was killed at Forkhill.

One thing that had changed, however, was the re-emergence of loyalist terrorist groups determined, as they saw it, to 'carry the war' to the IRA. From the early months of 1975 the Troubles took on a quite different character. Street demonstrations, riots, bombings and attacks on the security forces continued, but sectarian attacks were now being made by loyalist and republican groups. This was the case throughout Northern Ireland but was particularly so in Newry and the surrounding areas. Before the end of 1975, over thirty people had been killed as a result of terrorist violence. A community that had become accustomed to death was particularly shocked at the attack on the Miami Showband on 31 July. The van in which the band was travelling along the Loughbrickland road, not far from Newry, was stopped by members of the UVF. The band members were ordered out and then fired on by the gunmen.

The campaign of sectarian murders in the Newry area culminated in the deaths of ten Protestant workers ambushed at Kingsmills on 5 January 1976. As a result of this attack the SAS were deployed in Northern Ireland. (*Newry Reporter*)

225

Three of the band — Fran O'Toole, Brian McCoy and Tony Geraghty — were killed and the others injured. During the same incident, a bomb in the possession of the UVF men exploded prematurely, killing two of them — Harris Boyle and Wesley Summerville. The Miami Showband was one of the most popular in Ireland and the deaths seemed particularly senseless. This atrocity was the prelude to a summer of murder. Most of the killings were isolated attacks, but on 1 September 1975, following the murder of two Catholics a few days before by the Protestant Action Force, republican gunmen burst into the Orange Hall of Lodge number 630 at Tullyvallen, in south Armagh, and opened fire with machine guns, killing five of the occupants. The attack was claimed by the 'South Armagh Republican Action Force'.

There was some good news this summer, however. On 21 July the first Newry Canal Festival was opened, ironically at a time when due to a lack of rainfall water rationing had been introduced and the canal's level was low. August saw the announcements that a local firm, Ulcon, had secured an order worth £1.5 million and that Glen Electric planned an expansion, thus creating 150 jobs. Yet these made little impact on the fundamental economic problems. When Merlyn Rees flew in by helicopter to visit Newry and Warrenpoint on 27 October, the latest figures showed that there were 3,564 unemployed in the town.

A new security initiative was launched in October 1975, when roads into the Irish Republic were sealed off. Most people objected to this measure as many worked or owned land on the other side of the border and within a few weeks a number of the military barriers had been removed by local inhabitants. Despite the declaration of a ceasefire by the IRA in February, Merlyn Rees publicly admitted that there was no let-up in what he called the 'bandit country' of south Armagh — an expression that stuck. In a sinister development, on 20 December three people died in a no-warning bomb attack on Donnelly's public house in Silverbridge, near Crossmaglen, which was claimed by the Red Hand Commandos, a loyalist group. On 3 January 1976 another no-warning bomb was planted in the crowded Lough Inn in Camlough, on the outskirts of Newry, injuring fourteen people. On 4 January two Catholic brothers were shot dead in their home in south Armagh. On the morning of 5 January a minibus carrying ten Protestants to work was stopped at Kingsmills in south Armagh by armed men who ordered them onto the road and then shot them all dead. The attack was claimed by the South Armagh Republican Action Force, believed to be a cover name for the IRA. Everyone was stunned by the intensity of sectarian killings. No one could now doubt that open war had come to Newry and south Armagh.

The general feeling of tension was not eased by the arrival of the army's Spearhead Battalion or by the deployment of units of the Special Air Service (SAS). In Newry there was severe rioting, that went on for weeks, in response to the hunger strike of Frank Stagg, an IRA man in prison in England. February 1976 saw a renewed bombing campaign in Newry and on 1 March the post office was all but destroyed in an attack. Although the bombing continued, culminating on 25 April with incendiary attacks on Newry shops, causing an estimated £1 million-worth of damage, there was an abeyance in the sectarian assassinations following the minibus murders. On 15 April the first accredited action of the SAS took place when a patrol shot Peter Cleary, described as a 'wanted man'.

On the economic front in 1976, there was a public inquiry into the Newry Area Plan, which received submissions from various interested parties. The gasworks sank further into crisis as prices rose and consumption fell. Unemployment in Newry for 1975 stood at 3,982, and when the Bessbrook Products Company closed down in 1976, it meant not only the loss of the gasworks' biggest customer but a further 250 people 'on the dole'. In March 1976 the Northern Ireland Housing Executive announced that it was still owed £277,000 in the Newry and Mourne district from outstanding rent still being withheld because of the civil disobedience campaign and that there would be no amnesty.

The summer of 1976 was to be a long, dry one. In July it was announced that the number of unemployed in Newry stood at 3,687, which made it the second-highest for any town in Northern Ireland. Although the death toll in the Newry area decreased, the IRA's bombing campaign continued. Huge bombs were planted in Newry, the smallest being two hundred pounds. The Troubles claimed more innocent victims when Liam Prince, a local schoolteacher, was shot dead by the army near the border — the army said it was a 'mistake' - and twelve-year-old Majella O'Hare was shot by a soldier in Newry. Paratrooper Michael Williams was later charged with the manslaughter of Majella O'Hare and was acquitted in May 1977.

Horror at the continuing violence had given birth in Belfast to the Peace People. On 18 September the movement, led by Mairead Corrigan, came to Newry and an estimated twenty thousand people took part in a peace march. Undeterred by this display, the IRA had planted a bomb in an oil tanker, which temporarily halted the march, and then it planted another bomb outside a restaurant. In the following weeks there were more bombs in Newry, and another 'accidental' death, when an army patrol shot a man who was out duck hunting near Silverbridge. The army's behaviour in general continued to cause concern and at its monthly meeting in October the district council condemned the 'brutal interrogation methods' being employed in local army bases. Around this time also, some people in south Armagh began to voice complaints about the army taking over more land for bases and lookout posts. The trades council in Newry held a 'Better Life' rally on 18 November and on 21 November about five hundred people attended a second Peace People rally in the town.

After the blood-letting of 1976, the level of violence decreased. Across the whole of Northern Ireland, twenty-six people were killed in the first two months of 1977, compared to seventy-four in the same period in 1976. This year saw the beginning of the 'blanket protest' by republican prisoners in the Maze Prison (formerly Long Kesh), in which they refused to wear prison uniform and only wore the blankets from their beds. The efforts of the republican movement were concentrated on making political capital from this protest. Bomb attacks and killings, by republicans and loyalists, did, of course, continue and May saw one of the most mysterious cases, when Robert Nairac disappeared. Nairac, it transpired, was a captain in the SAS who had been engaged in undercover work in south Armagh. He lost contact with his base and was presumed killed by the IRA. However, despite intensive searches throughout Northern Ireland and the Republic, his body was never recovered. Although six men were later arrested in connection with Nairac's murder, the exact circumstances of his death were never uncovered.

The year 1977 was also the silver jubilee of the reign of Elizabeth II, and in the summer she visited Northern Ireland. Newry and Mourne, however, did not figure in her itinerary. In March the council had all but unanimously voted — only the two Republican Clubs councillors objected — to support any local body seeking aid to organise a celebration, although there would be no official event. There were some minor festivities in Newry, but in general the occasion was met by indifference or hostility.

The district council elections in May 1977 aroused little enthusiasm and the composition of the new council remained more or less the same. The SDLP retained its majority and John McEvoy was returned to the chair. In October much more attention was given to the elevation of Tomas Ó Fiaich as Archbishop of Armagh in place of Cardinal William Conway, who had died in April; in June 1979 Dr Ó Fiaich was made a cardinal and so became Catholic Primate of All-Ireland. At the time much significance was attached to the fact that Cardinal Ó Fiaich came from Crossmaglen, in the heart of Merlyn Rees's 'bandit country'.

Tomás Ó Fiaich was appointed Archbishop of Armagh in October 1977 and elevated to cardinal in June 1979. Many thought it significant that he came from Crossmaglen in the heart of Merlyn Rees's 'bandit country'. (*Belfast Telegraph*)

The violence still continued. There was a noticeable shift in IRA strategy, which moved from attacking 'economic targets' towards a concentration on the security forces. In 1978 over twenty security personnel and three civilians were killed in the Newry area. The economic situation did not alter much and unemployment stood at 3,834. In response to a government initiative, the local Alliance Party leader, Michael McVerry, was elected council chairman in what was hoped would be the first step in a rotation of offices among the different parties. However, the tide of events scuttled such ideas and the council again fractured along party lines. By now the Troubles had lasted ten years and there was still no end in sight. Government spokesmen talked of 'an acceptable level of violence' and the intention seemed to be to contain rather than to solve the problem.

The year 1979 began with a series of IRA attacks, culminating in the deaths of four RUC officers in a landmine explosion on the Millvale Road in April. In the same month the UK general election brought Margaret Thatcher and the Conservatives to power and many expected a new initiative from the new government. This year also saw the first direct elections to the European parliament. Northern Ireland was counted as one constituency, returning three members. The voting reflected the political make-up of the population, with two Unionists, Ian Paisley of the Democratic Unionist Party and John Taylor of the Ulster Unionist Party, and one nationalist, John Hume of the SDLP, winning the seats. In Newry itself two factories closed down, putting more people out of work. In south Armagh in July a Gaelic football park was taken over as a military base, and this prompted five thousand people to attend a protest rally. The following month people everywhere were shocked when the IRA killed eighteen paratroopers in an ambush at Narrow Water, near Warrenpoint. This was the largest death toll in any one incident in the current Troubles in Northern Ireland and it was widely believed that it would mark a watershed in the IRA campaign.

Hopes were raised when Pope John Paul II visited Ireland in September 1979. Many believed that a plea from the Pope could alter the course of events in the North, or that his visit would be the opportunity for a mutual gesture of reconciliation. Like so much else, the Pope's visit had little long-term impact and attitudes to him only highlighted the basic divisions that persisted between Catholics and Protestants in Ireland. When the Pope visited Drogheda in County Louth, many people from Northern Ireland went there to see him. Most travellers passed through Newry and at one point there was a huge traffic jam that stretched from south of the border to Banbridge. The following months saw more deaths in Newry. Attacks on business premises were renewed as grille bombs - explosives or incendiary devices attached to the security grilles over shop windows - were used on many commercial outlets. The year ended with the announcement that there were 5,265 people unemployed in Newry.

The following years were to see the continuation of the violence at different levels. Occasionally there were lulls but it rarely, if ever, ceased

The deaths of eighteen paratroopers in an IRA ambush in August 1979 was the security forces biggest loss in one attack and the highest death toll in any one incident in Northern Ireland up until then. (Army Information Service, HQNI, Lisburn)

However, other issues came to dominate the political scene and there was a shift in emphasis. The hunger strikes begun by Bobby Sands in the Maze Prison in 1981 touched Newry directly when local man Raymond McCreesh died after sixty-one days without food and water. His funeral was the occasion of a show of strength by the IRA and was followed by the worst rioting in years. The H-Block hunger strikes heralded a stormy and bitter time for the district council, especially when anti-H-Block candidates were elected to the council in July and October 1981. But the hunger strikes passed and in the end seemed to have had little effect. However, one important outcome was that the propaganda campaign resulted in Sinn Féin, the IRA's political wing, assuming a higher profile and from this time onwards it participated in local politics and elections.

A new initiative was launched in 1982 with the elections to the Constituent Assembly at Stormont. The principle behind the Assembly was that powers would be devolved to it as cross-party agreement was reached on the different areas of government. However, the Assembly was destined to flounder and fail as the intransigence of certain parties could not be overcome. There was a UK general election in 1983, which brought changes to Newry. As part of a redrawing of constituencies, in an attempt to redress the balance of representation, the town found itself part of the new constituency of Newry and Armagh. Despite these political developments, the violence went on and the year ended with unemployment in Newry standing at 40 per cent, the highest ever.

The legacy of the 1981 hunger strikes was felt during the local government elections in May 1985, when, for the first time, Sinn Féin gained seats on the district council. The deaths of nine members of the RUC in February, when the IRA launched a mortar-bomb attack on the police station, did little to diminish support for its political wing in Newry. The previous years had seen a general hardening of attitudes throughout Northern Ireland and a polarisation of politics. The gulf between nationalists and Unionists appeared to be unbridgeable. In the new council the SDLP were in a minority, having lost two seats. Sinn Fein, whose presence was objected to by the Unionists, took five seats.

Changes in government brought the Needham family back into Newry's story, if only indirectly, when Richard Needham, who had claim to the earldom of Kilmorey, was appointed the new parliamentary undersecretary of state for Northern Ireland in September. Although it had been many decades since the Needhams were involved in local politics, in his capacity as Minister of the Environment, Richard Needham did have ultimate responsibility for the Newry and Mourne District Council.

While Northern Ireland continued to be locked in confrontation, secret negotiations had been going on between the British and Irish governments, resulting in November 1985 in the signing of an agreement establishing an intergovernmental conference through which it was hoped to develop a common approach to the problems in the North. Reactions to the Anglo-Irish agreement were predictable: a welcome from nationalists, such as the SDLP; rejection by militant republicans, who saw it as an unacceptable compromise; and rejection by Unionists, who viewed it as interference by a foreign power in the affairs of Northern Ireland.

The Needham family re-entered Newry's history when Richard Needham (titular Earl of Kilmorey, Viscount Newry and Mourne) became the Northern Ireland Minister for the Environment. In March 1989 he donated the third earl's mantle of the Order of St. Patrick to the Newry museum. Also in the photograph are Matt McAteer (left) of the museum sub-committee and beside him, Eugene Markey, chairman of Newry & Mourne DC. (*Newry Reporter*)

The agreement had an immediate impact on Newry and Mourne District Council, which was now boycotted by Unionist councillors as part of an overall anti-agreement campaign. Unionist-controlled councils suspended all business and took to the streets in protest. However, when the annual election for council chairman came round in May 1986, the Unionist councillors in Newry and Mourne found a unique way of protesting. Only the SDLP councillors supported the agreement and since the district council elections in 1985, they could be outvoted by a combination of Unionists, Sinn Féin and Independent councillors. And this is precisely what happened, as all those opposed to the agreement voted against the party that supported it, electing two Independents as chairman and vice-chairman, Eugene Markey and Ciaran Mussen. So while other Unionists boycotted their councils, in Newry they remained to ensure that the pro-agreement SDLP would not be able to have its own way. This 'unholy alliance', as its critics called it, held for the following two years and the flamboyant Eugene Markey remained as chairman.

Whether or not the Anglo-Irish agreement proved to be a turning point in the Troubles, it altered the conduct of business in the district council and a further anti-agreement protest was made when all fifteen Unionist MPs resigned from Westminster, thus provoking a 'mini' general election. If the Unionists' intention was to show the strength of their support, their plan backfired in the constituency of Newry and Armagh. There was a straight fight between the sitting Unionist, Jim Nicholson, and Seamus Mallon of the SDLP, with the result that Mallon was returned as MP for the constituency. In the general election held the following year, Mallon retained his seat and in South Down, Eddie McGrady (SDLP) ousted Unionist Enoch Powell. As a historical aside, it must be mentioned that this occasioned the retirement of Powell from politics in Northern Ireland.

After the signing of the Anglo-Irish agreement, there were further attempts by the IRA to destabilise the region. In Newry and the surrounding areas its attacks increased and there were more deaths. In April 1986 the Irish National Liberation Army demolished the district council offices in two attacks — and they were not rebuilt until the following year. In May 1986 a six-hundred-pound bomb killed two policemen and a soldier at Crossmaglen. In June an electrical contractor, Terence McKeever, was shot dead by the IRA because he was working on an army base. In July three RUC officers were shot dead by masked men as they sat in their patrol car in Margaret Square. The extension of security posts throughout south Armagh led to protests at street level and at Westminster. The requisitioning of land for these posts and inconvenience caused did little to endear the army to the local population. In December 1986 there was another mortar-bomb attack on the RUC station, which fell short, injuring civilians and destroying nearby houses.

The Troubles are still with us and so we cannot draw any conclusions about their final impact on Newry. We do know that they have radically altered ordinary life and society in the town. During the years of the Troubles there have been many important changes in local government and parliamentary representation but there has also been an appalling economic decline and a rise in the number of unemployed. The combination of political disturbances and economic upheaval must leave many of the townspeople wondering if Newry can ever recover and again be the prosperous town it once was.

Enoch Powell first became MP for South Down in October 1974. He lost his seat to Eddie McGrady (SDLP) in 1987 and subsequently left the Northern Ireland political scene. (*Belfast Telegraph*)

IO

WILL THE YEW TREE FLOURISH AGAIN?

Will Newry ever flourish again? That is a question that many of its citizens have often asked over the last twenty years of civil disturbance, living in a town wracked by bombings and killings, with a poor economy and little work. Today the outlook seems little better: it is still a blackspot for unemployment; its streets are patrolled by British soldiers in full battle dress and police in armoured vehicles; no one any longer notices the noise of the helicopters that constantly circle above the rooftops. To any passing visitor Newry must seem a sorry place. But beneath this gloomy surface there are things happening that inspire hope. The Troubles have not been the whole story.

Although there are still some factories in the town there is a recognition, largely unspoken, that Newry's economic future lies in the retail industry and tourism. The town has always been important as a market centre for south-east Ulster and northern Leinster, and in this capacity it has assumed a new relevance in recent years. When the Irish Republic joined the European Monetary System in 1979 and so broke the link with sterling, the differentials in currency and taxation made Northern Ireland attractive to southern shoppers and it was not unusual to see coachloads of people crossing the border into Newry to buy everything from soap to stereos. As a tourist centre, Newry is ideally situated: it is on the doorstep of the Mourne Mountains, the Ring of Gullion and the Cooley peninsula. Despite the Troubles, some tourists do come to Northern Ireland and there is potential for growth. In 1986 visitors to Newry and Mourne spent £6 million, so although as yet there has been no comprehensive plan to develop tourism in the Carlingford Lough region as a whole, there is the basis of a profitable industry there.

In the town itself there are signs of regeneration. There are three industrial estates that already house some factories and hope to attract more, while Warrenpoint continues to grow as a port. Communications around the town have been improved by recent road building and a rail link has been restored with the reopening of a station outside the town. The housing stock has also been improved. In 1986 the Northern Ireland Housing Executive embarked on a £1 million programme to refurbish substandard accommodation. In appearance the old town is more attractive than it was in the 1970s. In 1981 the town centre around Hill Street officially became a pedestrian precinct. Despite some ugly modernisations, there have been conscientious attempts, particularly in Sugar Island, to preserve the architectural integrity of 'Old Newry' when erecting new buildings or converting old ones. Perhaps the most important sign of regeneration has been in the development of community groups and projects, aimed at improving the quality of life in the town at a social and cultural level. In 1987 the Newry and Mourne Civic Trust was established to act as an umbrella body for the different cultural and environmental groups and to take the initiative not just in maintaining the old but in promoting what is best in the new.

It is one of the most fascinating — and perhaps one of the most disturbing — aspects of present-day Northern Ireland that 'ordinary life' continues despite the upheavals and in this Newry is no different from anywhere else. The annual Newry Féis, for example, is still held every spring. This celebration of traditional music and dance attracts hundreds of participants and spectators. After being first staged in 1975, the Canal Festival has also become an established annual event, replacing the old Civic Week. Another favourite, also promoted by the district council, is the Newry and Mourne Arts Festival that is held each autumn. This brings to Newry first-class performers from all the different fields of the arts. The festival organisers have a talent for spotting rising stars, and many performers have gone on from Newry to appear at bigger and more prestigious venues, such as Edinburgh. Incorporated into the arts festival is the One-Act Drama Festival, which attracts the best companies from all over Ireland and has proved to be a most important event in the amateur drama calendar. Besides these, there are a number of community festivals held every year in different parts of the town.

The Newry Canal in the mid-1970s lies neglected – even the annual Canal Festival did not lead to its revitalisation. Not everyone saw its potential and some even wanted it filled in. (*Newry Reporter*)

The ship canal
continues to be used
for leisure activities
and hopes are high that
the whole waterway
from Newry to Lough
Neagh may be
reopened for leisure
craft. (*Newry
Reporter*)

The amateur tradition has always been strong in Newry. There are various groups catering for people of all ages and involved in all aspects of the arts. Many of these are long-established, dating back to the beginning of the twentieth century. They have often been an invaluable training ground for people wishing to pursue a professional career. For example, John Lynch, who starred with Helen Mirren in the film *Cal,* began acting with the local Newpoint Players. As the name suggests, Newpoint draws its membership from Newry and Warrenpoint. They have earned themselves the reputation of producing innovative, high-quality drama. On the musical side, the Newry Musical and Orchestral Society has been very successful. Every year its members provide a season of music and light opera and they have achieved the ultimate success of being awarded the prestigious Premier Trophy at the Waterford International Light Opera Festival. The town is also home to many more groups and choirs in the fields of classical, traditional and pop music.

The strength of support for the arts received official recognition when the town acquired Northern Ireland's first purpose-built arts centre. In 1981 the district council bought a site on Bank Parade, at what had originally been the town's Assembly Rooms, built in 1840, and which latterly had housed the offices of the inland revenue until it was bombed in 1972. The arts centre retained the 1840 facade but was completely rebuilt behind this, incorporating three galleries, an auditorium and two studios. In 1985 the building next door was also acquired by the district council and opened as the town's museum in 1986. Both the Newry and Mourne Arts Centre and the Newry Museum benefit from the Patrick Murphy Trust, which was founded on a bequest by a local businessman to the urban district council initially to alleviate the rates. After the reorganisation of local government in 1973, the courts decided that the new Newry and Mourne District Council could not benefit directly from the bequest and so the trust was established to oversee the spending of the fund on projects for advancing Newry, such as the arts centre.

It is not just the arts but also sport and leisure facilities that have benefited in recent years. In 1984 a large sports complex was opened at Patrick Street with all the amenities — from squash courts to indoor football pitches — that one would expect to find in any modern centre. Athletics and football have been encouraged; local sports clubs have been helped by grants from the district council and playing fields and running tracks have been opened in Newry and in surrounding areas. In 1986 alone, over £1 million was spent by the district council on various recreational facilities.

There has been strong local feeling against abandoning the Newry Canal. Since the closure of the ship canal, responsibility for it had passed to the Department of Economic Development. Although the sea lock gates remained closed and the inland locks had deteriorated, over the years the canal had been used by various leisure groups. However, the Canal Preservation Society received little support in its aim of achieving a complete reinstatement of the canal. The Canal Festival only held token events on the water and did not, in fact, encourage its greater use. Various reports had been produced at different times on what should be done with the canal; one report even suggested filling it in and using it as a car park. In 1978, the development agency Enterprise Ulster published a plan for its complete reinstatement and for it to be used as a recreational facility. After lengthy negotiations, in 1986 the district council assumed ownership from the Department of Economic Development for that section of the canal that lay within its jurisdiction, running about seven and a half miles inland. The district council then endorsed Enterprise Ulster's 1978 report and invited the agency to start work on the waterway, in the hope that other relevant local authorities would later co-operate in reopening the remainder of the canal as far as Lough Neagh. Strong arguments have been put forward that its reinstatement would make a significant impact on the tourist industry; activity holidays on the canal could prove to be an important local business and if, as has been proposed, a national museum of inland navigation were to be opened at Newry, it would attract visitors and provide employment. It is probable that a thriving leisure industry centred on the canal would have almost as significant an impact on the town as did its opening in 1742.

In July 1987 another valuable addition was made to the town when a new district library was opened in Hill Street. It has a lending library and a reference section, with additional rooms for use by local societies. In response to pressure from within Newry, the Southern Education and Library Board has now returned many of the books and papers of a local historical nature that had been removed to library headquarters in Armagh at the time of reorganisation, now making the reference section in Newry a useful source of information on local history.

The planting of two yew trees by Dr. Francis Brookes (third from right), Catholic Bishop of Dromore and the Rev. Mervyn Wilson (second from right), rector of St. Patrick's church, symbolised not only the optimism in the success of Clanrye/Abbey Developments but an enduring faith in the future of Newry. Also in the photograph are Paddy Magennis (front left), of Clanrye/Abbey Developments, and Eugene Markey (far right), chairman of Newry & Mourne DC. (Clanrye/Abbey Developments)

While new hopes were expressed for the canal, the end was in sight for another historic institution — the gasworks. Since the 1970s the gasworks had accumulated large debts and consistently failed to make a profit. Prospects of natural gas being piped up from the Kinsale field off the southern Irish coast failed to materialise and so the Northern Ireland Office decided to shut down the whole gas industry. Thomas McGrath, the last and longest-serving chairman of the district council gas committee, was bitter about the closure of the gasworks in April 1987. The building was later demolished.

As the fate of the gasworks was being sealed, a symbolically important building was being saved — the old Abbey Grammar School. It comprised a terrace of three Georgian town houses and their accompanying outbuildings, which had been built in the late eighteenth century by the Corry family. The Christian Brothers started to run a school there in the nineteenth century. It was given the name 'Abbey' because this was where the Cistercian abbey had once stood and where centuries earlier, as the story goes, Saint Patrick had planted the yew tree. The building was not only of architectural importance — being among the few surviving Georgian houses in the town — but the school was also situated in the oldest part of Newry, the very place where the town originated. By the mid-1970s the building had been vacated and it became derelict. The Department of the Environment proposed to clear the site for a car park but many local people thought it should be preserved because of its historical and architectural importance and, perhaps decisively, because it was where many of Newry's influential citizens had gone to school. In the end the Christian Brothers handed the building over to the Clanrye Community Workshop, a local youth training agency, on condition that it was restored and put to good use. The restoration work provided on-site training in a wide range of skills and gave the Clanrye workshop a permanent home but it was also envisaged that the restored building would become a focus for all community and cultural projects in the area. Clanrye/Abbey Developments was able to raise the £1 million needed to carry out the work and in 1987 the first phase of the restoration received an award, from a field of 140 entries, from the Royal Institute of British Architects. On 24 August 1987 the first phase was officially opened in a ceremony conducted by the Catholic Bishop of Dromore, Dr Francis Brookes, and the rector of St Patrick's Church, the Reverend Mervyn Wilson, in which they each planted a yew tree in the grounds. These trees not only evoked the memory of Saint Patrick but, like his planting of the original yew tree, they were symbolic of an enduring faith in the future of Newry.

It is tempting to be overly optimistic and only draw attention to the positive elements of the town's recent history. Developments in the area of commerce, from Norbrook Laboratories to the Buttercrane Shopping Centre, as well as in the area of culture, from the arts centre to the Clanrye/Abbey Developments project, do constitute a regeneration in Newry. However, the town continues to face enormous problems, most of them beyond the influence of local factors. The Troubles persist and Newry still has economic difficulties. The town has made world headlines because of the bombings and the killings there. There is also the low-level violence of robberies, hijackings, and punishment shootings. Ordinary life is disrupted by army and RUC checkpoints on the streets, search operations, and other security restrictions. There have been some signs of economic recovery and Newry does have its success stories, but any real achievement still lies in the future. The area has lost more jobs than those created by recent initiatives. In 1986, for example, Bessbrook lost its last contact with the linen industry when Ulster Weavers withdrew from the village. Emigration is now as common as it once was in the past, and many families in Newry have relatives working in England or America. Unemployment in the town remains unacceptably high: as Dr Brookes pointed out at the opening of Clanrye/Abbey Developments, 30 per cent of the adult population is without work, and among younger people the figure is 50 per cent.

If the history of Newry teaches us anything, it is that as yet no blow has been so severe that the town has not been able to recover from it. Since earliest times it has been on the frontier of many of Ireland's wars. It was completely destroyed when the Duke of Berwick put it to the torch in 1689, yet within a few decades it had become one of the wealthiest ports in Ireland and played an influential role in the nation's political affairs. Whether it was geographical and historical factors, or the determination of its people, that ensured the town's survival is not important, since those elements still hold true today and the present townspeople exhibit the same spirit of resilience that characterised their ancestors. Already there are signs of recovery and only the worst pessimist would claim that the yew tree at the head of the strand will not flourish again.

Epilogue

The years from 1989 to 2009 have seen many changes in Ireland in general, Northern Ireland in particular, and of course to Newry. The Troubles continued to affect the town. Between 1990 and 1998 when the Good Friday Agreement was signed around a dozen people – civilians, paramilitaries and security force members – were killed in or near Newry. Among them was Lance-Bombardier Stephen Restorick who was shot by an IRA sniper on 12 February 1997 while manning a checkpoint in Bessbrook. He was the last British soldier to be killed by the IRA before it declared a ceasefire for the second time. Few would have expected the optimistic note struck at the end of the first edition of *Frontier Town* to become reality so quickly with the IRA and Loyalist organisations declaring ceasefires in 1994 and then the Good Friday Agreement being reached in 1998. The subsequent political developments did not always run smoothly and it was to be some years before a stable executive was established in Stormont. However the final agreement involving the DUP for the first time led to a new executive with Ian Paisley as First Minister and Sinn Féin's Martin McGuinness as Deputy First Minister. On Rev. Paisley's retirement from politics in 2008, his deputy in the DUP, Peter Robinson, succeeded him as First Minister.

Newry politicians such as Isaac Corry and John Mitchel have played their part in national affairs. In that tradition, Conor Murphy of Sinn Féin is not only the MP for Newry and Armagh but also serves in the Northern Ireland Executive as Minister for Regional Development. Murphy had been a Newry and Mourne Councillor for eight years before being elected to the Northern Ireland Assembly in 1998 where he was his party's chief whip. He was a key member of the Sinn Féin negotiating team with particular responsibility for institutional issues and represented the party at the Hillsborough, Leeds Castle and St. Andrew's negotiations. His presence has ensured that Newry is never far from the top of the agenda in economic and regional development issues.

The town itself continued to flourish during the 1990s. In 1991 unemployment in Newry was estimated as being 26% of the workforce but by 2008 it had fallen to 2%. The development of the Celtic Tiger economy in the Republic and currency differences, especially after the introduction of the Euro in 2001, made Newry a very attractive place for people from South of the Border to shop. The extension of the M1 motorway from Dublin to just south of Newry in 2008 and the completion of the dual carriageway from Belfast have made it easily accessible from both these cities. This means that Newry is an advantageous place not just for retail businesses but for others also. Even despite the recent economic downturn that remains the case.

Another milestone occurred for Newry in March 2002 when as part of the celebrations of Queen Elizabeth's golden jubilee, Newry was granted city status alongside Lisburn. In the eyes of many this recognition was long overdue and not everyone in the town welcomed the fact that it took a charter of the queen to raise Newry to being a city. However, the elevation of Newry alongside Lisburn was unusual in the context of the United Kingdom since England, Scotland and Wales had only one town each granted city status in honour of the golden jubilee. It was widely believed, although never officially stated, that Northern Ireland got two cities in recognition of the 'two communities' and that Newry was chosen to represent the 'nationalist' community. The charter from Elizabeth II is on display in the new museum in Bagenal's castle not far from a reproduction of Newry's original royal charter from Murtagh MacLoughlin, High King of Ireland, in 1144.

It was the opening of the Newry Canal in the eighteenth century that set Newry on the road to prosperity and although neglected for decades the inland and ship canals are now seen as a key component not just of its identity but of future prosperity. The talk of re-opening Newry's canals seems more of a reality now as inland waterways was one of the cross-border bodies established under the Good Friday Agreement and one of the few areas where there appears to be all party support. Work has begun to restore the other canals in Northern Ireland, much of it paid for by the Irish government, and there is widespread recognition that the network would be incomplete without Newry. The Victoria Locks were modernised in 2008 and the ship canal is open as a leisure facility with some boats now being regular visitors in the Albert Basin.

Given that I came to Newry in 1985 to establish a museum there it would be remiss of me not to mention developments affecting it. The museum now has a new home on Abbey Way, the site of the original Newry abbey, on a hill overlooking the city. After its dissolution the abbey was taken over by Nicholas Bagenal who built a castle there. Bagenal's castle survived and in the nineteenth century was incorporated into the premises of McCann's Bakery. It was rediscovered when the bakery was closed down in 1996 and the district council acquired the site. It was seen as an opportunity for Newry and Mourne District Council to preserve and restore one of the most important aspects of the city's heritage. The building is of significance not just because of its history but also because it is the only known surviving Irish castle for which the original plans still exist in the National Archives in London. The District Council restored and developed the castle and an adjoining warehouse as the new museum. This flagship project aims to provide a top class museum service and be a focus for cultural, heritage and tourism activities.

Any visitor to Newry today would notice that it has changed much since 1989. It has grown in size and its appearance has altered particularly along the Albert Basin and the canal quays as old warehouses and yards have given way to shopping centres, offices and a hotel. The increased population has also given the city a more cosmopolitan atmosphere as many have come to settle here from eastern Europe and further afield. Ten years ago the town, as it still was then, had a homogenous appearance but now different faces are appearing on the streets and languages other than English and Irish are common. This new aspect to the city has meant there is a greater variety of shops and restaurants than ever before. The character of Newry has changed and while this may be unsettling for some, it is evidence of a new confidence and when we consider the international trading links that Newry had over the centuries, it fits in well with its heritage.

I end this epilogue with thoughts for the future. Despite the global economic downturn, the prospects for Newry are not too bleak and as always there is much optimism in the city, as we must now call it. Its position on the border, a frontier town, has enabled it to attract shoppers who come north in search of cheaper prices on all goods from the necessities to luxuries and this has cushioned Newry to some degree from the global recession. Once again the plan to build a bridge across Narrow Water linking Counties Down and Louth has been revived. However this time the project has been put out to tender and both governments in Dublin and London as well as the executive in Belfast support it. If it goes ahead it will fit in with ambitious plans to develop the Mourne Mountains and the Cooley Peninsula as a premier tourist region.

Newry is a very old town which has been through much in its nine centuries of history. Taken in this context present difficulties are not so major. In common with the rest of Ireland, the history of Newry was largely characterised by war and violence. The Good Friday Agreement has, we hope, put that part of our history behind us, and whatever problems which Newry may face in future will be peaceful ones.

BIBLIOGRAPHY

NEWSPAPERS AND MAGAZINES

Armagh Observer
Down and Connor Historical Society's Magazine
Dublin Newsletter
Frontier Sentinel
Mourne Observer
Newry Reporter
Neivry Telegraph

ARTICLES

Bourke, Cormac. 'Early Irish hand-bells', *Journal of the Royal Society of Antiquaries of Ireland,* vol. 110 (1980)
Brady, Ciaran. 'The killing of Shane O'Neill: some new evidence', *Irish Sword,* vol. 15, no. 59 (1982)
Burns, Gerry. 'Newry - the first town outside Belfast to fight for human rights', *Newry Reporter,* 2.6 January 1987
Davies, Oliver. 'Types of rath in southern Ulster', *Ulster Journal of Archaeology* (1947)
Day, Robert. 'A medal of the Newry Volunteers', *Ulster Journal of Archaeology,* second series, vol. 2. (January 1901)
Dornan, David *see* O'Driscole, Tom, David Dornan and Don Patterson Fenton, Roy. 'Fishers of Newry', *Ships Monthly,* vol. 17, no. 1 (January 1982) Fisher, John. 'The Newry Canal', unpublished essay
Fitzpatrick, Sean. 'The History of the Newry Fire Brigade 1877-1977', unpublished essay
Heaney, Ian. 'The legacy of Newry cinema and theatre', *Brass Tacks,* no. 39 (May 1988)
Hore, H.E. 'Marshal Bagenal's description of Ireland anno 1586', *Ulster Journal of Archaeology,* vol. 2 (1854)
Hume, A. 'Surnames in the county of Down', *Ulster Journal of Archaeology,* vol. 2 (1858)
Kerrigan, Paul M. 'Seventeenth-century fortifications, forts and garrisons in Ireland: preliminary list', *Irish Sword,* vol. 14, no. 54 (1980)
Lett, Henry. 'The dun at Dorsey', *Journal of the Royal Society of Antiquaries of Ireland* (1898)
McCutcheon, W.A. 'The Newry navigation: the earliest navigation in the British Isles', *Geographical Journal,* vol. 129 (1963)
MacLeod, Catríonia. 'An ale glass of the loyal Newry Volunteers, 1784', *Irish Sword,* vol. 15, no. 61 (1984)
MacNeill, T.E. 'Ulster mottes: a checklist', *Ulster Journal of Archaeology,* vol. 38(1975)
Maguire, W.H. 'Major General Ross and the burning of Washington', *Irish Sword,* vol. 14, no. 55 (1980)
Morris, H. 'Some Ulster ecclesiastical bells', *Journal of the Royal Society of Antiquaries of Ireland,* vol. 61 (1934)

Murphy, Leo. 'Action station: the story of Greencastle aerodrome', *Twelve Miles of Mourne,* vol. 3 (1989)

O'Driscole, Tom, David Dornan and Don Patterson. 'Joseph Fisher and Sons Limited, Newry', *Irish Shipping,* vol. 3, no. 2(1965)

Ó Nuallain, Seán. 'Irish portal tombs: topography, siting and distribution', *Journal of the Royal Society of Antiquaries of Ireland,* vol. 113 (1983)

Paterson, T.G.F. 'The County Armagh Volunteers of 1778—1793', *Ulster Journal of Archaeology,* third series, vol. 4 (1941)

Patterson, Don *see* O'Driscole, Tom, David Dornan and Don Patterson

Reid, T.E. 'Clontygora cairn, County Armagh', *Journal of the Royal Society of Antiquaries of Ireland,* vol. 67 (1937)

'Take it down from the mast' and 'The emerald pimpernel', *Cuisle na nGael,*uimhir 5 (1989)

Vinycomb, John. 'Newry', *Ulster Journal of Archaeology* (1898)

BOOKS, PAMPHLETS, REPORTS AND SURVEYS

Ancient Monuments of Northern Ireland: A Preliminary Survey, Belfast, His Majesty's Stationery Office, 1940

Annals of the Four Masters, Dublin, Hodges and Smith, 1848-61

Annals of Ulster, Belfast, Her Majesty's Stationery Office, 1887-1901

Archaeological Survey of County Down, Belfast, Her Majesty's Stationery Office, 1966

Armstrong, E.C.R. *Irish Seal Matrices and Seals,* Dublin, Hodges and Figgis, 1913

Bassett, G.H. *County Down Guide and Directory,* Dublin, G.H. Bassett, 1888

Beckett, J.C. *The Making of Modern Ireland,* London, Faber and Faber, 1966

Bessbrook, 1845-1945, Bessbrook, Bessbrook Spinning Company, 1945

Bradshaw, Thomas. *Bradshaw's General Directory of Newry, Armagh . . .,*Newry, Thomas Bradshaw, 1820

Brondsted, Johannes. *The Vikings,* Harmondsworth, Penguin, 1980

Buckland, Peter. *A History of Northern Ireland,* Dublin, Gill and Macmillan, 1981

Camblin, G. *The Town in Ulster,* Belfast, Mullan, 1951

Cambrensis, Giraldus. *Expugnatio Hibernica,* Dublin, Royal Irish Academy, 1978

Carlingford Lough, Carlingford, Carlingford Lough Heritage Society, 1980

Carville, Geraldine. *Norman Splendour: Duiske Abbey, Graignamanagh,*Belfast, Blackstaff Press, 1979

Colmcille, Father. *The Story of Mellifont,* Dublin, Gill, 1958

Coote, Sir Charles. *A Statistical Survey of the County of Armagh,* Dublin, The Dublin Society, 1804

Cordner-Pinkerton, Mrs (ed.). *The Open Window Annual 1899-1902,* Newry, Cordner-Pinkerton, 1902

Crawford, M.G. *Legendary Stories of Carlingford Lough,* Warrenpoint, V.G. Havern, 1985

Crossle F.C. *Volunteers and Yeomanry of the Newry District,* Newry, F.C. Crossle, 1906

Delany, Ruth. *The Inland Waterways of Ireland,* Belfast, Appletree Press, 1985

Deutsch, Richard and Vivien Magowan. *Northern Ireland 1968-1974: AChronology of Events,* 3 vols, Belfast, Blackstaff Press, 1973—5

Dillon, William. *The Life of John Mitchel,* London, Kegan Paul, 1888

Dolley, Michael. *Anglo-Norman Ireland,* Dublin, Gill and MacMillan, 1972

Doyle, J.B. *Tours in Ulster,* Dublin, Hodges and Smith, 1854

Elville, E.M. *English and Irish Cut Glass,* London, Country Life, 1953

Evans, E. Estyn. *Harvest Home: A Selection of the Writings of T.G.F. Patterson,*Dundalk, W. Tempest, 1951

Evans, E. Estyn. *Mourne Country,* Dundalk, Dundalgan Press, 1951

Exploring Living Memory Reminiscence Packs: 1 South Armagh; 2 Newry; 3 The Mournes, Living Memory Project, 1985—7

Fisk, Robert. *The Point of No Return,* London, Andre Deutsch, 1975

Gill, Conrad. *The Rise of the Irish Linen Industry,* London, Clarendon Press, 1925

Gilligan, Myles. *Newry,* Newry, Myles Gilligan, 1950

Gray, John. *City in Revolt,* Belfast, Blackstaff Press, 1985

Green, E.R.R. *The Industrial Archaeology of County Down,* Belfast, Her Majesty's Stationery Office, 1963

Gregory, Lady Augusta. *Cuchulain of Muirthemne,* Gerrards Cross, Colin Smythe, 1976

Gwyn; Aubrey and Neville R. Hadcock. *Medieval Religious Houses in Ireland,* London, Longman, 1970

Hadcock, Neville R. *see* Gwyn, Aubrey and Neville R. Hadcock

Hagan, Dennis *see* Sheridan, Tom and Dennis Hagan

Hall, Mr and Mrs S.C. *Hall's Ireland,* London, Hall, Virtue and Company, 1841-3

Hamlin, Ann (ed.). *Historic Monuments of Northern Ireland,* Belfast, Her Majesty's Stationery Office, 1983

Harris, W. *The Antient and Present State of the County of Down,* Dublin, Exshaw, 1744

Hayes-McCoy, G.A. *Irish Battles,* London, Longman, 1969

Hayes-McCoy, G.A. *Ulster and Other Irish Maps, 1600,* Dublin, Irish Manuscripts Commission, 1964

Hayward, Richard. *Border Foray,* London, Barker, 1957

Horsman, R. *The War of 1812,* London, Eyre and Spottiswoode, 1961

Irish Boundary Commission Report of 1925, Dublin, Irish Universities Press, 1969

Kenney, J.F. *Sources for the Early History of Ireland: Ecclesiastical,* New York, Columbia University Press, 1929

Keogh, Dermot. *The Rise of the Irish Working Class,* Belfast, Appletree Press, 1982

Knox, Alexander. *A History of the County of Down,* Belfast, Hodges, Foster and Company, 1875

Lewis, Samuel. *A Topographical Dictionary of Ireland,* Dublin, S. Lewis and Company, 1837

McCall, Hugh. *The House ofDownshire 1600-1863,* Belfast, Mullan, 1880

McCutcheon, W.A. *The Canals of the North of Ireland,* London, David and Charles, 1965

McGrath, Thomas. *Newry by Gaslight,* Newry, Newry and Mourne District Council, 1987

McLeod, W.W. *Motoring In Ulster,* Belfast, *Belfast News-Letter,* 1935

McNeill, D.B. *Coastal Passenger Steamers and Inland Navigation in the North of Ireland,* Belfast, Belfast Museum and Art Gallery, 1962

McNeill, D.B. *Irish Passenger Steamship Services,* London, David and Charles, 1969

Magowan, Vivien *see* Deutsch, Richard and Vivien Magowan

Malcomson, A.P.W. *Isaac Corry 1755-1813,* Belfast, Public Record Office of Northern Ireland, 1974

Maxwell, Constantia. *The Foundations of Modern Ireland,* London, Society for

Promoting Christian Knowledge, 1921

Messenger, Betty. *Picking up the Linen Threads: Life in Ulster's Mills,* Belfast, Blackstaff Press, 1988

Mitchel, John. *The Jail Journal,* London, Sphere, 1983

Moody, T.W. and F.X. Martin (eds.). *The Course of Irish History,* Cork, Mercier Press, 1967

Mulligan, Fergus. *Irish Railways,* Belfast, Appletree Press, 1983

Murphy, M.J. *At Slieve Gullion's Foot,* Dundalk, W.Tempest, 1940

Newham, Alan T. *The Bessbrook and Newry Tramway,* Blandford, Oakwood Press, 1979

Newry Aflame: The Official History of the Newry Fire Brigade, Newry, Newry Fire Brigade, 1977

Nowlan, Kevin B. (ed.). *Travel and Transport in Ireland,* Dublin, Gill and Macmillan, 1973

O'Connor, Rebecca. *Jenny Mitchel, Young Irelander,* Tuscon, Arizona, O'Conner Trust, 1988

O'Donovan, John. *Letters. . . of the County Down,* Dublin, Brown and Nolan, 1909

O'Donovan, John. *Miscellany of Celtic Society,* Dublin, Irish Archaeological and Celtic Society, 1849

O'Laverty, J. *Historical Account of Down and Connor,* Belfast, James Duffy, 1878

Ó Ríordáin, Seán. *Antiquities of the Irish Countryside,* London, Methuen, 1979

Otway-Ruthven, A.J. *A History of Medieval Ireland,* London, Benn, 1968

Plowden, Francis. *The History of Ireland from its Union with Great Britain inJanuary 1801 to October 1810,* Dublin, John Boyce, 1811

Reid, James Seaton. *The History of the Presbyterian Church in Ireland,* Belfast, Mullan, 1853

Schrier, Arnold. *Ireland and the American Emigration 1850-1900,* New York, Russell and Russell, 1970

Sheridan, Tom and Dennis Hagan. *Dirty Town, Proud People: A History of Church Street and Surrounding Areas,* Newry, Sheridan and Hagan, 1986

Small, John F. ('Newriensis'). *An Historical Sketch of Newry,* Newry, *Newry Reporter,* 1876

Smith, F. W. *The Irish Linen Trade Handbook and Directory,* Belfast, Greer, 1876

Stewart, A.T.Q. *The Narrow Ground,* London, Faber and Faber, 1977

Strahan, F.W. *The First Newry (Sandys Street) Presbyterian Congregation,*Newry, W. and S. Magowan, 1904

Stuart, James. *Historical Memoirs of Armagh,* Newry, Wilkinson, 1819

Thackeray, William Makepeace. *The Irish Sketch Book 1842,* London, Chapman and Hall, 1842

Wallace, Martin. *Northern Ireland: Fifty Years of Self-Government,* London, David and Charles, 1971

Warren, Phelps. *Irish Glass,* London, Faber and Faber, 1970

Watson, Raymond P. *Cath Saoirse An luir,* Newry, Raymond P. Watson, 1986

Wesley, John. *Journal of John Wesley,* London, Culley, 1909—16

Westrop, M.S.D. *Irish Glass,* Dublin, Allen Figgis, 1978

Young, Arthur. *A Tour in Ireland,* London, Whitestone, 1780

INDEX

252

Wyndham, Lord 74